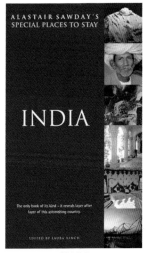

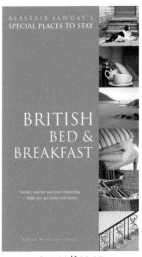

First edition
Copyright © September 2006
Alastair Sawday Publishing Co. Ltd

Published in 2006
Alastair Sawday Publishing,
The Old Farmyard,
Yanley Lane, Long Ashton
Bristol BS41 9LR
Tel: +44 (0)1275 395430
Fax: +44 (0)1275 393388
Email: info@specialplacestostay.com
Web: www.specialplacestostay.com

The Globe Pequot Press
P. O. Box 480, Guilford,
Connecticut 06437, USA
Tel: +1 203 458 4500
Fax: +1 203 458 4601
E-mail: info@globepequot.com
Web: www.globepequot.com

Design:
Caroline King

Maps & Mapping:
Maidenhead Cartographic Services Ltd

Printing:
Butler & Tanner, Frome, UK

UK Distribution:
Penguin UK, 80 Strand, London

ISBN-10: 1-901970-77-9
ISBN-13: 978-1-901970-77-7

A catalogue record for this book is
available from the British Library.

Paper and Printing: We have sought the
lowest possible ecological 'footprint' from
the production of this book, using super-
efficient machinery, vegetable inks and
high environmental standards. Our printer is
ISO 14001-registered.

The publishers have made every effort to
ensure the accuracy of the information
in this book at the time of going to
press. However, they cannot accept
any responsibility for any loss, injury
or inconvenience resulting from the
use of information contained therein.

ALASTAIR SAWDAY'S
SPECIAL PLACES TO STAY

GREEN
PLACES TO STAY

Contents

Alastair Sawday Publishing

Our main aim is to publish beautiful guidebooks but, for us, the question of who we are and how we inter-react is also important. For who we are shapes the books, the books shape your holidays, and thus are shaped the lives of people who own these 'special places'. So we are trying to be a little more than 'just a publishing company'.

New eco offices

In January 2006 we moved into our new eco offices. By introducing super-insulation, underfloor heating, a wood-pellet boiler, solar panels and a rainwater tank, we have a working environment benign to ourselves and to the environment. Lighting is low-energy, dark corners are lit by sun-pipes and one building is of green oak. Carpet tiles are from Herdwick sheep in the Lake District. We will sail through our environmental audit.

Environmental & ethical policies

We make many other, smaller, gestures: company cars run on gas or recycled cooking oil; kitchen waste is composted and other waste recycled; cycling and car-sharing are encouraged; the company only buys organic or local food; we don't accept web links with companies we consider unethical; we use the ethical Triodos Bank for our deposit account.

We have used recycled paper for some books but have settled on selecting paper and printing for their low energy use. Our printer is British and ISO14001-certified and together we will work to reduce our environmental impact.

In 2005 we won a Business Commitment to the Environment Award and in April 2006 we won a Queen's Award for Enterprise in the Sustainable Development category. All this has boosted our resolve to promote our green policies. Our flagship gesture, however, is carbon offsetting; we calculate our carbon emissions and plant trees to compensate. In future we will support projects overseas that plant trees or reduce carbon use.

Ethics

But why, you may ask, take these things so seriously? You are just a little publishing company, for heaven's sake! Well, is there any good argument for not taking them seriously? The world, by the admission of the vast majority of scientists, is in trouble. If we do not change our ways urgently we will doom the planet and all its creatures – whether innocent or not – to a variety of possible catastrophes. To maintain the status quo is unacceptable. Business does much of the damage and should undo it, and provide new models.

Pressure on companies to produce Corporate Social Responsibility policies is mounting. We are trying to keep ahead of it all, yet still to be as informal and human as possible – the antithesis of 'corporate'.

The books – and a dilemma

So, we have created fine books that do good work. They promote authenticity, individuality and high quality, local and organic food – a far cry from the now-dominant corporate culture. Rural economies, pubs, small farms, villages and hamlets all benefit. However, people use fossil fuel to get there. Should we aim to get our readers to offset their own carbon emissions, and the B&B and hotel owners too? That might have been a hopeless task a year or so ago, but less so now that the media has taken on board the enormity of the work ahead of us all.

We are gradually introducing green ideas into the books: the Fine Breakfast scheme that highlights British and Irish B&B owners who use local and organic food; celebrating those who make an extra effort; gently encouraging the use of public transport, cycling and walking.

Our Fragile Earth series

The 'hard' side of our environmental publishing is the Fragile Earth series:

The Little Earth Book, *The Little Food Book* and *The Little Money Book*. They consist of bite-sized essays, polemical, hard-hitting and well researched. They are a 'must have' for anyone who is confused and needs clarity about some of the key issues of our time.

This year we are also publishing *One Planet Living* and extracts from *The Little Earth Book* under the title *Earth, Air, Fire and Water*.

Lastly – what is special?

The notion of 'special' is at the heart of what we do, and highly subjective. We discuss this in the introduction. We take huge pleasure from finding people and places that do their own thing – brilliantly; places that are unusual and follow no trends; places of peace and beauty; people who are kind and interesting – and genuine.

We seem to have touched a raw nerve with thousands of readers; they obviously want to stay in special places rather than the dull corporate monstrosities that have disfigured so many of our cities and towns. Life is too short to be wasted in the wrong places. A night in a special place can be a transforming experience.

Alastair Sawday

Acknowledgements

This has been a fiendishly difficult book to put together. There are over 50 countries represented here – a monumental inspection task that speaks volumes for Richard's resourcefulness. We owe real gratitude to those many people who did the inspections, sometimes travelling uncomfortably in remote places. It is they who are opening our eyes to the impressively wide range of green initiatives all over the world.

Richard was supported throughout the project by Rachel Fielding, who has had a long career in travel publishing. In many ways this book owes its existence to her, for she gave wings to the idea and then ensured that it all happened. Thank you, Rachel.

We are lucky indeed to have Richard with us, for he has carved a niche for himself in the world of eco-tourism, judging the Responsible Tourism Awards and regularly writing on the subject for the *Guardian*. He has also written for *BBC Wildlife*, *Geographical*, *Resurgence* and *Green Futures*, and has authored several reports on eco-tourism for *Mintel International Publishing* - including *Sustainable Tourism in the Travel Industry*.

Alastair Sawday

Series Editor Alastair Sawday

Editor Richard Hammond

Managing Editor Rachel Fielding

Editorial Director Annie Shillito

Accounts Bridget Bishop, Christine Buxton, Sandra Hasell, Sally Ranahan

Editorial Jackie King, Jo Boissevain, Florence Oldfield, Maria Serrano, Kate Shepherd, Rebecca Stevens, Danielle Williams

Production Julia Richardson, Rachel Coe, Tom Germain, Rebecca Thomas, Allys Williams

Sales & Marketing & PR Siobhán Flynn, Andreea Petre Goncalves, Sarah Bolton

Web & IT Russell Wilkinson, Chris Banks, Joe Green, Brian Kimberling

Photo credits:

Entry 7, Amazon Yarapa River Lodge, Jana Lehmannova

Entry 10, Casa Andina Private Collection Suasi Island, Renato Bottini

Entry 11, Chalalán Ecolodge, Spanowicz/chalalan

Entry 12, Cristalino Jungle Lodge, Marcelo Breyne

Entry 102, Desert Lodge, ©PM-Image.ch

Entry 107, Chumbe Island, ©Peter Lange and ©Guido Cozzi

Entry 120, Phinda Private Game Reserve, ccafrica.com

Entry 150, Nihiwatu, Nihiwatu Resort – Indonesia

Entry 155, Paperbark Camp, Paperbark Camp – Jervis Bay

Entry 160, Awaroa Lodge, Abel Tasman National Park, NZ

We have done our best to acknowledge, where advised, photographers' images that have been given to us courtesy of owners of properties featured in this book, but we apologise if we have inadvertently omitted anyone from the credits.

I recommend you to Alain de Botton's *The Art of Travel*. It is touching, thoughtful, and elegant. One of his observations is: '*My mind and my body were to prove temperamental accomplices in my mission of appreciating my destination.*'
A charming way of putting something that all travellers know. I experienced it this year in the West Indies, where I had gone to revisit St Lucia; there I had met my wife, a fellow VSO, 38 years ago. The 'destination' had, of course, changed; my vision of it had not. I was, at times, depressed and frustrated. Then I met the fishermen with whom I had gone out to sea all those years ago, and was happy. Familiarity had rescued me, or was it the introduction of 'meaning' into the holiday?

This unusual new book encourages many worthwhile people and projects, and adds a dimension that can only add to your pleasure. To stay in a hotel that makes imaginative efforts to reduce its impact on the environment is like meeting an interesting and worthwhile fellow-traveller. Who would choose to swim in an oil-heated pool if there was a solar-heated alternative? To eat imported food if the local food was equally delicious? To stay in a hotel that ill-treated its staff if another, nearby, belonged to the community? Each of those alternatives, when chosen, adds something special to a holiday.

We once spent three months in India, travelling and exploring as travellers do. But our best day by far was with the director of a project among child tannery workers in Chennai. We learned more in that one day than in all the rest – and we loved every moment of it. This book is full of such opportunities. You can now have a terrific holiday while learning more than you thought possible, and while offering genuine support to the sort of people who deserve it.

Tourism must change. This book is now poised to do its bit. Your 'bit' is to find clever ways of getting to these places with the minimum use of air-travel, and to spend 'high-quality' time there rather than plan another quick trip! Go slow.

Alastair Sawday

Editor's acknowledgements

I would particularly like to thank Rachel Fielding for believing in this book from the start and for her help and advice throughout; Roger Diski and Judith de Witt of Rainbow Tours, for their suggestions for properties and for facilitating the inspection trip to the Seychelles; Amanda Marks, Tribes Travel, for her suggestions for properties and for facilitating the inspection trip to Jordan; Sinikka Ruotsalainen, Finnmark Tourism for facilitating the inspection trip to northern Norway; Dr Jonathan Keeling, BBC Natural History Unit, for his help in inviting colleagues to help with inspections; and Susie and Sam Pickering for their help in organising inspections in Australia.

I would also like to thank the following for their help: Alice Crabtree; Chris McIntyre; Christabelle Dilks; Deirdre Shurland, Director of the Caribbean Alliance for Sustainable Tourism; Edward Paine, Latin America Travel Association; Freya Pratt, Georgina Hancock, Discover the World; Harold Goodwin, International Centre for Responsible Tourism; Julie Middleton, Trips Worldwide; Laura Ell, formerly of The International Ecotourism Society; Michael Cullen and Nikki Tinto of i-escape.com; Rachel Dodds; Ronald Sanabria, Rainforest Alliance; Sarah Yearsley; Sofia de Meyer, Whitepod; and all the many inspectors and writers who have contributed to this book.

Inspections David Ashby, Ed Barnard, Claire Boobbyer, Renato Bottitini, Hannah Bullock, Jon Clarke, Jeanne Clenet, Shem Compion, Tina Cullen, Christabelle Dilks, Zoe Duby, Tim Ecott, Kirsten Gaymer, Jocelyn Gohary, Norm Goldman, Richard Hammond, Lorna Howarth, April Hutchison, Peter Hutchison, Jonny Keeling, Anabel Kindersley, Jane Koutnik, Jo Lane, James Lott, Andrew Marshall, Alison McGregor, Nadine Mellor, Piers Moore Ede, Jo Morton, Susie & Sam Pickering, Goyotsetseg Radnaabazar, Yasmin Razak, Alastair Sawday, Kate Shepherd, Joe Stevens, Lucy Tilney, Nikki Tinto, Geordie Torr, Rosie Walford, Heather Ward, Paul Woodman.

Writing David Atkinson, Judy Bastyra, Jo Boissevain, Vivien Cripps, Michael Cullen, Tory Dean, Stephanie Debere, Rachel Fielding, Nick Garbutt, Lydia Gard, Audrey Gillan, Lisa Grainger, Richard Hammond, Cathy Harlow, Steve Hartridge, Will Hide, Matthew Hilton-Dennis, Heather Holt, Jackie King, Robert & Daisy Kunstaetter, Nick Maes, Julian Matthews, Chris McIntyre, Jennifer Newton, Peter Nunn, Helen Pickles, Freya Pratt, Alex Robinson, Yolanda Rojal, Bram Rossman, Alastair Sawday, Kate Shepherd, Vicki Sleet, Francesca Syz, Cath Urquhart, Russell Wilkinson, Travis Winkler.

Richard Hammond

FROM YURT CAMPS IN THE ARDÈCHE TO COMMUNITY-RUN ECO LODGES IN BOLIVIA...

My first green adventure was in space. I was in a futuristic building in Ottawa, in a surround cinema where I was given an insight into what it is like to be transported into orbit with a group of NASA astronauts two hundred miles above the Earth's surface. As I acclimatised vicariously to zero gravity, the camera suddenly zoomed in on the Earth, through the upper atmosphere, through the clouds and rain, to the sweaty Amazon jungle then to plains of the Serengeti grasslands and other areas of incredible beauty before whizzing back to outer space. The film had a strong environmental message; the orbital perspective revealed the beauty of the Earth but also its fragility. I didn't know it at the time but it was a foretaste of what it would be like working on this book, which has taken me from the majestic Alps to eastern Canada, from the alternative Caribbean to the heavenly Seychelles. I have been lucky enough to have been welcomed into Berber homes in the Atlas Mountains, guided by Rastas through the rainforest in Dominica and to meet the largest giant tortoise on the planet. Space tourism might be the next big thing, but I don't think I'll be following anyone into the shuttle;

Photo Crescent Moon Cabins, entry 30

there's more than enough to hold my fascination here on mother earth.

One of my first inspections was in a very ancient and spectacular wilderness region of the Middle East. Feynan Eco Lodge lies at the foot of Wadi Dana amid the arid mountains of the southern Rift valley in Jordan. The Bedouin help run the lodge within the Dana Nature Reserve under the direction of Jordan's Royal Society for the Conservation of Nature (RSCN). The lodge is environmentally friendly, provides a source of income for the Bedouin and helps fund conservation of the reserve. It's an enlightened approach that is indicative of the range of places and inspirational people featured in this book, people who are leading the way in developing a better kind of tourism.

It is tempting to say that the interest in green travel is following hot on the heels of a renaissance in ethical consumerism. Fairtrade coffee has hit the high street, organic food is everywhere, and solar panels are fast becoming fashionable. Going on an environmentally friendly holiday used to mean pulling on your socks and sandals and heading for the nearest dry stone wall in Devon. Or for those with aspirations abroad, joining a band of well-meaning ecotourists and setting off – armed with the mantra *Take only photographs, leave only footprints* – to relatively remote places in the spirit of conservation. I've been on several conservation holidays – including mapping the beautiful coral reefs of Belize and monitoring bird nesting sites on an island off

Mauritius – and I can vouch for how enjoyable these types of holidays are and the excellent work they achieve. But times have moved on. Today being a green traveller is not just limited to conservation holidays, it has a wider remit – influencing the way we take city breaks to the way we spend our summer holidays. Conservation still has a crucial part to play, but going green is also about going easier on the environment and making sure your holiday somehow benefits the people that live in the destination, be they Berbers or Bedouin, Maasai or Maori. For it is just as possible to go green on a short break, to Andalucia for example, as on a three-week adventure to Bolivia, or on a trip to the Barrier Reef to tag turtles.

This is progress the planet can ill afford to resist. We've all seen favourite places ruined by the ravages of an unrelenting tourism industry – the white, sandy beach that has become overcrowded with package tourists; the remote mountain village that has become a backpackers' mecca; the quiet stretch of coastline that is now dominated with over-sized hotels all competing for the best view. As travel and tourism grow, the pressures on the environment and local communities, on a planet that is already stressed, are becoming more acute. Worldwide there are

Photo above Can Marti Agroturism, entry 86
Photo right Paperbark Camp, entry 155

some 700 million tourist trips each year, a figure which is set to reach one billion in the next decade as more people in the developing world – particularly from India and China – begin to travel. It's a sobering thought given the following:

• At the turn of the 20th Century the world population was just over one billion. In 1999 it hit six billion, and it is predicted to reach seven billion in 2012.
• Water use has been growing at more than twice the rate of the population increase during the last century. One billion people lack access to safe drinking water, 2.4 billion to adequate sanitation. By 2025, the United Nations predicts 1.8 billion people will live in countries or regions that will have an "absolute water scarcity" and two thirds of the world population could be under "water stress conditions".
• Over the last hundred years, the average global temperature has increased by about 1°C – a greater increase than in any other century in the last thousand years, the 1990s was the warmest decade on record, and 2002, 2003 and 2005 have been the hottest years ever.

The problems facing the planet are formidable, yet tourism can provide opportunities that can help make the world a little better. The industry is, after all, one of the largest in the world; 200 million people are employed in travel and tourism worldwide and the industry turns over US $7 trillion a year. In a world where two billion people earn less than £2 a day, tourism can play a significant part in poverty alleviation. The essential element of what sells a holiday is often related to its natural and cultural resources – something even the poorest countries have in abundance – the Masai Mara, the majestic Himalayas, wildlife-rich Madagascar, the marine life off Mozambique, the gorillas of Rwanda. For some developing countries, tourism may be the only or best export opportunity available.

Tourism can also help protect valuable natural and cultural sites. UNESCO's World Heritage List contains over 800 places; magnets for millions of tourists whose money helps contribute to their wellbeing. Elsewhere, vast areas of wilderness are now protected as parks or reserves, many of which are largely supported by tourism revenues.

There are a hundred other more prosaic reasons why travel is a positive thing: let's not forget the reason why we go on holiday – for fun! It's important we take time out to relax and recharge. Travel can broaden the mind, provide inspiration to millions of young globetrotters, (paradoxically) help one understand one's own culture, and it can be invaluable in promoting the understanding and appreciation of other cultures.

Yet the rise of green travel is borne not just out of the positives, but also from a desire to minimize the negatives. To the casual eye of the holidaymaker it can be difficult to see the full impact of the holiday on the destination, but insensitively managed tourism can cause environmental degradation: hotels built without proper sewage treatment, rubbish dumped in fragile areas and the diversion of scarce resources upon which local communities depend, such as local water supplies redirected to supply golf courses and hotel swimming pools. Frequently we see areas of great natural beauty displaced to make way for rampant mass tourism development.

Going Green

Twenty years ago a book such as this could scarcely have been possible, but there has been such a huge shift in awareness of environmental and social issues that green places to stay are popping up all over the world, from yurt camps in the Ardèche to community-run eco lodges in Bolivia, safari camps in East Africa to mountain lodges in Eastern Canada. And it is not just confined to holidays abroad; the Green Tourism Business Scheme (www.green-business.co.uk) is a certification scheme that recognises tourism-related businesses in the UK, such as hotels, travel companies and conference venues that are helping to improve the environment. It recently certified its 500th member.

Broadly speaking, the following three key considerations underpin a greener approach:

Environment and Conservation
Reduction of the impact of your stay on the environment – through minimizing the use of energy, reducing waste and pollution, and contributing to the conservation of biodiversity.

Culture
Respect of local cultures, contribution to the conservation of cultural heritage and traditional values, and promotion of cultural understanding.

Economic
Provision for long-term economic benefits to local people, through stable employment, local empowerment, and alleviating poverty. The idea is that tourism should be based upon the principles of fair trade.

Make a positive difference

The Travel Foundation is a charity that cares for the places we all love to visit.

By following this simple advice – wherever you are in the world – you can help make a positive difference to the lives of the people and places you visit. And help keep destinations special – for generations to enjoy!

Before you go:
Recycle your holiday brochures when you've finished with them, or pass them to a friend.

Remove any packaging from clothing, toiletries etc before you pack and recycle if possible.

Consider compensating for the environmental impact of your flight. Ask your airline if they are part of any 'carbon-offset' scheme or see www.climatecare.org.uk, www.futureforests.com or www.foc-uk.com for details.

On your holiday:
Please don't have your photograph taken with any 'wild' animals (such as lion and tiger cubs, monkeys, bears snakes and exotic birds).

Coral is extremely fragile and takes decades to grow. Don't step on or remove any coral when swimming or diving and avoid kicking up sand as it can suffocate and kill coral polyps.

Displaying expensive jewellery or cameras, particularly in very poor communities, may distance you from the culture you've come to experience.

Child sex tourism is a criminal offence in all destinations. To report an incident, contact Crimestoppers - if overseas +44 800 555 111 or 0800 555 111 in the UK (freephone). Or contact ECPAT UK (End Child Prostitution, Pornography and Trafficking) - www.ecpat.org - +44 207 501 8927.

Minimise waste by reusing plastic bags, bringing your own water filter bottle or purifier and taking your used batteries home with you.

Exploring the area:
Guidebooks are a useful source of information, but get 'insider' knowledge as well, by talking to local people and getting off the beaten track!
Use local guides and taxis when you need help getting about. This helps to support the local economy.

Hire a car only when you really need to. Use alternatives such as public transport, bicycles and walking - a great way to meet local people too.

Ask permission before taking photographs of people or their homes and don't be offended if they decline or expect to be paid for the privilege.

Please don't pick flowers and plants or collect pebbles and seashells.

Please think twice before taking part in any 'swim with dolphin' experience. There can be risks to both dolphins and people (including dolphins being injured by swimmers' jewellery or suffering infections caused by sun tan lotion).

Shopping:
Buy locally made products and shop, eat and drink in locally owned outlets during your visit. This can give enormous benefit to local people.

Always bargain with humour and bear in mind that a small cash saving to you could be a significant amount of money to the seller.

Please don't buy products made from endangered plants or wild animals, including hardwoods, corals, shells, starfish, ivory, fur, skins, teeth, reptiles and turtles. For more information on endangered species and the WWF-UK Souvenir Alert Campaign visit www.wwf-uk.org.

At your accommodation:
Turn down/off heating or air conditioning when not required. Switch off lights when leaving a room and turn the TV off rather than leaving it on standby.

Take quick showers instead of baths and inform staff if you are happy to re-use towels and bed linen rather than having them replaced daily.

Unfortunately the term 'eco' or 'green' has also been abused by some unscrupulous travel companies looking to make a fast buck out of using the label purely for marketing purposes. It can sometimes be hard to tell which hotel or travel company is telling the truth about its eco credentials and which is merely using the term as 'greenwashing'. We hope this book helps. All of the properties we feature have been visited and we are confident that they do represent a better kind of travel (see p.26 'what makes a place green').

If you're unsure whether your hotel or travel company is green, see p.36 for questions you can ask. Choosing a green place to stay is the first step in choosing a more responsible way to travel. There are also things we can all do on holiday to help support local communities – while our holidays might seem insignificant compared to the enormity of the global travel and tourism industry, a single trip can make a difference to someone's life... the mountain guide, the village market seller, the local community group that receives a share of the income from your visit. By buying locally – fruit and vegetables from local markets, drinks and souvenirs from locally owned outlets – you help share the tourism pound around. For more tips on how to be a more responsible traveller, see pp.16-17.

Flying and Climate Change

Green travellers that fly are hypocrites – the lot of them!
Flying to far-flung countries to stay in green places can bring great benefits to the destination, but can this be squared with the contribution the flight makes to climate change? Air travel is a significant part of our ecological footprint: by taking one return flight to New York, you'll be emitting as much carbon dioxide as you would by driving an average car for one year. And one flight to Australia will use up as much as all the energy to heat and power your home for up to six years. Consider this in the worldwide context: each year there are approximately 1.8 billion air passenger trips. The United Nation's Intergovernmental Panel on Climate Change says that aviation's contribution to climate change is currently about 3.5 per cent, which could rise to 15 per cent by the year 2050 if the growth of aviation continues unchecked. Many people have benefited from access to cheaper short-haul flights to Europe and long-haul flights to Africa, Asia and South America, but at what cost to the planet?

It's a thorny issue and not one easily resolved if you want to continue to see the world. We believe travelling more responsibly is a balancing act. This book provides examples of green

Public Transport

Just to give you an idea of how much you could save if you go by train rather than by plane, compare the two forms of transport in the table below.

CO2 emissions per passenger...

Journey	by air	by train
London-Edinburgh	3.5 hours 193 Kg/CO2	4.5 hours, 24 Kg/CO2
London-Nice	4 hours 250 Kg/CO2	8 hours by Eurostar+TGV 36 Kg/CO2
London-Barcelona	4.5 hours 277 Kg/CO2	Eurostar then overnight sleeper 40 Kg/CO2
London-Tangier	5 hours 435 Kg/CO2	48 hours by Eurostar, sleeper trains & ferry 63 Kg/CO2

Source: *The Observer*, 29 January 2006. See also www.seat61.com.
Times are centre-to-centre, each way. Kg/CO2 is for a return journey.

places to stay that are better for the environment and local communities at the destination. But choosing a green place alone does not necessarily mean that your holiday is 100% environmentally friendly, especially if you are considering flying to the destination.

Travelling by public transport is not only more environmentally friendly it can also give you much more of a feel for the country than if you speed in by airplane. En route to the Kasbah du Toubkal (entry 99), I took the ferry from Algeciras to Tangiers and then the train to Marrakech. Of course it took a lot longer than flying directly there, but arriving from Spain in to Africa by boat is a memorable

experience. And on the wonderful train journey down to Marrakech it wasn't hard to chat with locals and catch glimpses of Moroccan life – Berber farmers toiling in the fields or children playing in the sun; it gave me the feeling that I had experienced a little bit of the country before arriving at my destination.

Many countries have high speed rail links between cities as well as slower, regional lines that get to the more inaccessible places. Look out too for national coach companies, they are often a cheaper alternative to rail and can be surprising comfortable. Where possible we have included in the entries directions from the nearest train station and bus station. Also, at the back of the book, we have included a list of national rail and bus organisations to help you plan your trip. There is a great web site run by Mark Smith, known as The Man in Seat Sixty-One (www.seat61.com). It's an excellent resource for details on train travel on the continent. Did you know that in the summer there is a direct service from Waterloo to the Ardèche in the south of France? That from Paris every night there is a train to Madrid and Barcelona? Or that you can take a ski train to the Alps in winter? I also like his top tip: "never travel without a good book and a corkscrew"!

Carbon Offsetting

If you do fly then think about offsetting your carbon emissions. There are many organisations that help you calculate how much carbon is produced as a result of your flight and which suggest a financial contribution you can make, which they will then invest in green projects on your behalf to 'offset' this. A list of certified carbon offset organisations is provided by The Gold Standard carbon credit scheme, which is owned by a network of NGOs that are committed to implementing emissions reductions (see p.262).

Some say offsetting is a 'comfort blanket', which merely makes people feel better about the pollution their flights cause. If you're sceptical, do take a look at the policies of some of the companies that provide carbon offsets – it isn't all about planting trees! Climate Care for instance, uses the money to fund projects that provide efficient cooking stoves in Honduras and install energy-efficient light bulbs in Kazakhstan. As well as making savings in greenhouse gases, the projects also have wider benefits to the local communities and environment. With Climate Care, a return flight to Morocco, for example, will cost you just £5 to offset, whereas a return flight to South Africa would cost you £19.66.

Though carbon offsetting can be a useful tool, it doesn't offer a complete solution to the problems of flying. The bottom line is really that we should all be trying to reduce carbon emissions directly, by flying less and making other significant changes to our lifestyles to decrease our individual carbon output, and not just polluting the atmosphere and paying to offset our actions or consciences thereafter.

Tour Operators

Some tour operators are much more proactive in green issues than others. We have included a selection of operators you might use at the back of this book. The more enlightened ones have a policy or 'code of conduct' that outlines how they promote conservation of the environment and the cultural heritage of the areas they visit. Tribes Travel, for instance, promotes a series of Responsible Tourism itineraries: some are trips that have been set up with local communities who need the income from tourism to help sustain their traditional way of life; others involve particular local suppliers who use their profits benevolently to help build services such as local schools, health centres and water supplies. At Kahawa Shamba ('Coffee Farm' in Swahili; entry 106) in the beautiful foothills of Kilimanjaro, on a ridge overlooking the Weruweru Gorge, Tribes worked with Cafédirect, the charity Twin and the British government's Department for International Development to set up this community-based tourism project to help bring in extra income to the small-scale coffee farmers in the area.

There is no Fairtrade label for tourism, though projects such as that at Kahawa Shamba come close to it. It is possible though to find travel and tourism companies that have been eco-certified. There is no one global accreditation scheme for green or fair trade tourism, but there are individual schemes – at either the national or regional level – that recognise travel companies and projects that operate more responsibly. The campaigning charity Tourism Concern is working to produce a fair trade in tourism label – see p.22-23 for more details.

There are also a number of awards for ethical or sustainable tourism. The winners are often profiled in the national press travel pages, which provide a good source of information on the latest responsible holidays. Nihiwatu (entry 150), won the First Choice Responsible Tourism Award 'Best Hotel' category, for the work it has done to reduce poverty on the island of Sumba, in Indonesia. Since 2001, guests have donated over US$450k to projects through its Sumba Foundation, which has provided 22 water stations that produce clean water for 4,500 villagers.

Other organisations, such as The World Wildlife Fund for Nature and Friends of the Earth don't necessarily focus on green travel, but they are involved in some way with greener and more responsible living. Given the enormity of issues such as climate change and world poverty, the decisions we make about how we travel have to be integrated into a more responsible lifestyle, and so we recommend these organisations as sources for more information on these and other relevant topics.

When we take a holiday, it's not a simple activity that we're buying in to, but a lifestyle experience. We choose our holidays with great care. Where we go to, where we stay, what excursions we take, what clothes to take with us, what guide books to read. We're beginning to think how best to travel. Whether to offset and how best to do that is something we're also increasingly considering. Happily the idea that we might question whether our holiday will benefit local people and how best to handle tricky issues like bargaining so that we pay a fair price is also affecting our behaviour. But how many of us would buy into a fair trade holiday?

What is Fair Trade?

The Fair Trade Movement in Europe and in the UK has created a Fairtrade Label and ethical trading initiatives, which are designed to provide producers in developing countries with a fair share of the returns from the sale of their products. It is based on the principle that the terms of trade between industrialised and developing countries have historically created an inherent inequality and disadvantage for developing countries. This is due to higher costs being attached to products and services from industrialised countries while the prices that developing countries gain for their exported commodities are constantly low and even falling. The control over this system lies primarily in the hands of the seven richest countries in the world and is underpinned by international trade agreements.

Why Fair Trade in Tourism?

Tourism in developing countries is growing. From the package tour destinations in Southern Europe, such as Spain and Greece, long-haul package holidays from the UK are now extending to Africa, Asia and Latin America, with a strong emphasis on all-inclusive holidays, run by transnational tourism corporations. Existing historic inequalities in the terms of trade are now in danger of being re-enforced due to the fact that many of the developing countries have little or no tourism infrastructure or tourism expertise, and that poverty is a dominant factor in most of the tourism destinations in the South. This can mean that most of the profits from tourism flow back to the industrialised nations, and the people in destinations, who offer their natural, social and cultural resources to make the 'tourism product' successful, receive either an unfairly low return or suffer from a deterioration of their livelihood as a result of negative environmental, social and cultural effects from the tourism activity.

Fair Trade in Tourism aims to maximise the benefits from tourism for local people, ensuring that they are paid fair wages, given fair working conditions and there is a fair distribution of the income from tourism. It also supports the right of indigenous host communities, whether involved in tourism or not, to participate as equal 'stakeholders' and beneficiaries in the tourism development process.

In recent years there has been a huge transformation in national consciousness about fair trade and its ethical impacts on local producers. The UK now buys more fair trade goods than any other country. We have taken on the message that buying fair trade goods enables us as individuals to tackle international poverty. The Fairtrade Foundation tells us that worldwide sales of Fairtrade products rose by a third in the past year and that sales in the UK reached £200 million in 2005. This is a 40 percent rise in one year.

This extraordinary growth in sales indicates an increased demand from consumers for a much fairer and sustainable model of trade than the accepted norm. When we buy our Fairtrade bananas, we now have an understanding about how the purchase helps bring development to poor communities. We have learned to trust the label.

The same could be true for tourism and our holidays. Fair trade tourism would offer an alternative approach to conventional tourism, primarily because it will be a trading partnership focused on sustainable development for disadvantaged people working in tourism.

This is an extraordinary challenge to all of us. Everybody involved in our holidays, you, the customer, the tour operator and those providing our holidays in destinations that can, together, provide a far better opportunity for tourism to be fair to everyone.

Tricia Barnett
Director, Tourism Concern

Introduction

The notion of 'special' is of course subjective – and so is the portfolio of places in this book. As well as environmental and social responsibility (pp 26-34), there are few other hard and fast criteria for the kind of places we have chosen. We look for a place where you can sleep and relax in comfort, a setting which invites you to explore gorgeous coastlines or mountains, owners who fill you with joie de vivre (and good local, organic food). So you'll find a range of places (pp 39-40) – camps, beach huts, guesthouses, homestays, working farms, safari camps, romantic island hideaways and a few luxury hotels.

Many of the camps or buildings are special structures in themselves – yurts hidden away in the tranquil Andalucian countryside, white domed 'pods' high up in the Swiss Alps, remote igloo-shaped tents in the mountains of Patagonia, a tiny eco-cabin in Shropshire, recycled condominiums in the US Virgin Islands, high-tech adobe cabanas in Mexico.

In other cases, the trump card is its setting – a Ger camp in Mongolia's Gobi desert, a hotel near Lake Titicaca in Peru, a lodge in Jordan's ancient desert, a tropical hideaway in the Andaman Islands, even an organic retreat far from the madding crowd in Ibiza. But this alone is not enough, and those places which simply rest on their prime-location laurels don't make our grade.

Many of the places are off the beaten track. And while the more remote ones may take more than a full day to reach, we believe that travel is not just about arriving, but also about enjoying the journey. Slow tourism, if you like.

A few places are special because of an activity they offer – a boat trip with Ecoventura in the stunning Galapagos Islands, treks through the Peruvian rainforest from Yarapa River Lodge (entry 7), visits to a traditional Amerindian village at Surama (entry 5) in the Guyana rainforest, low-impact sports at Nipika (entry 56) in the Canadian Rockies, horse-riding across virgin landscape in Argentina at Huechahue (entry 20). Again this must be backed up by good organisation, and the knowledge that you've got a lovely home to come back to afterwards.

Photo Canvaschic, entry 87

Interior décor is also important. For us, 'special' means done with love, attention to detail, and respect for the bones of the place. Natural materials – stone walls, wooden or brass beds, canvas deck chairs – get the thumbs up; MDF cabinets and plastic garden chairs hurt our eyes. Simple, locally crafted pieces beat fancy imported stuff; aboriginal art says volumes more than the ubiquitous poster of Ayer's Rock.

Facilities come second to style. We'd swap a minibar filled with crisps and chocolate for a bowl of local fruit or olives. We'd prefer a single, refillable bottle of biodegradable shower gel to a basketful of toiletries which get half used and then thrown away. A varied, fresh and filling breakfast is better than an ill-equipped kitchenette. Give us homespun blankets, a good mattress, fluffy towels, candle-lit dinners and gorgeous views any day.

But the most crucial factor for what makes a place 'special' – which underscores all the others – is that the owners care about their place, about their staff, about their guests and about the environment. A little time and interest – How was your journey? Did you sleep well? What are your plans for today? – can go a long way. A broken light bulb or missing blanket are not a problem if they are rectified quickly and with a smile. Small touches, like a special local dish for breakfast, a hand-drawn sketch-map or a phone call to help you find out about public transport, can transform your stay. And this extends to the surroundings. We expect staff to be able – indeed to want – to tell you all about their region, to recommend the best places to eat, visit, swim or hike.

Many of those selected are owner-, family- or community-run. Where outside staff are employed, we expect to see the owners imparting a sense of pride and belonging to their colleagues. We observe how owners treat other guests as well as their staff, and how they respond to our suggestions. The best places are always keen to improve. Most are small enough to make you feel like a house guest, not a number.

The community-run places in this book extend a particularly warm and friendly welcome – the indomitable Lena Florry at Damaraland (entry 114) in Namibia, the Berber smiles at the Kasbah du Toubkal (entry 99) in Morocco, the herders' sharing tales of encounters with snow leopards at Himalayan Homestays (entry 131), and the legendary (if a little quirky!) hospitality of the Bedouin at Feynan Eco-Lodge (entry 122) in Jordan.

Introduction

But as with all travel, along the way you may also meet quick-buck greed and laissez-faire shoulder-shrugging – though we hope, not in the places we've chosen. What you won't find in this book are places which neglect the local touch or ride cheaply on the green wave.

What Makes a Place Green?

We have selected places based on our opinion of how special they are and whether they go the extra mile to minimize their impact on the environment, contribute to conservation and benefit local communities.

Location, location...

First impressions count. Situation, architecture and construction are important to us, technically and aesthetically. We like places that complement the scenery rather than stick out as eye sores; we prefer buildings that use local materials in tune with the surroundings, that minimize noise and harsh lights, and are designed to complement the natural vegetation. We love the new Chic-Chocs Mountain Lodge in Quebec, Canada (entry 58) for the way it perches discreetly on the side of a mountain within the Matane Wildlife Reserve, rather than lording over it.

Energy, Water and Waste

An impressive commitment is shown by owners to energy conservation by limiting their use of water and reducing waste. Some have worked it out as they've gone along through trial and error – some methods are improvised (and just about work!), others are ingenious. Many owners have bought clever gadgets and expensive equipment while others have decided instead to invest in long-term energy saving techniques. In all cases, being 'green' goes much further than just using use low-energy light-bulbs.

Jill at Trelowarren (entry 68) in Cornwall has installed a huge woodchip Bison boiler, which she estimates will generate 300kW of heat from 350 tonnes of wood produced by coppicing the forests on her estate: not only will it significantly reduce the cost of heating the whole development using fossil fuels, but it will also bring back the sustainable economic use of her woodland. She says it costs £45 per tonne to cut and chip the wood for use in the boiler, giving an output figure of 1.2p kW/hr compared to 2.8p kW/hr for an oil-fired boiler. She expects her 600-acre estate will be carbon neutral in two years.

Of course not all owners have the resources to build and operate large-scale woodchip boilers, but use of other alternative energies,

such as solar panels and wind generators, are fast becoming economically viable and many owners have substantially reduced, in some cases eliminated, their reliance on fossil fuels. In certain instances using alternative energy isn't practical, so owners have instead bought their energy from suppliers that have themselves channelled power from alternative energy sources. Our offices have super-insulation, solar panels and a wood-pellet boiler but we still need energy to run our computers so we buy extra electricity from Good

Energy (www.good-energy.co.uk). We are particularly impressed with owners who measure their achievements and try to improve their environmental performance each year. Limiting the use of water is something that is relatively easy

to measure over time. Some of the water-saving devices we have come across include low-flow or dual-flush toilets, low-flow showerheads, optional towel and linen cleaning programmes and the use of rainwater for cleaning and gardening. Polite notices asking you to minimise water use while showering do not upset us at all – quite the contrary. And sometimes the crudest methods are surprisingly effective – Gloria at Toadhall Bed and Breakfast in Canada (entry 57) puts a brick in her water tank, which she estimates saves her 1,500 litres of water a year. She has also imposed a minimum stay of two nights on environmental grounds – so that she doesn't have to wash linen for guests who only stay for one night.

Swimming pools are fun but they're often an indulgence; they use large amounts of water, require huge amounts of energy to heat and are often chemically treated to ensure they meet health and safety requirements. We prefer natural swimming pools, the sort pioneered in Austria and increasingly popular in Italy, Switzerland, and Germany. A wall below the surface divides the pool into two zones – one for swimming and the other for marsh plants and sand, which act as a natural filter for cleaning the water and prevent algal growth.

Air-conditioning

We make no bones about our dislike! We prefer places that allow for natural ventilation, such as Zandoli Inn in Dominica (entry 29) where the clever design of the building lets sea breezes from the Caribbean waft in to the light and airy rooms. We do however realise that some travellers rely on air-conditioning so we have marked (through gritted teeth!), the ⼈ symbol for those places that provide it. The Orchid Hotel in Mumbai, India (entry 135) has an innovative device for limiting the amount of air-conditioning used. Press the 'green button' on the master control panel in the room and you'll increase the thermostat of the air conditioner by two degrees. Savings in electricity are calculated, and you're issued with a certificate that shows you how your voluntarily participation has conserved energy.

Waste management is not the prettiest subject, but is one of the most important environmental issues faced by owners. For guests, out of sight is out of mind, but the effect of poor waste management can have enormous consequences for human health and pollution, especially on marine environments. There are many effective methods of treating waste in a more environmentally friendly manner: composting toilets, natural wastewater treatments that use vegetation to break down wastes,

aerated filters, biological contactors, ultraviolet disinfection, ionisation (which uses an electrical current to kill off harmful organisms), sand filtration, and reverse osmosis (a form of filtration that purifies wastewater without using chemicals). We haven't provided a listing in the quick references at the back of this book for those places that manage their waste well (most do), but if you would like to be pointed in the right direction for a good composting toilet, we recommend Black Sheep Inn in Ecuador (entry 1), Ongajok Mountain Farm in Norway (entry 61) and Chumbe Island in Zanzibar (entry 107) . You may be surprised to find how clean they are; modern composting toilets are as comfortable as a standard toilet, they smell far less and use little or no water. And if you really want to go back to basics, try the long drop at Himalayan Homestays (entry 131); pure class!

Reduce, Re-use, Recycle is the mantra that underpins many of the places in this book. Clearly labelled recycling bins in rooms are often provided for paper, tin, glass, plastic, while some of our owners go to extraordinary lengths to re-use and re-cycle glass, cans, clothes... anything they can. One of our favourite places is Crescent Moon Cabins in Dominica (entry 30) – almost everything is made from recycled parts, even the coffee roaster is made from an old car windscreen motor.

Many environmental features employed by owners are not immediately obvious to guests, or are informal, sometimes understated, yet hint at the owner's genuine commitment to the environment. We were intrigued to find the wide sandy path at Awaroa Lodge in New Zealand (entry 160) was actually made out of ground bottles, and we were charmed by the welcome pack at Pacuare Lodge in Costa Rica (entry 48), which includes a biography of local guides and staff. We love finding those light green touches that speak volumes – a collection pot for used batteries for recycling, biodegradable soap in the shower, hand-held solar lanterns to help you find your way back to your room.

Many owners encourage guests to use public transport and car-sharing, perhaps for transfers to the train station or airport. Vanessa and Les at Strattons in Norfolk, England (entry 71) offer a 10% reduction to anybody who arrives by the sole use of public transport. Places that lend or hire bikes are marked with the 🚲 symbol.

Some owners have formalised their commitment in the shape of an environmental policy – O'Reilly's Rainforest Retreat in Queensland (entry 151), Australia publishes a 35-page Environmental Management Plan, which sets out a clear agenda for "preserving the unique natural environment surrounding us, so that friends, family and guests may enjoy it, as we do, now and into the future". The Orchid Hotel (entry 135) produces 40-page guide that shows how it is "setting a new standard of environmental responsibility by conserving natural resources; educating, enlightening and motivating our staff; and cultivating community relationships."

We look to see if owners provide guests with information about local history and culture. Every place has its own story to tell and we love reading and hearing about how a place has grown, spiritually as well as physically. Anne Jno Baptiste at Papillote Wilderness Retreat (entry 28) has a remarkable story to tell: she and her husband rescued the Roseau valley following the devastation caused by Hurricane David in 1979 and the delightful nooks and crannies of her fabulous retreat are a charming legacy of their work.

We also like to see owners show you how you can help do your bit for the environment and help with their efforts to limit the use of energy and water. Some provide guided tours or informal presentations over a glass of wine, others pin a polite notice on the back of the door urging you to switch off the lights when you leave the room, or to hang up only those sheets and towels that you want washing. And we like to know how guests can learn about the local environment and wildlife. How frustrating it can be to arrive in the most beautiful spot, but not know a thing about it! The best interpretation techniques are those that show you how to get the most of the activities and surroundings. Long lists of plant names and wildlife turn us off, we prefer hints on how you can find that elusive hornbill, a voice of experience that predicts where the game will be that day, a wink and a nudge on where to find an overgrown track that leads to a little-used beach, or a practical tip for where is the best place to swim on an incoming tide.

Conservation

Many of the places we have selected are near to protected areas and owners actively help in conserving wildlife and the environment. Bird Island in the Seychelles (entry 125) has provided the nesting ground for over 1 million sooty terns, Ionian Eco Villagers on the island of Zakynthos in Greece (entry 95) has preserved one of the last nesting sites of the loggerhead sea turtle, and Damaraland in Namibia (entry 114) has ensured the survival of one of the country's first wildlife conservancies. By staying in these and other places in the book, you will be helping with their conservation work.

Social Responsibility

We have not selected a place solely on its commitment to the environment, for what makes a place green is also a strong connection with local culture and communities, especially in areas of great poverty. We like to know whether places are owned or managed by local people, whether local staff are involved in the running of the place, if there is a policy for training them, and whether the property increases the economic benefit of tourism to the local community. If the owner organises activities or trips to the local area, we ask if they employ local guides rather than expatriates or people shipped in from elsewhere. Jungle Bay Resort and Spa in Dominica (entry 27) employs a local electrician part-time as a handy man and part-time as a nature guide.

In many of our places owners employ mainly local staff, buy food from local suppliers, and encourage guests to take part in locally organised cultural activities. Forced after-dinner 'traditional' dances make us feel uncomfortable, we prefer sitting round a fire hearing tales of encounters with snow leopard or lion. At Amazon Yarapa River Lodge in Peru (entry 7) you are encouraged to trade crafts with locals rather than pay cash for goods, at Robin Pope Safaris Nkwali Camp in Zambia (entry 108) you are given the opportunity to swap a night at the comfortable safari camp for a night in a mud hut at nearby Kawaza village, where many camp staff come from. Don't miss these opportunities, for they can stay long in the memory.

We are delighted to include a number of community-based enterprises. At Chalalán Ecolodge in Bolivia (entry 11), the indigenous Quechua-Tacana community manages the lodge, and at Kapawi Ecolodge & Reserve in Ecuador (entry 2), the indigenous Achuar people run the lodge in partnership with a private tour operator. In 2011, the reserve is due to be handed over to the Achuar people. This kind of community-based tourism makes a real difference to the lives of local people – at Himalayan Homestays guests are invited to stay on a rotational basis so that income is shared around, and at Shiwa Ng'andu Manor House in Zambia (entry 110), a country crippled by poverty, 100% of the 80 staff are local indigenous people, many of whom are unskilled general workers,

who help with all the game walks, accompany horse rides and take guests on hill walks.

Agritourism

We have also selected a few places where farmers have diversified into tourism – popular across Europe, particularly in Italy, and a growing movement in other continents. We love Casa del Grivò in Italy (entry 89) where Toni and Paola produce their own organic Tocai, Verduzzo and Refosco wine. Estancia y Bodega Colomé in Argentina (entry 15) produces the world's highest altitude wine – reason enough to visit!

We set great store by places that grow their own food, preferably organically. Crescent Moon (entry 30) is a model of self-sufficiency and provides all its own food – fruits and herbs from the garden, vegetables from a huge greenhouse "minimizing the time between plant and plate", and has its own chickens and goats (the cleanest looking goats we've seen!). Many of our green places source their fresh food locally, from friends, village markets, local fishermen, and so bring economic benefit to local communities.

Luxury

We do think it is possible for a place to be green and luxurious, though we've only been convinced of it at a few places. Frégate Island in the

Seychelles (entry 127) is extraordinary - you may encounter rich Russian oligarchs speeding around in electric-powered buggies, but the owner of the island has planted over 60,000 trees, reintroduced the magpie robin, and returned the island almost to its pre-coconut plantation days of 200 hundred years ago. In the Maldives, the plush Banyan Tree Vabbinfaru (entry 128) has set up an excellent marine biology laboratory for reef and fish conservation, and Turtle Island Resort (entry 166), the exclusive setting for the film 'Blue Lagoon' – has for 12 years overseen over 1000 cataract operations for local people and built two budget resorts now run by local people.

Some places encourage philanthropy. The 'Berber Hospitality Centre' at Kasbah du Toubkal in Morocco (entry 99), not only creates employment for the rural villagers but also charges guests a 5% levy for the local Imlil Village Association, which has used the funds to buy an ambulance and build a village Hamman. Nihiwatu (entry 150) on the island of Sumba in Indonesia established The Sumba Foundation funded by voluntary donations and has more than halved the occurrence of malaria in the surrounding area.

Owners

In some cases, it is the owner's enthusiasm that has won us over. Some have made great sacrifices to set up their green place to stay, taking a gamble and investing in expensive environmental technology. Sofia de Meyer traded in her life as a London City solicitor to find ways to discover the mountains with a variety of low impact activities, eventually setting up Whitepod close to where she grew up in the Swiss Alps. Her 'eco-philosophy' is inspiring. Jem Winston spent a decade saving money from his job as a London taxi driver to set up his patch of paradise at Three Rivers Eco Lodge in Dominica (entry 26). The workshops he now runs, showing others on the island how to go green, are a model in the Caribbean. Other owners in this book have struggled against the ravages of mass tourism or with jealous competitors who try to portray green as extreme.

But above all else – what counts the most – is that the owners have thought through their impact on the environment and how they can benefit the local community. When such a commitment shines through, we are convinced it makes a place all the more enjoyable to visit.

A few questions to ask owners to see if their place really is green:
• Ask if they have a written green policy; this should describe how they minimise their impact on the environment, benefit conservation and local people.
• Ask them how the property was built; did they use local materials?
• Ask if they grow their own food or source food locally; is it organic?
• Ask them how they source their energy for heating their building; do they use alternative energies?
• Ask how they treat their waste water; do they use environmentally friendly systems?

• Ask if they provide recycling facilities and use biodegradable detergents
• Ask if they provide information and advice about wildlife, local cultures and customs
• Ask if they employ people from the local community; are the owners local?

Practicalities

Maps

The maps in this book show the rough location of our green properties and are designed to be used as an overview, obviously not as road maps for navigation. Each property is labelled with an entry number and colour coded according to its international region.

Time difference

See p.268 for time differences relative to GMT.

Passport, Visa, Health and Insurance

Make sure your passport is up to date and check whether you need a visa for entering a country. A passport valid for six months from the date of entry is required for the United States and some other countries. You should check passport and visa requirements with the consulate or embassy of the country you plan to visit. Also check what vaccinations you need at least six weeks before you go and consider whether you need to take extra health precautions.

Photo Himalayan Homestays, entry 131 by Jonathon Keeling

Arrange vaccinations via your local doctor or contact Masta www.masta.org for immunisation – and anti-malarial advice.

For UK and other EU nationals travelling in Europe there is a new 'European Health Insurance card', EHIC (the replacement for the E111, which is no longer valid), which entitles you to reduced-cost, sometimes free, medical treatment when necessary while you're in a 'European Economic Area' country, Iceland, Liechtenstein, Norway and Switzerland. You can apply through www.dh.gov.uk/travellers (delivery within 7 days), by calling 0845 606 2030 (delivery within 10 days) or by picking up a postal application form at any UK Post Office (though applications via this route may take up to 21 days). Also, make sure your insurance is up to date, valid for the entire trip, for any activities you have in mind and that it covers everyone in your party.

Driving and Maps

If you are planning to drive, make sure your driving licence is current and valid. In some countries you will need to have an international driving permit as well as your UK licence. Be aware that in many countries there are on-the-spot fines for traffic offences. The maps at the front of our book are designed as an overview to help locate our special places but are not for use as road maps. If you are planning to drive, get a good map such as a Michelin one: clear and accurate, they also show nature parks and ancient sites. For detailed walking maps, consult a specialist bookshop such as Stanfords (www.stanfords.co.uk). For locally-led Green Map projects worldwide, which highlight an area's natural and cultural resources, see www.greenmap.com.

Travel Documents

Keep, separately from the originals, copies of your passport (including any visa pages), insurance policy, driving licence and ticket details. You might find it useful to scan these documents and send them by email to a web-based email address, such as hotmail or yahoo, so you can retrieve them from an internet café abroad, though bear in mind not all public-access computers allow you to access attachments.

Money

The following countries use the euro: Austria, Belgium, Finland, France, Germany, Greece, Italy, Ireland, Luxembourg, The Netherlands, Portugal and Spain. The UK, Denmark and Sweden do not! Elsewhere, check whether it is legal to take local currency out of the country or bring it in as you may need to change money at your point of arrival. You may be asked when leaving to change any foreign currency cash you have left into hard currency – at a relatively unfavourable rate, so aim to have as little as possible in your pocket when you get to the airport.

Communication
Email & fax: Almost all entries in this guide have an email address; many have a fax number.
Telephone: The numbers printed include the country code, denoted by (+). Calling internationally: Dial 00 then the country code and the area code (omitting the zero in brackets where appropriate).

Electricity
Current varies around the world, so check whether you will need an adaptor for your plugs and a transformer for 110-volt appliances.

In some countries power cuts are not infrequent, particularly outside the cities, and some places have an electricity supply only at certain times of the day. Also, many green places run partially or fully off their own generators – be they solar, wind or oil (as back up) – so be sensitive to any instructions provided on the use of electricity. Lighting may also be planned for its capacity to create atmosphere rather than to make things visible, so take a good torch – it may help you find the way back to your room!

Noise
Though many of the places in this book are off the beaten track, not all are far – or indeed protected – from street noise so consider taking ear plugs.

Water
Local people might drink the water from their wells or from their taps when they know it is safe but it is advisable to stick to bottled water until you are acclimatised.

Know Before You Go
The Foreign and Commonwealth Office publishes an excellent travel advisory section on its web site (www.fco.gov.uk/travel), including a 'Know Before You Go' campaign dedicated to helping travellers plan their trip overseas. Incidentally, if you happen to be travelling when

your vote is required back home, read the section: 'Keep your vote!'

It is not easy to place properties into fixed categories – safari camps may be 'under canvas' but they may also be hotels! We have tried to categorise each property according to the description that best illustrates its most obvious feature, but where more than one category applies, we have included two descriptions.

Eco lodge – sounds like a generic term but a place should only be described as this if it fulfils the main criteria of true ecotourism (see pp.26-36) – it should minimise its impact on the environment (for example if it is made out of sustainable building materials and has a low carbon output through environmentally sensitive design and use of alternative technology to fossil fuel, such as wind, solar or hydro power), provide direct benefits for the conservation of local biodiversity, and provide tangible financial benefits and local empowerment for the local community. The best examples of an eco lodge also provide some kind of interpretation facility to help guests understand about the local environment, wildlife and culture. We believe if a place calls itself an eco lodge it must keep tightly to these ideals. If you come across any

place that calls itself an eco lodge but clearly isn't, please let us know.

Hotel – This category covers everything from wilderness lodges to island hideaways. They are usually small (up to about 25 rooms – for it's difficult to justify how hotels larger than this can be environmentally friendly), with presence and character but with widely differing levels of comfort and price. That said, we have included a few larger hotels, less intimate, but chosen for some specific quality of history, atmosphere, setting and what we consider to be a genuine commitment to environmental and social responsibility.

Beach hut – can vary from a hippy shack to a lavish hotel room. Take lungfuls of fresh salty air, feel the warmth of fine sand underfoot, or drift into a lazy sleep to the sound of lapping waves.

Cabana (mostly used in Central and South America) – is a cabin (usually) by the sea, lagoon or lake, though it can also be used to describe a small changing room by a swimming pool.

Working farm or vineyard – these are enterprises that have diversified into tourism. Owners are usually happy for you to get a closer look at their farm animals or vines, but you should ask first. And keep an eye on the dinner table for their produce!

Homestays – tend to be family homes where you get a taste of traditional life. Remember you are in their home, so it is important to respect the customs of the family. Friendships are easily formed over sociable dinners.

Guest houses – tend to be smaller and less anonymous than hotels, but less intimate than homestays. They are often private houses that have been partially converted and may or may not have a restaurant, room service or telephones in the rooms.

Safari camps cover rooms or tents or both, often in protected areas such as wildlife reserves or national parks. Meals and safaris are often included in the price. They vary: some are rustic and basic, others are smarter, decorated with leather-clad interiors, while others still are lavish and surprisingly contemporary with all the mod cons.

Under canvas – The standard of luxury varies – some tents have four-poster beds and en suite showers, others are very simple. Be warmed by camp fires and dine by candlelight.

Yurt (or Ger) – Round, wood-framed and self-supporting structures traditionally used by the nomadic people in the wild steppes of Central Asia. Think Genghis Khan.

Tipi – More like the Wild West, similar to a 'wigwam', a tall, tilted cone-shaped canvas shelter, often with a central log fire controlled by smoke flaps at the apex, used by the 'People of the Plains' in North America.

Disabled and limited mobility
Provision for the disabled obviously varies throughout the world. We have indicated with the 𝝠 symbol those places that have basic ground-floor access while the ♿ symbol indicates those places that have full and approved wheelchair facilities for at least one bedroom and bathroom and access to all ground-floor common areas

Types of Rooms
We give the total number of single, double, twin or triple rooms, tents, cabins, huts, suites, apartments and cottages. (Extra beds are often available for children.) Rooms vary

Photo left Bird Island Lodge, entry 125
Photo right Nihiwatu, entry 150

enormously; in one you may find a simple mattress on the floor, or thin mattresses on top of each other in The Princess and the Pea style, in another a gloriously comfortable double bed with organic sheets, while a pricier room may have luxurious orthopaedic bedding.

Double means a room with one double bed. Twin means a room with two single beds. Twin/double means that the room can be made up either as a double or a twin (often using 'ziplock' beds); lodge rooms quite often have two double beds. Triple means either a double and a single bed, or (occasionally) three single beds. Family room means a room sleeping three or four or more, normally in one double and one or more single beds, or occasionally

two double beds. Studio means a bedroom with kitchenette, normally in a single space; it may or may not have a sitting area. Suite means a room with an inside sitting area, normally separate from the bedroom. Apartment means a bedroom (or more than one) with a separate sitting room and/or kitchen.

Some rooms have extra sofabeds; this is what we mean by 'suites for 2-3', 'apartments for 2-4' etc. Many places can supply extra folding beds (usually small; if you intend it for an adult, check first). All bedrooms are assumed to have an en suite bathroom, unless otherwise mentioned. Where an entry reads '4 + 2' this means 4 rooms plus 2 self-catering apartments/villas/cottages.

We have included two photos of the property in each entry – usually one exterior photo that shows the property in its setting, and one smaller photo that shows one of the bedrooms or a dining/living area. Two pictures cannot tell the whole story so if you take a peek at web sites – all of our entries have them – you will get a fuller picture.

Prices

There is a massive range in this book. Unless we specify otherwise, prices are per room/apartment/villa per night. Most of our chosen places offer breakfast, and many also offer lunch and dinner. Hotel/guesthouse prices include breakfast (except where breakfast prices are listed separately below); self-catering prices exclude all food. If we give a range, it means either that some rooms are more expensive than others or that some seasons are more expensive than others, or both. If breakfast is not included, its price will appear under Meals. Many places offer terms for children, half or full board, long stays, etc., or package deals with activities, spa treatments, etc. Ask when booking. Published at the end of 2006, the prices printed here are liable to be altered at any time and most are likely to be changed for autumn 2007. Some prices are quoted with local taxes included, others not. You may find these are levied per guest per night added to your bill. The same goes for VAT. Some places also ask for guests to make a contribution to a foundation or charity, which will be added to your bill unless you let them know you do not wish to make the donation.

Price Bands

Owners have given us their prices in sterling, US dollars, euros or local currency. To save confusion, we have added a price band in sterling that ranges from A (under £25) to G (over £250). The letter code is printed at the bottom of each entry and the breakdown is shown on the inside back page.

Seasonal prices and special deals

Be aware of price differences in low and high season – they can change dramatically. We mention the high season period in the price section, so if you are going out of season, prices may be lower. Don't be afraid to ask for special deals for longer stays.

Meals

Where lunch and dinner are not available, we have tried to indicate the nearest restaurants.

Ratings for Environmental Technology and Social Responsibility

We have included a score out of 100 for each place in this book, based on how we judge their use of environmental technologies (ET, denoted by a green band) and their social responsibility (SR, denoted by a red band). We invited owners to tell us about their green credentials but we also used feedback from people who visited the property so that we could make up our own mind. It's an inexact science, our ratings are subjective, but we hope it gives an idea of why these places were chosen. In some instances a place has scored highly for use of environmental technologies but rates lower on its social responsibility. Or vice versa. But no place falls down too heavily on either as we believe no place can truly be green unless it goes some way to limit its impact on the environment and follows some sort of agenda towards benefiting the local community.

Low Impact Activities

Below the write up for each entry, where relevant we have provided bullet-pointed details on the flora and fauna that can be seen near or at the property; names of nearby sites of natural and cultural interest; and details of low-impact activities, such as hiking and canoeing. Because of the sensitive locations of many of the places in this book, it is important you choose only those activities that are recommended by the owners and go with local operators that the owners recommend. There are plenty of unscrupulous travel companies who claim to offer 'ecotourism' but in fact are just after a quick buck. Remember others will follow in your footsteps, so tread lightly!

Alcoholic drinks

Many places sell beer and wine, others allow you to bring you own (BYO); some do not specify but this does not always mean no alcohol. Those places that do have a license to sell alcohol are marked with the ₫ symbol. In Islamic countries, the situation is delicate. For instance, in Morocco, some places will neither sell alcohol nor accept that guests

bring it in. However, many guest houses and small hotels may provide wine with meals but do not have a licence so cannot announce the fact. On the other hand, they want you to drink their wine – which can be good and interesting – rather than bring in something from the local supermarket. So please understand this before arriving with bags of clanking bottles and asking for a corkscrew.

Communication, booking, cancellation

It can be quite difficult to contact some of the remote places in this book. Just because a place has an email address doesn't necessarily mean the owners will respond immediately to your enquiry. In some cases the owners only have access to email once a week, so while your booking is important to them, they might not get the chance to reply to your enquiry immediately. Be patient!

Some of the places featured in this book don't have the facilities to deal with bookings, so they leave it up to tour operators to deal with the administration. For these entries we have recommended in their contact details a tour operator through which you can book your stay.

Do also bear in mind the difference in seasons between the Northern and Southern Hemisphere: for instance, in Australia, the end of the

summer season is April when owners might go away for some respite after a long and busy period; and January might be the popular time to book a holiday, but in Australia it is the peak of the season so owners might be too preoccupied dealing with guests to respond immediately to booking enquiries.

Sending an email is usually the more practical option, and almost all owners/staff speak enough English to answer a simple reservation query. Those with fluent English speakers are marked with (Hello) symbol. Faxing is also fairly reliable.

Most places will require a written reservation (fax or email). Some smarter hotels will need credit card details as a guarantee. Those places that only accept cash are marked with a 🪙 symbol – when staying at these (perhaps remote) places make sure you have sufficient cash to pay for your stay and any transport to get you there and back.

When booking, check the cancellation policy (or ask what it is, if in doubt); if you are making a financial commitment, consider taking out travel insurance at this early stage in case of unexpected cancellation and loss of deposit.

Arranging transfers

Some owners may offer to collect you from the nearest airport, train or bus station and drop you off there after your visit. When travelling to the more remote places this can be essential. When booking, make sure you check whether there is an additional charge for this service and do liaise with the owner over exact timings, in both directions if relevant. We recommend that you re-confirm the exact details (particularly your arrival transfer), nearer the time of your stay in case there have been any changes to flight arrival times or local public transport timetables.

Subscriptions

Owners pay to appear in this guide. Their fee goes towards the cost of inspections (every entry has been visited by a member of our team before being selected), of producing an all-colour book and of maintaining a sophisticated web site. We only include places and owners that we find positively special. It is not possible for anyone to buy their way into our guides.

Internet

www.specialplacestostay.com has online pages for all of the green places featured here and from all our other books – around 5,000 Special Places in Britain, Ireland, France, Italy, Spain, Portugal, India, Morocco, Turkey and Greece. There's a searchable database, a taster of the write-ups and colour photos. For details see p.270.

Disclaimer

We make no claims to pure objectivity in choosing our Green Places to Stay. They are here because we like them. Our opinions and tastes are ours alone and this book is a statement of them; we hope that you will share them.

We have done our utmost to get our facts right but apologise unreservedly for any mistakes that may have crept in. Feedback from you is invaluable and we always take note of comments. With your help and our own inspections we can maintain our reputation for dependability.

You should know that we do not check such things as fire alarms, swimming pool security or any other regulations with which owners of properties receiving paying guests should comply. This is the responsibility of the owners.

Stay in Touch

We love hearing about your experiences – good and bad – and your comments make a real contribution, be they on our report form, by letter or by email to info@sawdays.co.uk. This book is a first edition – please let us know about new green places for the future.

And finally

In many cases the owners of the places featured in this book have invested in green technologies – often at great expense (though this is becoming less of an issue) – and have integrated with local communities – or indeed are run by local communities themselves – yet they have not had the recognition they deserve. There are numerous places that call themselves 'green' or 'eco', yet standards differ throughout the world, and to the casual eye it can be difficult to separate those truly green places from those that are greenwash. We have visited every one of the places in this book and are confident they meet our criteria. We hope that in featuring these places in this book we will help bring them your custom and the recognition they deserve.

Richard Hammond

Photo Tiger Mountain Pokhara Lodge, entry 129

NORTH AMERICA
Entries 55–59

Arctic Ocean

EUROPE
Entries 60–97

Atlantic

Ocean

THE CARIBBEAN
Entries 23–31

CENTRAL AMERICA
Entries 32–54

Pacific

Ocean

SOUTH AMERICA
Entries 1–22

Regional maps appear immediately before the
first entry in each colour-coded section.

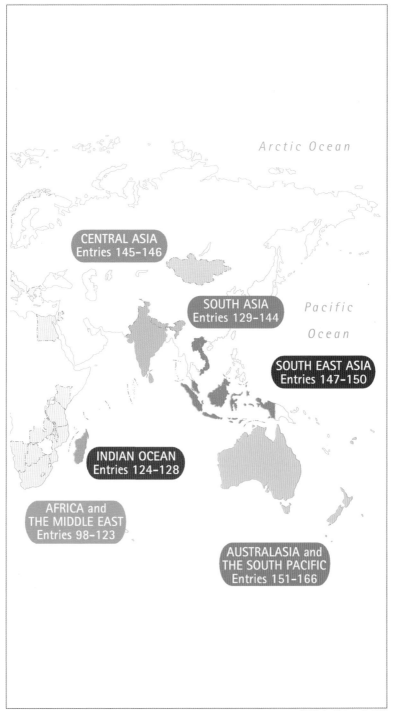

Arctic Ocean

CENTRAL ASIA
Entries 145–146

SOUTH ASIA
Entries 129–144

Pacific

Ocean

SOUTH EAST ASIA
Entries 147–150

INDIAN OCEAN
Entries 124–128

AFRICA and
THE MIDDLE EAST
Entries 98–123

AUSTRALASIA and
THE SOUTH PACIFIC
Entries 151–166

south america

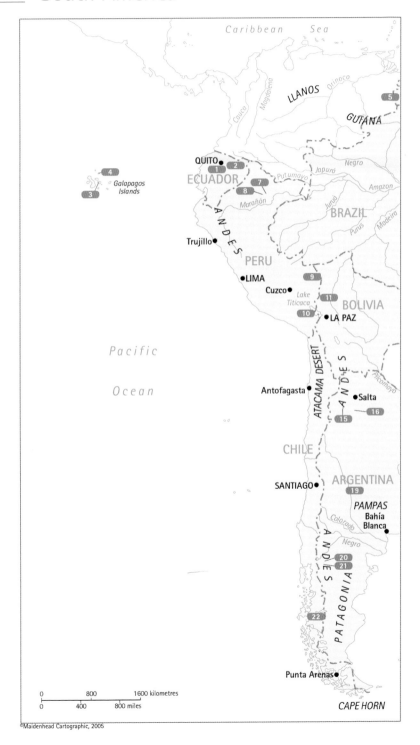

Caribbean Sea

LLANOS

Orinoco

GUIANA

Magdalena

Cauca

QUITO ●
1 **2**
ECUADOR
8 **7**
Putumayo
Marañón
Japurá
Negro
Amazon
Juruá
BRAZIL
Madeira
Purus

4
Galápagos
Islands
3

ANDES

Trujillo ●

PERU

● LIMA
Cuzco ●
Lake
Titicaca
9
11
10
● LA PAZ
BOLIVIA

Pacific

Ocean

ATACAMA DESERT
ANDES
Pilcomayo

Antofagasta ●
● Salta
15
16

CHILE

SANTIAGO ●
ARGENTINA
19

PAMPAS
Bahía
Blanca ●
Colorado
Negro

ANDES
20
21

22

PATAGONIA

Punta Arenas ●

CAPE HORN

0   800   1600 kilometres
0   400   800 miles

Black Sheep Inn

PO Box 05-01-240, Chugchilán, Cotopaxi

Whether you arrive trekking through the breathtaking Río Toachi canyon, riding the roof of a local bus, or in comfortable private transport, the dramatic Andean scenery leaves an indelible first impression. Then it's the personal feeling of the place, a feeling nurtured over the years by owners Michelle and Andy. It's all in little touches like the herbal teas available throughout the day in the dining/common room, where you can curl up with your warm cup and watch the mist drift through the valley. Accommodation is comfortable, either in private rooms with their own fireplace, or in simpler dorms. The vegetarian cooking is delicious, and many ingredients are harvested from the organic garden. What makes the Black Sheep 'green' goes well beyond composting toilets, for the inn has had an important effect on a particularly poor, neglected rural community. *10-15% discount to cyclists.*

- Self-guided & guided hikes; horse riding; mountain biking
- Pumas, hawks, forest falcons, hummingbirds, swifts
- Iliniza Ecological Reserve & cloud forest; indigenous Andean markets; Laguna Quilotoa

The lodge is a permaculture demonstration site.

rooms	9: 3 twins/doubles, 6 triples/quads, all sharing showers; 1 bunkhouse for 10.
price	Half-board US$60. Triple $81. Quad $100. Single $43. Bunkhouse $20 p.p.
meals	Half-board only. Lunch box US$3.
closed	Never.
directions	Along Sigchos-Chugchilán road, 3hr drive from Pan-American H'way & Latacunga. Bus: Quito-Latacunga (2 hrs), Latacunga-Chugchilán (4 hrs).

Andres Hammerman & Michelle Kirby

tel	+593 (0)3 281 4587
email	info@blacksheepinn.com
web	www.blacksheepinn.com

Eco lodge

B

Kapawi Ecolodge & Reserve

Amazon, c/o Canodros S. A., Urb. Sta. Leonar, Mazana 5, Solar 10, Guayaquil

One of the most remote places in the book. Here, near the Ecuadorian and Peruvian border on a major tributary of the Amazon, it's a ten-day hike to the nearest town. You are in Achuar Territory, home to 4,500 indigenous Achuar people, some of whom have a hand in running the lodge in partnership with private tour operator Canodros. In accordance with the Achuar's ancient building techniques, not a single nail was used to build the 20 thatched-roofed cabañas lining a small lagoon. It's an eco lodge in the true sense: all electricity is solar powered, so too are the showers which have biodegradable soap. The rooms are screened to keep out the insects. Sit outside on a wide terrace and drink in the sights and sounds of the thick jungle or enjoy freshly brewed coffee while birdwatching in the early morning from the dining room's beautiful veranda.

- Hiking (3 ability levels) & night hiking; canoeing; birdwatching; rainforest lectures; Achuar village visit
- 200 mammal species (jaguar, pink river dolphin), 540 bird species (Muscovy ducks, brown jacamars)

rooms	20 cabins for 2 or 3.
price	Full-board US$650 p.p. for 3 nights (based on 2 sharing). Additional $10 Achuar community fee.
meals	Full-board only.
closed	Never.
directions	By air only: fly Quito-Shell-Kapawi (1.5 hrs in all), then 10-min hike through village followed by 15-min canoe ride to lodge. Note: flight delays possible due to rains.

	Canodros
tel	+593 (0)4 251 4750
fax	+593 (0)4 228 7651
email	canodros@canodros.com
web	www.kapawi.com

In 2011, the reserve will be handed over to the Achuar people, providing an alternative to Amazon destruction.

Eco lodge

Finch Bay Eco Hotel
Punta Estrada, Puerto Ayora

Imagine a hotel manager who persuades a guest to move her sunbed so that a seven-year-old child can have an unimpeded run into the pool! That's what you might expect of Xavier, head of Finch Bay's truly delightful staff. The other great thing about this place is the area around the pool and bar. Overlooking a small pretty beach and shallow lagoon, flanked by rocks and mangroves, it's the definitive sundowning spot. The hotel is quiet and secluded, well away from the hustle of Puerto Ayora across the bay. Painted to blend in with the scenery, the rooms are a series of cheek-by-jowl little 'bungalows', each with its own balcony. They're fresh, clean and modern, with lava rock and locally turned wood incorporated into the décor. Though not the greenest hotel we've visited, it's certainly a cut above the rest in Galapagos and its introduction of a blackwater treatment plant will have a valuable impact on the island.

- Guided wildlife excursions; kayaking, snorkelling & scuba diving; cycling
- Lava herons, egrets & finches viewable from patio
- Galapagos is home to two UNESCO World Natural Heritage Sites

rooms	21 cabins for 2.
price	US$284.50.
meals	Lunch & dinner, 3 courses, US$22.
closed	Never.
directions	Fly to Baltra on Santa Cruz; bus to Puerto Ayora (30 minutes); water taxi across bay. Hotel arranges transfers on request.

Drinking water is turned off at night & reinstated in the early hours to conserve fresh water.

Xavier Burbano
tel   +593 (0)5252 6297/6298
email   operaciones@finchbayhotel.com
web   www.finchbayhotel.com

Hotel

Ecoventura: Yachts 'Flamingo', 'Letty' and 'Eric'

c/o Galapagos Network, Miami, Florida, USA

No surprise that people target the Galapagos for the wildlife. It was the 13 finch types identified by Charles Darwin that played a pivotal role in his theory on the origin of species: that flora and fauna, far from being immutable, are created through natural selection. And how better to visit these 'enchanted islands' (actually the peaks of underwater volcanoes) than by cruiser? Built in 1991, these modest-sized vessels are well-kept, shiny and comfortable, and have been certified by the Smart Voyager Programme, which recognises operators that run low impact trips to the islands. Cabins are peaceful, even though those on the lowest deck. The captain eats with his guests, and the staff – most from the mainland, just a handful from the Galapagos – are charming and eager to please. Recycling is de rigeur, external lights are yellow to deter insects, cleaning products are biodegradable. The islands Fernandina and Genovese are fabulous. Bring your hiking boots! *15% tip is the norm.*

- Snorkelling with sea lions; wildlife tours (max. ten people per guide)
- Finches, albatross, blue-footed boobies, flightless cormorants, great frigates, giant tortoises, iguana

rooms	10 cabins: 3 doubles, 5 twins, 2 triples.
price	Full-board 7 nights US$2,450-$2,995 p.p. Triples $2,300 p.p. Singles $3,775.
meals	Full-board only.
closed	Never.
directions	Flight to San Cristóbal; transfer to boat at nearby dock, organised by company.

Experienced guides know their wildlife, and are knowledgeable about the islands' unique ecosystem.

	Reservations
tel	+1 305 262 6264
fax	+1 305 262 9609
email	info@galapagosnetwork.com
web	www.ecoventura.com

Eco lodge

Surama Village
Surama Village

A traditional Amerindian village in the heart of the rainforest. If you're in search of your inner intrepid-explorer then getting here is part of the adventure. The dirt road isn't so much rutted as crevassed and as your van lurches from one pot hole to the next, plumes of small green butterflies spring into the air. You may pass men on bicycles going out to hunt peccary with bows and arrows. At the village, you are very much part of the (mainly Makushi tribe) community and are encouraged to visit the school (blank notebooks for teachers and pupils make welcome gifts), drop in at the house of the local shamen and watch people pounding cassava. The wooden huts are basic, but dry and cool, and the food is local, simple and delicious. The Surama people have identified ecotourism as a sustainable way to use their land and the guides' passion and knowledge is outstanding.

- Dawn hiking (led by Surama guides) & canoe trips
- Giant river otters, tapir, tira, spider monkeys, harpy eagles, jaguars, armadillos, anteaters, capybara & fish-eating bats
- Iwokrama International Centre for Conservation & Development

rooms	4 huts for 2 (twins).
price	Full-board US$110. Singles $60. Many possible itineraries/packages.
meals	Full-board only.
closed	June-August.
directions	Pre-organised by 4x4 through the rainforest.

Income from the tours goes directly to community projects.

Eco lodge

	Sydney Allicock
tel	+592 (0)227 7698
fax	+592 (0)226 2085
email	info@iwokramacanopywalkway.com
web	www.wilderness-explorers.com/surama_village.htm

Entry 5

B

Rock View Lodge
Annai, North Rupununi

Where the jungle meets the grasslands, you'll be greeted off the 12-seater plane by Colin (an English ex-agricutural volunteer) and his local Amerindian, Makushi-speaking staff. Colin's love for Guyana is evident in the art collection and library in the main ranch house, where you can drink at the Dkota Bar with the local Amerindian community. Rooms in two guest houses are simply, comfortably furnished, and there's a wonderfully tempting pool in the shade of the cashew trees. Barbecued meat (Brazilian style) is cooked on a wood-fire grill under mango trees, and other simple, home-cooked meals such as chicken and duck with coconut milk (with fresh fruit and vegetables from the garden) are served in the dining room in front of the field where vultures warm their wings on the fence. Adventure is all around, but you could just curl up in the benab on a hammock, listen to the hummingbirds and drift into a deep, remote sleep.

* Birdwatching; nature trails; boat trips; horse riding with vaqueros (local cowboys)
* Tapir, giant anteater, capybara, giant otter, agouti, birds, laba, turtles
* Karanambu Ranch; Iwokrama Forest; Pakaraima Mountains; Surama village

rooms	8: 4 twins, 2 family, 2 triples. Also hammock & tents.
price	Full-board US$150. Triple $210. Singles $95. Includes activities; without $60 p.p. Camping $10.
meals	Full-board only.
closed	Never.
directions	Fly from Georgetown to Annai; airstrip 200m from Lodge. Car & bus from Georgetown (420km) & Lethem (110km). New bridge on border with Brazil will improve links.

Colin Edwards
email   info@rockviewlodge.com
web   www.rockviewlodge.com

The lodge helps operate the 154m (33m high) Iwokrama Canopy Walkway.

Guest house & Eco lodge

Entry 6

Amazon Yarapa River Lodge
c/o Av. La Marina 124, Iquitos

Local management, local materials, local ideas, deep in Peruvian rainforest.
The focus of the centre is on research and education (it's a partnership between
Charles Mango – an ophthalmologist from New York – the people of Jaldar village
and Cornell University) but that doesn't take anything away from the quality of
the stay; in fact, it adds to it. Their work brings you closer to nature, and when
you hold a pigmy marmoset monkey in your hand you'll know in an instant what
environmental responsibility is all about. The only road is the Amazon tributary
flowing alongside; the only disturbance is the occasional sound of a paddle slicing
through the water from a hand-carved canoe, or the blast of air from a breaching
pink dolphin. The roofs and walkways are thatched and provide a natural cooling
system from the tropical heat, and 95% of electricity is generated by solar power.
Guides from the village will show you not how they live off the land, but how
they live with it. *Minimum stay three nights.*

- Guided hikes; canoeing; plant identification walks; birdwatching
- Monkeys, pink dolphins, hoatzin birds, caimans, giant Amazon water lilies

rooms	23: 15 twins/doubles sharing bathrooms; 8 bungalow suites for 2.
price	Full-board for 3 nights. US$700 p.p. Singles $800. Bungalows $760 p.p. Singles $860. Includes tranfers & guided tours.
meals	Full-board only.
closed	Never.
directions	Pick-up from Iquitos. Transfer to boat up Amazon, to Yarapa river; 110 miles (3.5 hrs) to Lodge.

The lodge (with the local village &
Cornell University) has created a 60,000
acre surrounding reserve.

	Charles Mango
tel	+011 5165 223320
mobile	+51 65 993 1172
email	yarapariverlodge@hotmail.com
web	www.yarapariverlodge.com

Eco lodge

E

Tahuayo Lodge

Tahuayo River, c/o Amazonia Expeditions, Av. La Marina 100, Iquitos

Kerosene lamps in the relaxation rooms, torches in the bedroom and river water (warmish!) for showers. Nudging the Tahuayo river, in a clearing in the forest, are six thatch and stilt buildings connected by pathways. Come for the greatest diversity of flora and fauna in the world in the Reserva Comunal de Tamshiyacu-Tahuayo. Stay a year and you won't be short of things to do – canoe trips into the flooded forest from February to May, swimming with pink dolphins, night boat trips to view southern constellations, visits to Fair Trade projects and medicinal plant hikes all year round. They run a flexible, indeed exemplary, adventure ecotourism programme thanks to helpful, knowledgeable and well-organised staff. Bedrooms have four-posters, soft mattresses and mosquito nets – the essentials – while relaxation comes in the form of generous and convivial buffet meals, a basic bar, and books and guitar in the delightful, conical Hammock Room.

- Huge canopy zipline; boat trips to visit Bora Indians; fishing for piranha; hiking
- 16 species of primates, tree frogs, tropical fish, crocodiles, butterflies & 533 species of bird

rooms	14 cabins: 3 doubles, 8 twins, 3 family. 3 dormitories for 4. Shared showers.
price	Full-board US$1,295 p.p. for 7 nights. Includes private guide & excursions.
meals	Full-board only.
closed	Never.
directions	From Iquitos, 4hr riverboat ride. Transfers from Iquitos airport to riverboat by Amazonia Expedition staff.

Guests are invited to donate summer clothes, first aid materials & vitamins to local villages.

Dr. Paul Beaver

tel	+1 813 907 8475
fax	+1 813 907 8475
email	amazonia.expeditions@verizon.net
web	www.perujungle.com/lodge.html

Eco lodge

Entry 8

Posadas Amazonas

c/o Av. Aramburu 166, Dep. 4b, Miraflores, Lima 18

You're so close to nature at this open-plan lodge at the heart of the Peruvian rainforest you are advised to follow two simple rules: don't keep any food in your luggage and always check under the bed at night. The rooms have only three heat-regulating clay and cane walls; the front is open to the jungle canopy beyond a waist-high veranda. Beds are shrouded in mosquito nets and fittings furnished from jungle materials: wood, palm and wild cane. Dinner is candlelit in a communal dining hall and the living room is a lofty open house thatched with palm leaves. The ethos is based on maintaining the ecological balance of the forest and you're encouraged to learn about your surroundings on guided nature trails, and about the life of the indigenous Ese Ejas people through classes in indigenous crafts. *Minimum stay two nights.*

- Rainforest-canopy tours; ethno-botanical excursions to Centro Ñape; night walks
- Monkeys, giant river otters, turtles, hoatzin, macaws, 32 species of parrot, 90 of frog
- Tambopata National Reserve; Tres Chimbadas; parrot clay licks

The lodge is part-owned by the indigenous community of Infierno.

rooms	30 doubles/triples. Cold water showers only.
price	Full-board US$205. Singles $157.50.
meals	Full-board only.
closed	Never.
directions	Fly from Lima or Cusco to Puerto Maldonado, transfer from airport to Tambopata river port (40 mins), motorised canoe upriver (45 mins); 15-min walk from river to lodge.

Kurt Holle

tel	+51 (0)1 421 8347
fax	+51 (0)1 421 8183
email	postmaster@rainforest.com.pe
web	www.perunature.com/lodgespa.php

Eco lodge

Casa Andina Private Collection Suasi Island

Isla Suasi, Lago Titicaca, c/o Av. Meliton Porres 392, Miraflores, Lima 18

Come to be marooned on a private island. This charming low-key resort on Lake Titicaca, managed by a young hotel chain committed to showing the Andean way of life, is rustic, remote and peaceful. Suasi Island, with its low-slung stone, wood and thatch buildings, its food sourced from Puno, its Peruvian décor and its eucalyptus-log fires, is inspired by a pre-Inca age, and staff – courteous, flexible, friendly – are Titicaca-born. Among terraced gardens full of wild flowers and roses, hammocks and herbs are two rustic lodges. In the first, bar and dining areas are on the ground floor and bedrooms above. In all, comfort and cheer – from feather duvets on big beds and gorgeous lake views, bathrobes, hot water bottles and eco-friendly shampoos. A distant suite is connected by walkie-talkie. No pool, but a library and games room, sauna and massage, delicious fresh food and heavenly night skies. *Island entrance fee of $12 goes to wildlife conservation.*

- Beach walks & canoeing; hiking; birdwatching
- Vicunas, alpacas, Andean mountain cats; 87 species of bird including cormorants
- Titicaca & its islands – legendary birthplace of the Inca empire

rooms	25: 9 doubles, 13 twins, 2 triples, 1 suite for 2-4.
price	Full-board US$230. Triple $345. Singles $150. Suite $414-$828.
meals	Full-board only.
closed	Never.
directions	By boat from Puno's main port, or by bus or taxi around the lake (2.5 hrs).

Water is pumped from the lake & heated using solar power.

Juan Stoessel

tel	+51 (0)1446 8848
fax	+51 (0)1445 4775
email	jstoessel@casa-andina.com
web	www.casa-andina.com/suasi

Hotel

Chalalán Ecolodge
Bolivian Amazon, Madidi National Park

Managed entirely by the indigenous Quechua-Tacana community, Chalalán is pioneering Bolivia's fledgling community-based ecotourism industry. Buried in the vaste swathe of the wildlife-rich Bolivian Amazon, the pristine Madidi National Park lies at your doorstep. Knowledgeable guides and themed nature trails encourage you to learn about wildlife behaviour and medicinal qualities of the plants. The low-impact, wood and palm cabins are simple and rustic, but perfectly comfortable. Wash away the day's expedition, then soak up the sunset over Lake Chalalán from a deckchair or hammock outside your cabin. Traditional dishes are served in a central dining hall (with a flourish of handcrafted table decorations) and include 'dunucuavy' – catfish cooked in leaves. Washed down with a drop of red from the Bolivian wine-growing Tarija region, being green never tasted quite so good.

* Guided nature trails; wildlife exploration; boat excursions on the River Tuichi
* Monkeys, caimans, turtles, tapirs, jaguars, white-lipped peccary, hoatzin, macaws
* Madidi National Park & jungle town of Rurrenabaque

A share of the profits is paid to the 74 families of San José de Uchupiamonas.

Eco lodge

rooms	6 cabins: 3 doubles; 3 rooms for 2-3, sharing bathrooms.
price	Full-board (4-days, 3 nights) US$325 p.p. Twin/triple $295p.p. Singles $345. Includes transfers & activities.
meals	Full-board only.
closed	Never.
directions	By dugout canoe up the Beni and Tuichi rivers, 5 hrs from gateway village of Rurrenabaque.

Reservations

tel	+591 (0)3 892 2419
mobile	+591 71282697
email	info@chalalan.com
web	www.chalalan.com

Cristalino Jungle Lodge
Cristalino State Park, Mato Grosso

This remote lodge hides in a private rainforest reserve on a bend of the Cristalino river – a tributary of a tributary of a tributary of the distant Amazon. From the floating dock (sheltered by a mushroom-shaped thatched *palapa* and towered over by giant tropical trees), a long winding path leads you to the discreet wooden cabins in a garden of palms and fruit trees. Spacious bed and living areas have hardwood chairs, large beds draped with mosquito nets, and six-foot-high glass walls. Huge bathroom mirrors are framed in hardwood commodes and there are deliciously powerful showers. Food is simple and hearty with staples such as beans, rice, potatoes and salads accompanying fried chicken and stewed beef or very tasty, sweet-water fish. The visionary Vitoria has done much to protect the surrounding area of rainforest and raise the awareness of the biological importance of the region. *US$25 per visitor is donated to the Cristalino Ecological Foundation.*

- Trekking; river swimming & canoeing; birdwatching at dawn from 50m-high observation tower
- Over 570 species of bird & 1,800 of butterfly; a tapir clay lick

rooms	11: 2 cabins for 2-3, 4 cabins for 2-4. Dorm with 5 rooms for 2.
price	Full-board US$320-$380 for 2. Dorm $240. Includes transfers & activities.
meals	Full-board only. Buffet-style meals.
closed	Never.
directions	Flights weekdays (1.5 hrs) Cuiabá to Alta Floresta or overnight coach; transfer to Teles Pires river (1 hr); boat to lodge (30 minutes).

	Vitoria Da Riva Carvalho
tel	+55 66 35127100
fax	+55 66 35212221
email	info@cristalinolodge.com.br
web	www.cristalinolodge.com.br

The lodge's conservation & community work is being used as a model for ecotourism development in the region.

Eco lodge

Pousada Picinguaba
Rua G, 130, Vila Picinguaba, 11680–000, Ubatuba SP

Hike to a waterfall or laze in the gardens; paddle upriver or chill in the spa. The ever charismatic Emmanuel is the driving force behind this deliberately small off-the-beaten-track hotel that manages so effortlessly to marry Brazilian charm with French chic. And the setting is sensational, by a rainforest that tumbles into a turquoise bay splashed with fishing boats. Bedroom 'luxuries' extend to a mosquito netted bed, a chilled beer in the mini bar, a balcony with a hammock, a small shower… and a jacuzzi and a sea view for the suite. Convivial evenings start with passion-fruit caipirinhas (pricey but tasty), followed by candlelit tables for two, ocean-fresh fish, tropical fruits and unexpectedly delicious Brazilian white wine. No mobiles, no TV, and, when electricity fails, no hot water – but fresh food, local smiling service and DVDs and coffee-table books galore. Stay as long as you can: it's fabulous. *Minimum stay three-six nights according to season.*

* Private schooner for snorkelling & fishing trips off deserted islands
* Parati for cobbled streets, colonial houses & quirky eateries

rooms	10: 9 twins/doubles, 5 with extra bed; 1 suite.
price	Half-board Discovery Package, 4 nights €1,436. Suite €1,997. Includes activities & car from Rio or São Paulo.
meals	Half-board. Lunches/tea available.
closed	Never.
directions	Car or bus to Parati; 30km south tiny road signed Vila Picinguaba. Final 250m on foot (staff carry bags).

They recycle everything & encourage the community to do the same.

	Emmanuel Rengade
tel	+55 12 3836 9105
fax	+55 12 3836 9103
email	booking@picinguaba.com
web	www.picinguaba.com

Hotel

Pousada Vida Sol e Mar

Praia do Rosa, Ibiraquera District, Box 108, 88780-000, Imbituba SC

Surfers create a buzz at weekends in season. Otherwise 'Rose Beach' is a wild, natural place – a couple of beach shack bars on a perfect crescent of soft sands, with dunes behind. The resort, run by a charming Argentinian family, is perched on the hillside above; you swim in the lagoon or the hotel pool. Below are seven beautiful, rustic-chic villas, rented in whole or in part. Some have their own pool, others a close-up view of the sea, all blend harmoniously with the landscape. Chunky river stones, Brazilian woods, colour-washed tables, sweeping glass, natural linen. Balcony decks with loungers and perfect kitchens add pizzazz: if you're on a higher floor, you're guaranteed one. Hire a cook, dine in the laid-back hotel restaurant above (fish stews, fillet steaks, divine puddings) or hot-foot it to one of the village restaurants over the hill. Yesterday's whale hunters are today's guides, and the whale-watching tours are the best in the area. *Minimum stay four-seven nights according to season.*

- Whale-watching safaris (July-Nov); surfing school; horse riding
- Trips to sleepy La Laguna for dolphins & the tiny Whale Museum

rooms	29 + 7: 29 doubles. 7 villas for 2-10.
price	US$72-$180. Villas $140-$180 for 2.
meals	Lunch US$25. Dinner US$25. Self-catering in villas.
closed	Never.
directions	From Florianópolis south on BR101; after 70km, left to Garopaba City; 2nd rd signed to Praia do Rosa (after IPIRANGA gas station); 6km to a dirt road; straight for 1km. Signed on corner.

	Enrique Litman
tel	+55 48 3355 6111
fax	+55 48 3355 6111
email	tvsm@terra.com.br
web	www.vidasolemar.com.br/ingles

5% of hotel income goes to Brazil's Right Whale Institute, & the support of two volunteers.

Hotel & Self-catering

Estancia y Bodega Colomé
Ruta Provincial 53 Km 20, Molinos, Prov. Salta

You'd never know this was new, the mellow-stone finca that blends so serenely into its surroundings. Here, in the foothills of the Andes, this bodega produces the world's highest altitude wine: reason enough to come. The scenery is spectacular, the gardens boldly planted, the estate run bio-dynamically. It is unusual to find such luxury with such minimal environmental impact and the self-sufficiency is inspiring – all thanks to the energy, love and rare vision of Ursula and Donald Hess. Nine rooms wrap themselves around a courtyard open to the sky: tall shutters, sweeping tiles, ancient ceramics, modern art, private terraces. Bathrooms are Swiss, in testimony to the owners' origins. Zen-like water sculptures add movement and sound. The dining room is decorated in spicy colours, its huge window overlooking an ancient algarrobo tree. Add a cosy bar, a roaring wood fire, a big table, home-grown foods, delicate flavours, fine wines… exceptional.

* Llama introduced to generate income from meat & wool
* Valles Calchaquies for villages, scenery & high-quality weavings

rooms	9: 7 doubles, 2 twins/doubles.
price	US$220.
meals	Lunch US$16. Dinner $17.
closed	Never.
directions	From Salta (4hrs, 226km) towards Cafayate; in Cerillos right to Cachi; at Parque Nacional Cardones signed Colomé; left to Seclantás; at Molinos follow signs. Bus Salta-Molinos (07.00 daily), taxi, or ring.

Visionary owners have transformed the lives of the 56 families on the estate – & introduced welfare.

	Ursula & Donald Hess
tel	+54 (0)3868 49 4044/49 4200
fax	+54 (0)3868 49 4043
email	info@estanciacolome.com
web	www.estanciacolome.com

Hotel

Finca Santa Anita
Coronel Moldes, Prov. Salta

Leave the tourist trail and head for a rare and wonderful experience on a
traditional tobacco finca. On this vast plain framed by densely forested mountains
you share the remarkable lives of Valentina, Carlos (the local mayor) and their
six delightful children in a colonial-columned, sun-filled house. Join them on
horseback through algarrobo and molle trees; raft on the powerful Juramento
river; cycle through the plantations; return to rustic bedrooms with their old
wood stoves intact and the sweet smell of Valentina's distinctively delicious
cooking. Learn how prize-winning goat's cheese is made (taste it too!) and
discover the principles of biodiversity in the organic kitchen garden. Carlos and
Valentina are utterly engaged in the protection of local culture and community:
civic pride is a priority, lively fiestas are funded. Fantastic for adults *and* children –
and great value, particularly if you self-cater in the barns.

- Horse riding, cycling, trekking & river rafting
- Dique Cabra Corral

rooms	5 + 2: 2 doubles, 3 twins. 2 barns for 2-7.
price	US$50. Barns $70.
meals	Lunch US$8. Self-catering in barns.
closed	Never.
directions	From Salta city, Ruta Nacional 68 south direction Cafayate. At Coronel Moldes, take rd signed Dique Cabra Corral. Follow signs to Santa Anita. From Salta city, no. 5 bus.

	Carlos & Valentina Lewis
tel	+54 (0)387 490 5050
mobile	+54 387 5683 1089
email	clewis@salnet.com.ar
web	www.santaanita.com.ar

Carlos has introduced a
self-sustainable kitchen garden
scheme for local families.

B&B & Self-catering

Rincón del Socorro

Los Esteros del Iberá, Prov. Corrientes

Your hosts are young, funny, charming, thoughtful, widely travelled and will do anything for you. Leslie is a celebrated horse whisperer, Valeria was Argentina's top dressage rider, Celia is the perfect guide. Far more than just an eco lodge, this is conservation in action – the biggest such project in Argentina. So the exotic garden merges into savannah and the wildlife comes to you: capybaras hop about the lawn, herons, pelicans and alligators circumnavigate the lake. As for the lodge, it's a 1900s estancia wonderfully adapted to pull in the views. Bed-sitting rooms are wooden and warm, huge sepia photographs add style, old floor tiles are impeccably restored. The adobe and thatch cabins are charming; the public rooms (chocolate, cream, splashes of red) brim with wildlife books; the food is organic, simple, exquisite and surprising. It is a privilege to be in an area of such virgin beauty, and among such inspiring people.

- Guided boat trips & horse riding by day; owl safaris by night
- Giant ant-eaters, giant otters & marsh deer are being re-introduced

Cattle farming is being eliminated as tourism funds conservation & employment.

rooms	9: 1 twin, 5 triples, 3 cabins for 2.
price	Prices on request. Discounts for children. Activities included.
meals	Full-board only.
closed	Never.
directions	5 hrs from Posadas: Rte 14 SE for 100km; 30km after Virasoro, right to Rte 40 for 150km; right 30km past Pellegrini; signed. Daily flights to Posadas, transfers available.

Leslie & Valeria Cook
tel   +54 (0)3782 497073/11 5032 6326
email   info@delsocorro.com
web   www.rincondelsocorro.com

Eco lodge

Yacutinga
Andresito

Imagine tree trunks curving up beams, lianas and seed pods for decoration, and treetop platforms for butterfly-gazing. Charlie trained as an architect and his harmonious open spaces invite as much nature in as possible. Exotic gardens with open bar and small pool beckon, yet you are deep, very deep, in secondary rainforest where native species (and medicinal plants) are being studiously reintroduced. Each of the scattered lodges has four spacious suites with constant warm water, a cosy woodburner, a mosquito-netted porch and a rustic simplicity: rag rugs on earth-red floors, woven blankets on comfy beds, colourful bottles inserted into north-facing walls. Everyone congregates round the fireplace at night: a great spot for drying out clothes, a glass of wine and a chat before simple, delicious dinner. Welcoming staff are excellent guides and bring nature and the culture of the indigenous Guarani alive. *Minimum stay two nights.*

- Scheduled floating trips & walks accompanied by forest guides & local Guaranis
- Cappucine monkeys & 562 species of butterfly
- Spectacular Iguazu Falls are 120km down river but only accessible from Puerto Iguazú

rooms	20: 6 doubles, 14 triples in 5 lodges.
price	Full-board US$385 p.p. for 3-day, 2-night package. Includes excursions.
meals	Full-board only.
closed	Never.
directions	Transfer from Raices Argentinas (Puerto Iguazú) through Argentine Provincial Urugua-I State Park. Switch to 4x4 truck to Iguazú river. Navigation in motorboats for 45 minutes. Jeep transfer to Lodge.

Excellently monitored reforestation programme; every guest gets to plant a tree.

	Carlos Sandoval & Micki Steffen
email	yacutinga@yacutinga.net
web	www.yacutinga.com

Eco lodge

Entry 18

Estancia Los Potreros
Casilla de Correo 4, La Cumbre X5178WAA, Córdoba

The gracious old estancia sits on top of the world, its 6,000 acres stretching over several mountain chains – wild beauty as far as the eye can see. The warm, charming, very English family share their deep love of this place where trees, pampas grasses and wild flowers support a rich bird life; delight in telling you about their Paso Peruano horses and their Aberdeen Angus cattle, over dinner, as organic food and fine wines flow; and accompany you on daily rides. (Beginners are made as welcome as the experienced.) From wide open hilltops to steep tree-studded gullies the terrain is exceptional, for both experts and beginners. They recycle bottles, cherish the ranch's spring water, care tenderly for their staff and keep the stocking rate to a level that allows grasses to regenerate. Bedrooms are charming, old-fashioned, beautifully maintained; warm beds, baskets of logs, wool rugs, private terraces. A relaxed, family, country-house feel.

- Riding gaucho (cowboy) style; involvement in the life of a working farm
- Exceptional birdlife
- Discover the wild Sierras of Córdoba

rooms	11: 7 twins/doubles in main estancia, 3 in home 300m away, 1 cottage for 2.
price	Full-board US$260 p.p. Includes activities.
meals	Full-board only.
closed	Never.
directions	Coach from Buenos Aires to Rio Ceballos, nearest town, then taxi. Fly to Córdoba, 45km away, 1 hr by taxi. Owners will arrange taxis.

Energy is 90% wind- or solar-generated & trees are planted every year.

	Kevin Begg
tel	+54 (0)3548 452121
mobile	+549 3548 (15) 566628
email	bookings@ride-americas.com
web	www.ride-americas.com

Guest house

Huechahue
A.E.12, Junin de los Andes, 8371 Neuquen

Watch the *criollo* being broken in, round up the cattle. Grandfather-in-law bought the land, Jane runs the estancia and friend Yvonne helps looks after guests. Come for log fires, big sofas, huge windows and warm, generous, life-loving Jane who makes it so harmonious and so homely. Snug in a little valley, miles from anywhere and as safe as houses, Huechahue is as authentic as can be. Bricks come from local clay, saddles from the farm's cattle, and sheepskins (which make the riding so comfortable) from the sheep. Two veranda'd outbuildings guard cosy, spacious, pretty bedrooms with polished wooden floors and – Argentinian rarity – duvets. Views sail over lavender and roses, orchards and trees to the distant steppes of the Andes. Everyone eats together, round a home fire or by a wide swathe of Patagonian river: beef and venison for meat-lovers, tasty quiches for vegetarians, wine and beer for all. The scenery is ravishing. *Children over 10 welcome.*

- Exploring the virgin landscape by horse
- Great place to watch condors
- Mapuche reservations & Lanin National Park

rooms	8: 7 twins/doubles, 1 twin.
price	Full-board US$270 p.p. Includes activities.
meals	Full-board only.
closed	May-August.
directions	Buses to Junin de los Andes drop guests off by estancia entrance, collected by staff. 50km from Chapelco airport, 200km from Bariloche airport, 25km from Junin de los Andes. Directions on booking.

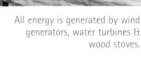

	Jane Williams
tel	+54 (0)2972 491303
fax	+54 (0)2972 491303
email	huechahue@anylink.com.ar
web	www.huechahue.com

All energy is generated by wind generators, water turbines & wood stoves.

Homestay

Peuma Hue

Cabecera Sur Lago Gutiérrez-PNNH, Km 25 Ruta 40, Bariloche

Gallop through pristine forest on a noble horse; return to dogs snoozing by the fire. And sit back with a cocktail as you watch the sun setting over Lake Gutiérrez and the shadows creep up the mountain. Evelyn, warm, generous and in love with life, is guardian to this sacred place. Indeed, she has resurrected the surrounding area and introduced electricity and roads. Peuma Hue is a rare place of connection – with animals, environment, people, oneself. Glorious Nature is virtually untouched and the estancia has been harmoniously conceived: walls hewn from huge tree trunks, tiles inspired by cave paintings, rugs hand-woven and glass ceilings open to the magnificent peak of Cerro Catedral. Swap tales over a heart-warming dinner. Indigenous species are being reintroduced, produce is organic from the kitchen garden or locally sourced, alternative energies are on their way. Exceptional place, inspirational people, and all who stay here long to return.

- Guided treks on foot & horse; kayaking & fishing; mountain ropes; healing massages, tango classes!
- Argentina's biggest national park, Nahuel Huapi, surrounds you

rooms	7 twins/doubles, 1 triple, 1 cabin for 2-4, 1 cabin for 6-7.
price	Full-board for 1, 3 or 7 days. US$375-$642. Singles $284-$375. Includes activities. B&B only $103-$133p.p.
meals	Full-board only.
closed	15 May–30 June.
directions	Buenos Aires to Bariloche: bus 18 hrs, flight 2 hrs. Ruta 40 towards El Bolsón, 25km; 3.5km along gravel road.

Every member of staff shares the owner's eco-spiritual & humanist vision.

Guest house

	Evelyn Hoter
mobile	+54 9 2944 501030/504856
fax	+54 (0)2944 457349
email	info@peuma-hue.com
web	www.peuma-hue.com

Patagonia EcoCamp

c/o Don Carlos 3219, Las Condes, Santiago

The journey here makes you feel like you've come to ends of the earth, but it's worth every step of the way to witness one of the most epic locations in the world. A stronghold of the puma, the Torres del Paine National Park has unique wildlife. Condors soar over the magnificent Andean mountains while herds of guanaco (wild relative of the llama) roam the foothills. A strong ecological ethos runs through the running of the camp, from the sustainable design of the igloo-shaped tents to the use of solar and wind energy. The brightly painted tents (not to everyone's taste!) look impressive and are compact and cosy inside, connected by wooden boardwalks to the warm and friendly dining area where a huge picture window opens out to the mountains beyond. The weather, like the mountains, can be dramatic, but take advantage of the many adventure activities here for this is a part of the world you'll remember for a long time. *Package trips only.*

- Guided walks; horse riding, hiking
- Puma. grey fox, Magellanic woodpecker, Darwin's rhea, huemul deer (national symbol of Chile), waterfowl, dondor

rooms	15 tents: 10 twins, 3 doubles, 2 triples.
price	Full-board from US$823 p.p. for 4 days. Includes activities & transfers.
meals	Full-board only.
closed	15 April-September
directions	Morning flight from Santiago to Punta Arenas (07.45: 4 hrs). Private transfer (370km) to EcoCamp & Torres del Paine National Park arranged Sun, Mon & Wed at 12.30.

The camp does not burn any fossil fuels.

	Reservations
tel	+56 (0)2 232 9878
fax	+56 (0)2 232 8954
email	trips@ecocamp.travel
web	www.ecocamp.travel

Under canvas

Entry 22

caribbean

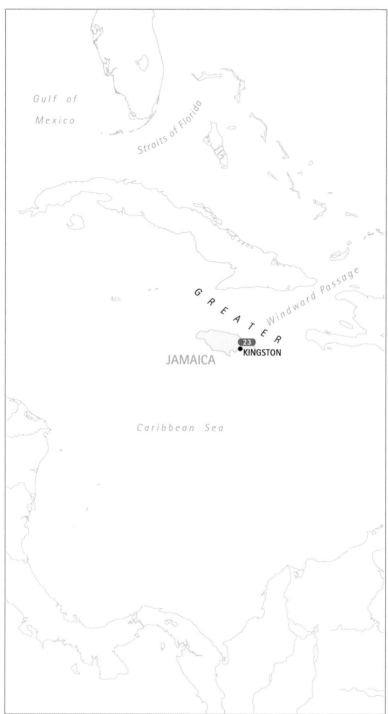

Gulf of
Mexico

Straits of Florida

G R E A T E R

Windward Passage

JAMAICA

23 KINGSTON

Caribbean Sea

0   500   1000 kilometres
0   250   500 miles

Atlantic

Ocean

LEEWARD ISLANDS

US VIRGIN ISLANDS   24
● CHARLOTTE AMALIE

ANTILLES

LESSER ANTILLES

GUADELOUPE ● BASSE–TERRE   25

DOMINICA ● ROSEAU   26
27–30

Caribbean Sea

CASTRIES ●
ST LUCIA   31

WINDWARD ISLANDS

LESSER ANTILLES

Hotel Mocking Bird Hill

Hotel Mocking Bird Hill, P.O. Box 254, Port Antonio

High in the hills of Portland you're far from the hustle and bustle of mass tourism (though expect a party or two on a Friday and Saturday night – this is Jamaica!). All is bright and breezy: white and blue fabrics, hammocks and wrought-iron railings allow natural air conditioning. Barbara and Shireen are committed to the environment and their communities. They use an anaerobic waste-water treatment plant, heat water by solar energy and clean with non-toxic products. Their holistic approach extends beyond the boundaries of the property and they encourage you to explore the local area. Though you'll need some persuading: the rooms are simple and stylish, there's a gorgeous swimming pool and you'll be treated to some of the best home-cooked food on the island (the choice of bread alone at breakfast is outstanding). And there's a generous locally made 'eco-spa body-care' package.

- Hiking in the Blue Mountains & Rio Grande; birdwatching with guides; diving
- Jamaican woodpecker & oriole, red-tailed hawk, striped-head tanager, ringtail pigeon
- Reach Falls; visits to coffee estates & community tourism initiatives

They use vinegar & soda as cleaning products & re-cycle bottles to irrigate the garden by drip feed.

Hotel

rooms	10 twins/doubles.
price	Garden View US$165.50-$295. Seaview $220-$355.
meals	Half-board US$58-$65 extra p.p. Breakfast from $21. Lunch & dinner from $40.
closed	September.
directions	10-min drive from Port Antonio, coast rd east towards Frenchman's Cove; 1st right after Jamaica Palace hotel; 5-min drive up hill. From Kingston, through Drapers, 1st left.

Barbara Walker & Shireen Aga

tel	+876 (0)993 7267/7134
fax	+876 (0)993 7133
email	mockingbird@zeroiq.com
web	www.hotelmockingbirdhill.com

Maho Bay Camp
PO Box 310, Cruz Bay, St John, USVI 00831-0310

An all-American tented camp and condominium resort in a tranquil and beautiful corner of the Caribbean. The pragmatic use of eco-technology is the vision of the charismatic, white-bearded New Yorker Stanley Selangut who pioneered North American ecotourism in the 1970s. Although Stanley is now seldom seen on the island, the environmental ethos among his young and enthusiastic staff remains essentially the same. The tented camps, some with wonderful views of island, are scattered within lush foliage and connected by raised wooden walkways that span the hillside. A handmade curtain separates the sleeping area from the living room, sheets and blankets cover twin beds, while at night you may hear rain tiptoeing on the canvas. No running water in the tents, and cold water (only!) showers are in a separate shared block. The condominium studios, with king-size bed, kitchenette and tiled private bathroom, are made almost entirely of recycled materials and run on solar and wind power.

- Yoga; watersports; guided hikes
- Mongoose, iguana, pelicans & frigate birds

rooms	Maho Bay Camps: 114 tent cottages for 2-3, sharing showers. Harmony Studios: 12 for 2-3.
price	Maho: US$80-$130. Singles from $56. Harmony: $120-$230. Plus 8% USVI tax.
meals	Self-catering. Restaurant & beach café. A la carte entrées US$14-$22.
closed	Never.
directions	11km taxi ride from Cruz Bay harbour.

Glass & paper are recycled as saleable art.

	Augusta Daniels
tel	+1 340 776 6226
fax	+1 340 776 6504
email	reservations@maho.org
web	www.maho.org

Self-catering & Tented Camp

Le Parc aux Orchidées

Trou Caverne, 97116 Pointe Noire

Magic and medicine on the slopes of a tropical volcano. Other places on this butterfly-shaped French Caribbean island have borrowed the word 'ecotourisme' simply to spice up their marketing – not so here. Richard, Valérie and family share their delight in a place intimately in tune with its environment. The Gautiers have left behind a rat race of metropolitan medicine – she an ex-nurse, he a former pharmacist – to pick up where Jean-Claude Rancé, the Parc's creator, left off. It's a point of pride for the local community and a place of fascination for guests. Wake up in your neat little bungalow amid the dew-drenched leaves of a tiny jungle, buzzing with hummingbirds and crowded with colour. Water, heated by solar panels, flows from the mountain to the freshwater pool and jacuzzi. Learn of neglected Creole medicine, hidden in the abundant plant life that envelops you here. Green and serene.

- Guided tour of the park; coffee & cocoa plantation visits; snorkelling & diving
- Orchids, hummingbirds, butterflies, geckos & nocturnal frog chorus
- Soufrière volcano; Réserve Cousteau; Saut d'Acomat

Orchids by the hundred!

rooms	2 bungalows: 1 for 2, 1 for 2-5.
price	€300-€650 p.w.
meals	Self-catering.
closed	Never.
directions	From Pointe-à-Pitre, take route de la traversée over Basse Terre. At end of rd turn right for Deshaies. Through Pointe Noire and uphill. Parc signed on left after school.

Richard & Valérie Gautier

tel	+590 38 56 77
fax	+590 38 56 77
email	contact@parcauxorchidees.com
web	www.parcauxorchidees.com

Self-catering

Three Rivers Eco Lodge
PO Box 1292, Newfoundland Estate, Rosalie

Crossing the eponymous three rivers to this wonderfully lush green patch of paradise is like a rite of passage. Within walking distance of the beach, natural pools and towering waterfalls, the hardest decision you'll have to make is which type of accommodation to choose: string up a hammock, hide away in a treehouse or go for one of the more comfortable cabins. The incredibly hard-working Jem is an ex-London cabbie who fell in love with the island on a backpacking trip and has returned to build this award-winning eco-friendly enterprise, run entirely from hydro and solar power, on a former banana plantation. The rooms are basic, clean and comfortable – all part of the 'back to nature' experience, and there's a genuine community atmosphere: dine together around a large table and share transport to many of the island's fabulous natural attractions. If there's early evening rainfall, hundreds of fireflies twinkle like stars you can almost reach at dusk. Outstanding.

- Walking, diving, whale-watching, horse riding & Community Life package
- Three Rivers Falls; Emerald Pool; Freshwater Lake

rooms	4 cottages for 3; 3 forest cabins & 1 tree house for 2-3; 1 dorm for 6; hammocks & tents.
price	U$40-$70. Dorm $20 p.p. Hammock $10. Camping $15 in own tent, $30-$35 in hired. Plus 10% tax.
meals	Full-board additional $40 p.p.
closed	September.
directions	From Melville Hall airport right over bridge, through Marigot, 40 mins to Pond Casse; left at roundabout.

Jem Winston

tel	+1 767 446 1886
fax	+1 510 578 6578
email	info@3riversdominica.com
web	www.3riversdominica.com

The lodge organises 'sustainable living' workshops for the local community.

Eco lodge

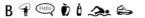

Entry 26

Jungle Bay Resort and Spa
PO Box 2352, Roseau

It is rustic and naturally elegant. At the jungle's edge, the cottages face out towards the wild Atlantic and, although free standing, have the creaking swagger of treehouses (or even birds' nests!); they're built on wooden posts and tucked between a canopy of cedar, gomier and galba trees. Inside, there are Pacific-style platform beds – one king-size or two doubles – and wonderful semi-outdoor en suite showers where you can wash among nature with Ecossential natural soap and sing along with the forest birds. The 55-acre resort is more upmarket than most places on the island (with a Spa du Soleil and two large yoga studios) but it has retained the local feel that defines Dominica. The food is deliciously Creole (with wonderful combinations of fruit drinks, such as sorrel and passion fruit) served on the deck of the circular restaurant overlooking a volcanic rock swimming pool and the sea beyond.

- Hiking; ocean kayaking, whale-watching, snorkelling & diving
- Sperm whale, blue-headed hummingbird & lesser Antillean bullfinch
- Sara Sari Falls; Victoria Falls; Champagne Beach; Boiling Lake

rooms	35 cottages for 2.
price	US$199-$249 p.p. Includes airport transfer, activities & spa.
meals	Full-board only.
closed	Never.
directions	Transfer from Melville airport included.

Ex-banana plantation workers are employed as guides & for handywork.

Sam Raphael

tel	+1 767 446 1789
fax	+1 767 446 1090
email	info@junglebaydominica.com
web	www.junglebaydominica.com

Hotel

Papillote Wilderness Retreat

PO Box 2287, Roseau, 00109/8000

From the moment you enter the Roseau Valley and see the towering Trafalgar Falls you know this is somewhere special. Anne and her husband Cuthbert Jno. Baptiste helped rescue the valley following the devastation caused by Hurricane David in 1979, and the quirky walkways and delightful nooks and crannies are a charming legacy. Anne has created a world-class tropical garden and believes gardens are where truly responsible tourism lies. Be ravished by two-tiered waterfalls, dozens of tree ferns, cacaos, breadfruits and cool mountain streams. She has made sure their ethos remains true to guests' pleas "to keep it just as it is". The rooms are clean and have large beds, and there are four gorgeous natural hot spring baths you can soak in before enjoying genuine Caribbean food on the terrace with wonderful views of the valley. The unsightly hydro power plant nearby is unfortunate – but don't let that put you off. The place is a gem.

* Peacocks, tree frogs, lizards, land crabs
* Trafalgar Falls; Ti Kwen Glo Cho; Titou Gorge

rooms	7: 3 doubles, 4 suites.
price	$110-$125. Singles $100.
meals	Half-board extra $35 p.p.
closed	September & October.
directions	4 miles east of Roseau, up well-travelled road beyond village of Trafalgar.

This world-class tropical garden is an inspiration for nature conservationists.

	Anne Jno Baptiste
tel	+1 767 448 2287
fax	+1 767 448 2285
email	papillote@cwdom.dm
web	www.papillote.dm

Guest house

Entry 28

Zandoli Inn

PO Box 2099, Roseau

An eco-architectural delight – and a wonderfully open-planned solar-powered country inn, 80-foot above the sea. The sturdy beds are made out of local Gommier wood (the same used for local canoes) and there's no need for air conditioning in the remarkably airy rooms, where the wooden jalousie windows provide prime sea views across to the arching Grand Bay. Cook Marlene prepares the freshest Dominican ingredients, such as a carrot-coconut muffin and fillet of fresh fish from the nearby fishing village of Fond St Jean. It's easy to miss the trail that leads away from the terrace through six acres of forested garden where Linda – with a glint in her eye – has planted a variety of citrus, cashew and date palm trees. Enjoy a contemplative moment on the bench at the far end of the trail where there are wonderful undisturbed views of the sea. En route, dip in a swimming pool perched at the top of the cliff – or climb down to the rocks where the more intrepid can jump into the tide below.

- Hiking; swimming & snorkelling
- Dubique Waterfalls; Morne Anglais Mountain; Grand Bay

rooms	5 doubles.
price	US$145.
meals	Breakfast from US$10. Lunch from $10. Dinner $25–$40.
closed	Possibly in September (hurricane season).
directions	From Roseau 30-min drive, 2km past Grand Bay on right before Fond St Jean. By bus from Roseau to Grand Bay (pick-up arranged on reservation).

The rooms are designed for natural ventilation instead of air conditioning.

	Linda Hyland
tel	+1 767 446 3161
fax	+1 767 446 3344
email	zandoli@cwdom.dm
web	www.zandoli.com

Hotel

Crescent Moon Cabins

PO Box 2400, Roseau

A lesson in self-sufficiency. There are wind and hydro generators, all utility water is spring-fed through a ram pump, the food is all home grown, and almost everything else in this fabulous rainforest retreat is made from recycled parts; even the coffee roaster is made from an old car windscreen motor. The food deserves a bright green tick too: Jean and Ron – he a chef for 20 years in Pennsylvania – grow fresh ingredients in their enormous greenhouse for dishes such as pumpkin and breadnut ravioli (homemade pasta) and chipolte pepper sauce with ice cream made from their own goat's milk. The cosy cabins, built from local wood, have a hammock strung out on the balcony with panoramic views of the rainforest and the distant sea. You can walk to the coastal village of Massacre (described by Jean Rhys in *Wide Sargasso Sea*) then return for a soak in the stone plunge pool among the mango, pawpaw and almond trees. The ambience and ethos are inspirational.

- Ornamental flowers, fruit trees, culinary herbs & medicinal plants, all labelled
- Hiking to Middleham Falls; Boiling Lake; Morne Trois Pitons National Park

rooms	4 cabins for 2, each with extra bed.
price	US$115.
meals	Breakfast US$8. Lunch $6-10. Dinner $30.
closed	August.
directions	1hr south on Imperial Highway to Sylvania, take road on right signed Crescent Moon Cabins.

All food, herbs & soap are produced on site.

	Ron & Jean Viveralli
tel	+1 767 449 3449
email	jeanviv@cwdom.dm
web	www.crescentmooncabins.com

Eco lodge

C 🦽 Hello 🍷 🍼 🏊 👟

Balenbouche
P.O. Box 707, Vieux Fort

The wind sighs in the trees, hummingbirds shimmer among flowers, the dogs cavort at your feet and you may wonder if you have awoken from a long sleep. The serenity emanating from the house, the grounds and the remarkable trio of Uta and her two daughters takes you by the heart. You may sleep in one of four cottages, invisible among the trees and foliage. Each has a ravishing combination of colour, simplicity and elegance. You have space and comfort, yet stimulus too, for there are imaginative flourishes everywhere: an open air shower next to a luxurious bathroom, chairs swinging from beams, bold splashes of colour. The main plantation house, old and dignified, has dark wooden floors, antique furniture, white tablecloths, books and breezes. You eat the best food on the island, on the veranda among plants, white wooden railings and walls, on handsome tablecloths – and exquisitely presented. Leave your pretensions behind. *Minimum stay three nights.*

- Swimming, walking, reading, writing: recover your creativity
- The Pitons; wild & empty beaches a short walk

rooms	4 cottages: 1 for 4-6, 1 for 4, 2 for 1-2.
price	US$90-$190 for 2. Additional guests $20. Singles $70-$80. $570-$1,200 per week.
meals	Light lunch US$15. Dinner $20.
closed	Never.
directions	20 mins from Vieux Fort/Hewanorra airport. Half-way between Laborie & Choiseul, near village Piaye. Estate off main rd on side facing ocean. Local minibus route.

Their 'green-ness' lies in their aesthetic & their resistance to over-commercialisation.

	Uta Lawaetz
tel	+1 758 455 1244
email	info@balenbouche.com
web	www.balenbouche.com

Guest house

central america

Tijuana

Mexicali

Ciudad Juárez

Hermosillo

Chihuahua

Red River

Colorado

Rio Grande

Rio Bravo del Norte

Gulf of California

SIERRA MADRE OCCIDENTAL

SIERRA MADRE ORIENTAL

MEXICO

Monterrey

León

Guadalajara

Querétaro

MEXICO CITY

Puebla

Rio Balsas

Acapulco

Pacific

Ocean

0	500	1000 kilometres
0	250	500 miles

©Maidenhead Cartographic, 2005

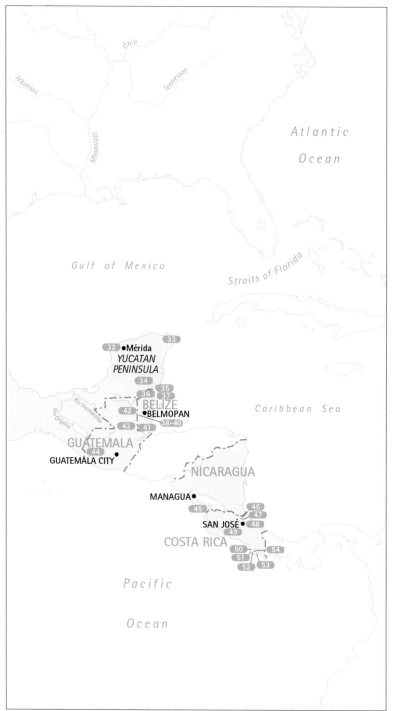

Ohio

Arkansas

Tennessee

Mississippi

Atlantic

Ocean

Gulf of Mexico

Straits of Florida

32 ●Mérida   33
YUCATAN
PENINSULA

34

35
36   37

Río Usumacinta

42   *BELIZE*
●BELMOPAN

Río Grijalva

43   41   38–40

Caribbean Sea

GUATEMALA

44   ●

GUATEMALA CITY

NICARAGUA

MANAGUA●

45   46
47
SAN JOSÉ ●   48
49

COSTA RICA

50   54
51
52   53

Pacific

Ocean

Hotel Eco Paraíso Xixim

Km. 10 de la Antigua Carretera a Sisal, Municipio de Celestún, Yucatán

Daydream to the click-clack of geckos and the put-put of the odd boat.
With fauna, dune flora and creepy crawlies at every turn — insects are
'relocated' not exterminated — nature lovers will be in heaven. For the rest:
flat sands, warm sea, huge skies and organic meals (catch your own fish).
On three miles of white sands on the virgin side of the peninsula, 15 cabanas
built of hi-tech adobe nestle up to each other between the first and second
dunes, with club house and pool a flip-flop away. Almost all have stunning sea
and sunset views. Interiors are simple, circular, light and cool. Co-ordinated
beds and sofas lie on terracotta floors, ceiling fans hang from lovely open-thatch
roofs where geckos perch. No need to fight over the hammocks, each porch
has two. "The guest comes first — always!"

- Dawn tours of flamingo bio-reserve at Celestún, kayaking
- Sea birds, sea shells, iguanas & geckos
- Trips to nearby Maya ruins: Uxmal, Kabah, Sagil

rooms	15 cabanas for 2.
price	US$144-$178. Singles $125-$152. Half-board $176-$210, singles $141-$168.
meals	Half-board option. Lunch/dinner US$19.
closed	Never.
directions	10km north of Celestún. Pick-up on request. Bus from Mérida (2.5 hrs).

Multi-stage desalination process for
drinking & washing water; grey water
goes to gardens.

Hotel

Jaime Solis
tel   +52 988 916 2100/916 2060
fax   +52 988 916 2111
email   info@ecoparaiso.com
web   www.ecoparaiso.com

Sian Ka'an Visitors Center

Sian Ka'an Visitors Center, Tulum Highway, Boca Paila Km.17, Z.C 77780

All you hear is the faint hum of the wind turbine and the chirp of the osprey. You are deep in mangrove and orchid forest but not so far that you can't walk to the deserted – beautiful – beach. Camp life centres round the thatched dining platform, entirely candlelit at night, and the open reception below with seating, maps and small shop (buy your organic insect repellent here). Brave the swaying turbine and climb to the platform for breathtaking views of the lagoon and the sea. The huts, built of local zapote wood, are simple: a curtain over a circular window, a mosquito net over a comfortable bed, a planked door, a warmish shower. This government-run centre is staffed by charming Mayans; the naturalists come from further afield but are training locals to take over. Our delightful guide took us kayaking in the lagoon and guided us on bikes through the jungle – avoiding poisonous bark trees on the way.

- Night-time summer beach tour to see turtles; kayaking in the wetlands; snorkelling on the reef
- Beautiful Maya cliffside ruins at Tulum (15km)

rooms	6: 2 doubles, 4 suites for 2-4 (with bunks).
price	US$62-$75. Suites $82-$95.
meals	Breakfast US$7. Lunch $9. Dinner $11. No alcohol.
closed	Never.
directions	From Cancún, H'way 307 to Tulum, then Boca Paila; pass entrance to Sian Ka'an Reserve; cont. 9km. Bus to Tulum, taxi/pick-up/cycle. Boat through wetlands.

	Kenneth Johnson
tel	+52 998 842 3145
mobile	+52 998 845 1548
email	info@ecotravelmexico.com
web	www.ecotravelmexico.com/mapasiankaan.htm

10% of profits help fund conservation of the Biosphere.

Eco lodge

Entry 33

Villas Ecotucan
Bacalar, Quintana Roo, Yucatán

Gregarious, hands-on, family-friendly Arturo sets the mood; Sophie makes sure it all works. This is a fun, organic, slightly chaotic oasis in an otherwise arid region of Mexico. The lake is the big draw – one vast, freshwater, aquamarine *laguna*. Dotted about the gardens and orchards are mini 'Maya' temples and six cottages: picturesque structures with open-thatch roofs and a spartan eco simplicity. Beds are made by a friend in Bacalar, sheets are clean and unworn and bathrooms (cool showers) are basic. The most spectacular lake views are from the airy restaurant/bar, and the food, when it happens, is good. (Arturo's barbecues are legendary.) But meal times are erratic, in keeping with the spirit of the place, there are no menus and the nearest restaurants are in Bacalar. A great little place for laid-back nature lovers, with character.

- Boat trips on the lake, kayaking & birdwatching
- Armadillo, possum, spider monkeys & 2,170 species of bird
- Mahahual beach for white sands, snorkelling, diving, souvenir shops

rooms	6: 5 family for 4, 1 family for 3.
price	US$45. Singles $30.
meals	Lunch & dinner available.
closed	Rarely.
directions	At Km27.3 on highway. 5km south to Bacalar. Bus, then walk 1km. Pick-up available. Cycling possible.

Everything is solar powered, from path lights to washing machines.

Arturo Borrego & Sophie Viswanathan
tel	+52 0983 834 2516/120 9096
email	ecotucan@yahoo.com
web	www.villasecotucan.info

Eco lodge

Balamku

Mahahual, Quintana Roo, Yucatán

Balamku combines North American style with eco sense – thanks to the Canadian owners, warm, engaging and passionate about how responsible tourism should be done. This is a chilled retreat and one of a new breed of resort on the Costa Maya. They are doing as much as they can on their own patch – replanting mango, papaya and banana, and they encourage you not to be wasteful with water, to leave hair dryers unplugged – and push you, gently, into the community and encourage you to support the local restaurants and attractions. Two beach restaurants are a stroll away, the reef even closer. 'Twixt the (still little used) sand road and the sea, enveloped by bougainvillea, hibiscus and palms, the two-storey *palapas* have pure Caribbean views. Solid, circular, tile-floored, high ceilings and breezy, they are a pleasure to nap in; throws are Maya, beds are perfect and lots of Mexican art. And, with breakfast and bar beneath the owners' home but no dining, peace reigns supreme.

- Snorkelling, diving, kayaking – winds permitting; birdwatching
- Orioles, jays, hummingbirds, tanagers, warblers & sea birds
- Chinchorro Coral Reef (1 hr); Maya ruins

rooms	10 palapas for 2-3.
price	US$70-$75. $10 extra person. Singles $65-$70.
meals	Packed lunch available. Café/restaurant 0.5km.
closed	Never.
directions	4.5hr drive south from Cancún, 5.7km south of Mahahual. Take beach road to Xcalak. Buses twice daily. Taxis available.

Used water supports constructed wetlands, toilets are low-flush and waste is filtered into composting units.

	Carol Tumber & Alan Knight
tel	+52 983 839 5332
email	information@balamku.com
web	www.balamku.com

Eco lodge & Beach hut

Entry 35

Chan Chich Lodge

Gallon Jug Estate, Orange Walk District

Fifty-two jaguar sightings a year – not bad. The remote lodge and its lovely, lush, part-topiary'd gardens, aglow with toucans and parrots, is set amid the unexcavated ruins of a Maya city. On a peninsula severed from the mainland by three defensive moats, it is a site with spectacular views. And they don't miss a trick, from margaritas by the pool to wellies for muddy pathways. Breakfast is big enough to see you through the heartiest trek, the guides are superb, the wildlife stupendous (mozzies apart). After a wholesome and delicious dinner, return to a huge teak bed with billowing pillows, wooden slat windows bound by mosquito nets, a big bathroom beautifully lit, a veranda hung with hammocks, a ceiling fan, a minibar. Such is your luxury thatched cabana for two (twice as nice as the 'regular' for four). The villa is even grander. Ocellated blue and orange turkeys peck about the grass in the afternoon light, fireflies flicker at night, May is the perfect month to go.

- Guided wildlife trails, also at night
- Maya sites of Aguateca & Dos Pilas accessible by boat & horse

rooms	13: 12 cabanas for 2 or 4; 1 villa for 4.
price	US$205-$280. Singles $175-$240. Villa $795-$895. Plus 9% tax. Full-board $440-$520 for 2. Includes tours & tax.
meals	Packages US$70. Plus 9% tax.
closed	September.
directions	36 miles from Blue Creek. Ask for map at booking (3.5 hr drive from Belize City). Gallon Jug airstrip 15 minutes from lodge.

A 20-year hunting ban is beginning to see the return of previously threatened species.

Eco lodge

Anne Lees

tel	+501 (0)223 4419
fax	+501 (0)223 4419
email	reservations@chanchich.com
web	www.chanchich.com

Salamander Belize

Salamander Hideaway, PO Box 120, San Pedro, Ambergris Caye

Kick off your shoes on arrival – and forget them till you leave. Hans, German, is married to Elsa, Belizean; she cooks and he looks after you. They and their staff are delightfully hands-on. The palms sway, the warm winds blow, the sands are raked daily and the surf murmurs on the reef… you could be on a private desert island. No cars, just the odd boat slipping by. The simple-chic wood-and-thatch cabanas, facing jungle or sea, are on stilts to catch sea breezes and have fun, part-open-plan bathrooms and bedrooms. Cosiness and privacy are yours. Make friends later in the big rustic open-roofed lodge, where dining/sitting room, terrace and bar beautifully merge. No night life or TV, just a juice and cocktail bar and ocean-fresh fish. The food is an abundant, delicious mix of Belize and Mediterranean. The garden glows with local flora and hummingbirds, and the turtle grass is kept in the sea.

- Kayaking to the reef, fishing & snorkelling; Blue Hole dive site 2.5hrs away by boat
- Manatees, turtles, crocodiles, bats; huge variety of fish & bird life; orchids
- Lamanai & Altun Ha jungle river adventure; marine reserves

rooms	8 cabanas for 2 (3 with extra futons).
price	US$140-$160.
meals	Breakfast US$12. Lunch $14. Dinner $25 or full meal plan US$45 (plus taxes).
closed	September.
directions	Pick-up from San Pedro, 16km south. Or boat from San Pedro (25 minutes).

The lodge is 100% power self-reliant thanks to solar panels & a wind generator.

	Hans Wagenhaus
tel	+501 (0)209 5005
fax	+501 (0)209 5005
email	info@salamanderbelize.com
web	www.salamanderbelize.com

Eco lodge

The Lodge at Chaa Creek

PO Box 53, San Ignacio, Cayo

Every room has a view – acrefuls of lush, pristine forest in the foothills of the Maya Mountains. This resort is immaculate, its buildings and landscaping groomed to the nth degree. When Mick and Lucy Fleming built their first cottage 20 years ago they could hardly have known it would become Belize's best-known model of sustainable tourism. Furniture is made from sustainable hardwood, bay palm thatch is locally grown, veggies come from their organic farm – and the treetop suites (with jacuzzis) are sensational. Expect colourful tiles, fresh flowers, thick towels, eco luxury; wake to toucan chatter and the occasional howler monkey. The villa and cottages are close but screened, there's no pool for the kids but hundreds of trips and the guides are walking encyclopedias. After a day visiting Maya temples, bliss to return to the spa on Butterfly Hill.

- Swimming, horse-riding, mountain biking & sunset canoeing
- Blue Morpho Butterfly Breeding Centre on site, Maya Temples, The Belize zoo

rooms	23: 17 cottages for 2; 5 suites; 1 villa for 6.
price	US$150. Suites $350-$450. Villa $450.
meals	Breakfast US$10. Lunch $10. Dinner, 4 courses, $32.
closed	Never.
directions	From San Ignacio take Benque Viejo road for 8km. Signed. Pick-up can be arranged. Cycling possible.

Waste glass is ground on site for building purposes & cans used as concrete refill.

Eco lodge

	Mick & Lucy Fleming
tel	+501 (0)824 2037
fax	+501 (0)824 2501
email	reservations@chaacreek.com
web	www.chaacreek.com

duPlooy's Jungle Lodge

PO Box 180, San Ignacio

There's a strong eco policy here and it's getting stronger. In 1988 Judy duPlooy discovered the old riverside farm and moved in with husband and five daughters, added tropical splendour, running water, a dining room/bar – and opened to guests. Now there are 20 cottages linked by a canopied boardwalk on stilts and the marvellous Belize Botanic Gardens – an orchid-rich jewel in a remarkable crown. The gardens are blissful to stroll, but visit in style and hire a horse and buggy. Judy, über-manager, is as committed as ever, and daughter Heather oversees the environmental features – roofs are tiled not thatched (palm is unsustainable here), vehicles are shared, food fairly sourced and every last thing composted or recycled. Your bedroom will be large, light and airy, its tiled floors and solid furniture adding a colonial feel. This is an old-style place run with passion. Let nature chirrup you to sleep.

- Canoe or horse rides to Louisa's Farm for lunch
- Belize Botanic Gardens; Tikal park & ruins; Aktun Tunichil Muknal sea caves

rooms	20 cottages for 2-4, 1 suite for 3-6, 1 suite for 4-8, 1 house for 3-8.
price	US$145-$185. Suites $275-$495. House from $275.
meals	Breakfast US$10. Lunch $12. Dinner $24. Meal deals available.
closed	Never.
directions	From San Ignacio, on western highway towards border with Guatemala at Benque; signed. Bus from Belize City; taxi, cycling and pick-up possible.

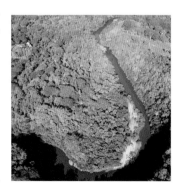

Corn plates & sugar cups are provided for picnics.

	Judy duPlooy
tel	+501 (0)824 3101
fax	+501 (0)824 3301
email	judy@duplooys.com
web	www.duplooys.com

Eco lodge

D

Maya Mountain Lodge

PO Box 174, San Ignacio

Come for the range of activities and tours, and for delightful, compassionate owners. Suzi and Bart run an eco-activity centre up above San Ignacio – enclosed (but not hemmed in) by tropical foliage and an edible plant trail. It is perfect for naturalists, adventurers and families. In compact thatched cottages and a Jerry-built-style lodge are clean, simple bedrooms with basic en suite showers and hammock-strung porches. They overlook a pool surrounded by chemical-free, compost-rich gardens and tropical rainforest. 'Mr Bart' talks with humour and insight on a wide range of issues, is an active local lobbyist and advises you on excursions – perhaps horseback trails into the jungle, archaeological tours to Maya sites or canoeing around Barton Creek Cave. Good local cuisine; bring your own alcohol. The price reflects the simplicity. *Active Adventures tours last three to seven days.*

- Iguana, kingfishers, toucans, otters, porcupine & jaguarundi
- Belize Zoo, opened 1991, protecting indigenous animals & birds

Tours emphasise the protection of the cultural & natural heritage.

Eco lodge

rooms	2 small doubles, 5 rooms for 2-5; 8 cottages for 2-6.
price	US$49-59. For 2-5 $79-$99. Cottages $99-$119. Plus 19% tax.
meals	Breakfast US$8. Lunch $10. Dinner $18.
closed	Rarely.
directions	From San Ignacio, left after petrol station onto Cristo Rey Road. Signed. Or bus to San Ignacio, then taxi. Cycling possible.

Bart and Suzi Mickler

tel	+501 (0)824 2164
fax	+501 (0)824 2029
email	info@mayamountain.com
web	www.mayamountain.com

B 🎣 💬 🍴 🏊

The Lodge at Big Falls
PO Box 103, Punta Gorda

In a clearing in a jungle, where hummingbirds hum and raptors soar overhead, is an intimate, peaceful eco lodge. Rob and Marta, fun and full of energy, came here three years ago and are passionate about this unspoilt corner of Belize, home to the English-speaking Maya. Committed but laid back, they have an excellent working relationship with their Maya staff and foster local enterprises (and you can visit village homes and try your hand at making tortillas). Six cabanas are dotted alongside the Rio Grande, each private, each an amble from the lodge where food, drink, internet and pool beckon. Octagonal in design to catch the breezes, your rooms are simple, spacious and smart. Magical open showers face compost-fed private gardens, laundry is line-dried, hammocks grace verandas and food is as delicious as you'd expect. At sunset flocks of parrots fly overhead, and exotic moths and butterflies descend. Superb.

- Tube-swimming in the river & under waterfalls
- Montezuma's oropendula, keel-billed toucan, laughing falcon... 215 bird species in all
- Maya sites at Lubaantum & Nim Li Punit

rooms	6 cabanas: 2 for 2, 2 for 3, 2 for 4.
price	US$125-$155. Triples $140-$180. Singles $95-$125. Children under 12 free.
meals	Lunch US$12. Dinner, 3 courses, $27.
closed	Never.
directions	29km north of Punta Gorda. 800yds off southern highway at Big Falls; well-signed. Pick-up available. Buses run to top of trail.

No iguana hunting allowed! Landscaping is indigenous and disturbance minimal.

Eco lodge

	Rob & Marta Hirons
tel	+501 (0)614 2888
mobile	Skype: lodgeatbigfalls
email	info@thelodgeatbigfalls.com
web	www.thelodgeatbigfalls.com

D 🔥 🌴 💬 🐾 🍷 🏊 🚲 ⛵

Chiminos Island Lodge
Southwestern Petén

You can see the lagoon from your jungle perch – but the lagoon can't see you. This Maya-built 'island' is thick with jungle and jungle noise: howler monkeys, toucans, parrots, eagles… and the odd snake and creepy-crawlie. But you couldn't be safer or snugger in your reclaimed-mahogany and thatch bungalow on stilts; it is open sided, deeply romantic and – you'll be glad of this – mosquito-protected. Solar-lit walkways weave through the jungle floor as you pick you way across raised tree roots to the lodge itself where food, drink, hammocks and floating dock await – and friendly (mostly Spanish-speaking) staff. The bungalows, all ultra secluded, with lagoon views, are warmly rustic inside: tree trunks for tables; weavings for colour; swing doors that open to big hot showers; balconies for sunsets and views. We love this place.

- Fishing, snorkelling, kayaking & hiking
- Jungle hardwoods include mahogany, ceiba & cedar
- Farmer's horse & cart transports you to Maya sites

rooms	6 bungalows for up to 5 (1 with 2 doubles).
price	Full-board $170. Singles $85.
meals	Full-board only.
closed	Never.
directions	60km from Flores Mayan World airport in Santa Elena. Bus from Flores to the river at Sayaxché. 1.5hr boat ride from Sayaxché. Water taxis.

All proceeds go directly to the lodge, its staff and the local community.

Eco lodge

Juan Carlos Pinto
tel	+502 2471 0855
fax	+502 335 2647
email	info@chiminosisland.com
web	www.chiminosisland.com

Hotel Ecológico Finca Ixobel

Popún, Petén, Zona 6 Barrio Ixobel

Here, in a small corner of the Petén jungle on the Maya route amid limestone hills, this pine forest retreat (American-owned and managed by Guatemalans) is the place to unwind. The finca prides itself on the candlelit, family-style suppers with homemade organic salads and vegetables from the fields (the carrot cake from the bakery is a sought-after sweet treat!). Come also for river tubing and the exciting and challenging cave trips in the grounds of the property. At night, retire to a hammock under the stars, to ping pong, pool, or to the bar to sup a Gallo. Choose between camping, *palapas* with hammocks, dormitories and bungalows with private bathrooms. But, the real adventure is a night in a tree house (to be exact, a cabin on stilts). Keel-billed toucans and green parrots call Ixobel home as well as the many small mammals that scamper across the grounds.

- Caving; horse riding; jungle trekking; inner-tubing; visiting Mopan waterfalls
- Toucans, parrots, armadillos, squirrels, tepescuintle, snakes, iguanas
- Maya city of Tikal (2 hrs); replica of Maya cave of Naj Tunich, glyphs from AD750

rooms	12 rooms for 2-6, some sharing baths; 9 treehouses for 2-5; 3 bungalows for 2-4. 2 dorms for 7-9; 1 suite for 2-5; camping.
price	Q80-Q270 for 2. Dorms Q30 p.p. Camping Q22 p.p.
meals	Breakfast Q10-Q32. Lunch Q17-Q40. Dinner Q30-Q55.
closed	Never.
directions	Buses from Flores or Rio Dulce & from Guatemala City pass by entrance. 15-min walk.

	Carole Ann DeVine
tel	+502 5892 3188
fax	+502 7927 8590
email	info@fincaixobel.com
web	www.fincaixobel.com

The Finca supports a tourism development association in the southern Petén region.

Hotel & Self-catering

Entry 43

Uxlabil Atitlán

Barrio Xacal, San Juan la Laguna, Sololá

A short stroll from unspoilt San Juan, overlooking the "loveliest lake in the world", is Uxlabil. It may be a touch rough around the edges and more hostel than hotel but it is surrounded by terraces, boardwalks and medicinal herbs and every window gets a view. Rooms are fun, rustic and authentically Guatemalan: white textured walls, a hotch-potch of furniture, vibrant lighting, the odd hand-painted chair. The basin is in the bedroom, the loo is in the shower and the communal terraces face west. Eat in at least once and book the day before; the fish, shellfish and home-grown veg are not to be missed and the cooking is popular with the locals. Miles from the backpacker crowds of Punafachel, all that will disturb you here is the odd water taxi circumnavigating the lake. Come for peace and (as yet) undiminished views – in fact, it's all so lovely it's on the point of being discovered. Staff look after you quirkily but comfortably – in Spanish.

- Trekking up volcanoes; canoeing; swimming off sandy beaches
- Santiago Atitlan, a Tz'utujil Maya lakeshore village

rooms	12: 8 twins/doubles, 2 family rooms, 2 bungalows for 4.
price	US$35-$48. Family US$60. Bungalow $73. Singles from $20.
meals	Lunch US$5. Dinner $6.
closed	Never.
directions	By bus 175km from Guatemala City; by boat 25 mins from Panajachel.

Guests are actively encouraged to visit San Juan's weavers who use earthy plant-based dyes.

Reservations

tel	+502 5990 6016
fax	+502 2366 9555
email	atitlan@uxlabil.com
web	www.uxlabil.com

Hotel

Morgan's Rock Hacienda and Ecolodge
Near San Juan del Sur,

Mahogany, cedar, eucalyptus, guapinol, laurel and walnut… the tropical woods that were used to build these cabanas were sourced from responsibly managed trees. Inside: simple luxury. A huge bed and a sofabed, a solar heater, an outdoor shower, a deck for sunsets, a ceiling fan, crisp linen… for seclusion and views, choose the cabanas on the ridge. An amazing suspension bridge (butterflies flutter, birds chatter, monkeys swing) and 100 steps take you down to the hacienda; a further 180 steps and you're on the Pacific. Once there: bliss. No undertow, warm sands, protected sea turtles and waves that could knock you over. Return to convivial cocktails, just-squeezed juices and ample portions of delicious food served by a truly charming and enthusiastic local staff. Bay, pool, forest trails and butterfly farm are yours for free; kayaking and bodyboarding come at a price. Be lulled to sleep by the wind in the trees and the breakers on the beach.

* Estuary kayaking at sunrise (see herons, firecatchers, egrets) & fishing
* Giant sea turtles; charming, colonial Granada; Lake Nicaragua & Ometepe Island (2 volcanoes)

rooms	15 cabanas for 2 + extra sofabed.
price	Full-board US$170-$195 p.p. Singles $205-$240.
meals	Full-board only.
closed	Never.
directions	10 miles from San Juan del Sur. About 3 hrs from Managua airport. Also accessible from San José & Liberia in Costa Rica.

Over 1.5 million hardwood & fruit trees have been planted in the last four years & wildlife introduced.

	Marcela Gómez
tel	+506 232 6449
fax	+506 232 6297
email	info@morgansrock.com
web	www.morgansrock.com

Eco lodge

E

Laguna del Lagarto Eco Lodge
Boca Tapada

They tempt the toucans with bananas at seven – watch them while you breakfast. Early to rise, early to bed – you are perfectly at one with nature here. Remote even for the jungle, this is for serious rainforest fans, and the journey to get here is all part of the adventure. You're put up in a cluster of plain wooden cabins next to the restaurant: simple beds, screened windows, ceiling fans, shared verandas. Settle into a comfy rocking chair with a borrowed book (on wildlife – of course), swing in a hammock with a forest-and-lagoon view, aim the telescope at the birds. The birdlife here is remarkable, so much so that the lodge is a magnet for biologists in search of the Great Green Macaw. For such a remote place, the commitment to recycling paper, plastic and bottles is admirable – and we were struck by the attentiveness of the staff, prepared to take guests on impromptu walks and delighted to arrange trips according to preference – while sticking to the carefully marked trails.

- Birdwatching trips upriver to the Nicaraguan border
- Toucans, caymen, monkeys, iguanas & poison-dart frogs

The owners are protecting the rainforest & refuse to sell to loggers.

Eco lodge

rooms	20 cabins: 18 for 2, 2 for 3-4.
price	US$50.75-$68.20. Triple $58.65-$79. Singles $38.46-$51.55.
meals	Breakfast US$6. Lunch $7.40. Dinner $12.50.
closed	Never.
directions	Bus from San José to Pital then bus to Boca Tapada. 7km from Boca Tapada, 4x4 can drive straight to lodge. Owners arrange transport from airport (3.5 hrs) or village.

Kurt & Vinzenz Schmack

tel	+506 289 8163
fax	+506 289 5295
email	info@lagarto-lodge-costa-rica.com
web	www.lagarto-lodge-costa-rica.com

Finca Rosa Blanca Country Inn

APDO, 41-3009 Santa Barbara de Heredia

Teri and Glenn have created one of Costa Rica's most recognised eco-friendly places to stay. Perched among guava and mango trees on a hilltop not far from the quiet suburbs of San José, there are wonderful views of coffee plantations and rolling countryside, particularly from huge windows in the dining area, and best of all from the suite terrace on the top floor. The stylishly converted main building has an eclectic, artistic elegance, decorated with murals, paintings and sculptures made by local artisans. Light and airy rooms, not particularly large, are adorned with colourful (but not garish) bedspreads and rugs. Glenn and Teri are locally acknowledged as experts in conservation and work with the local community in a recycling scheme for all non-organic waste. The hotel is likely to be busy in high season, but doubtless there will always be a relaxed and peaceful atmosphere. The pool is sublime and you can stare at the valley for hours.

- Horse riding; Café Britt coffee tour; hiking
- Butterflies, birds & over 300 fruit trees
- Barva Volcano National Park; Ark Herb & Botanical Garden

rooms	9: 3 doubles, 3 for 3-4; 1 suite with separate bathroom; 2 villas for 6
price	US$200-$250. Suite $300. Villas $270.
meals	Lunch US$15. Dinner, 4 courses, $40.
closed	Never.
directions	15-minute drive from San José International Airport. Hotel/bus station/airport transfer on request.

Spring-fed swimming pool is ionised rather than chlorinated.

	Teri & Glenn Jampol
tel	+506 269 9392
fax	+506 269 9555
email	info@fincarosablanca.com
web	www.finca-rblanca.co.cr

Hotel

Pacuare Lodge
El Bajo del Tigre, Turialba

The ultimate eco adventure. As you approach this authentic yet stylish rainforest retreat the complex dense jungle may be unfamiliar at first, but soon you will become its intimate friend. Cattail-thatched wooden cabins (rafted in by Cabacar Indians from a sustainable reforestation project) are far enough apart to provide privacy among the riverside wild gardens. Simple natural colours create an almost luxurious feel to the basic rooms: simply a bed, two small tables and curtains that draw across mosquito netting panels. Water is piped from local tributary streams to the bathrooms where biodegradable soap is de rigeur. As the nocturnal wildlife begin to stir, dine upstairs in the main *palapa* where freshly made food is served in candlelight against the flickering shadow of the forest. Plates are furnished with a beautiful grasshopper garnish made from woven grasses. *Children over 12 welcome.*

- Guided hikes; white-water rafting; rainforest-canopy tour
- Toucans, orapendulas, kingfishers, hummingbirds, Morpho butterflies
- Cabecar Indian village in Pacuare Protected Zone

rooms	13: 9 cabins for 2; 4 tents for 2, sharing showers. Extra beds available.
price	Full-board from US$259 p.p. Includes local transport & guide.
meals	Full-board only.
closed	Never.
directions	Arrival by raft along Pacuare river or by 4x4 through forest with short walk at end. Details on booking.

The welcome pack includes a biography of the much-valued local guides & staff.

Eco lodge

	Daniel Peyer
tel	+506 225 3939
fax	+506 253 6327
email	lodge@junglelodgecostarica.com
web	www.junglelodgecostarica.com

F 🔵 🐾 🍾

Inn at Coyote Mountain

Calle La Tabla de Piedades Sur, San Ramon, Alajuela

Up the spiral stair in the tower to one of the most stunning panoramas in Costa Rica – it's worth paying the extra for the 'observatory' suite! The other bedrooms – all lofty, all large – open to a Moorish courtyard where fountains play and swallows swoop. No air conditioning, no fans: the modern hacienda has been carefully designed to be cool in the summer and warm in the winter. Once here, you will pretty much stay put – the 4x4 van does not come cheap – but there are guided walks within the reserve and orchids and wildlife aplenty (flycatchers, hummingbirds, sloths, coyote). Visitors are enchanted by the peace, the setting and the food. Start with a margarita by the fire, move onto four gorgeous Spanish/Creole courses served at a big friendly table (or privately on the veranda). Sophisticated bedrooms display textiles on walls and floors, huge bathrooms, delicious beds. No need for room keys: staff are trustworthy, courteous and caring.

- Creole cookery courses; massages; guided tours of reserve
- Day trip to Arenal Volcano – five mini-eruptions per day

rooms	4: 2 doubles, 1 twin, 1 suite.
price	Half-board US$149-$169. Suite $229. Plus 18% service on meals & drinks.
meals	Breakfast US$20. Lunch $20. Dinner $40.
closed	Never.
directions	59km (1.5 hrs) north of Juan Santamaria Airport nr San José. Bus from San José to San Ramon, 17km away, then 4x4 taxi.

Wind turbine on site & all grey water channelled to the orchard.

	Reservations
tel	+506 383 05 44
fax	+1 800 980 0713
email	info@cerrocoyote.com
web	www.cerrocoyote.com

Eco lodge

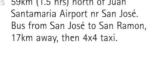

La Cusinga Lodge

A.P. 41-8000, San Isidro del General

Surely the Garden of Eden must have been like this! The heart-stopping beauty of the rainforest, the empty, enticing beaches, the tumbling diversity of wildlife… The Costa Rican family who own and run this remote reserve are determined to preserve its perfections. Ox carts are used instead of tractors, energy is hydro- or solar-powered and there's no swimming pool to squander precious water – but with the Pacific on your doorstep why should you want one? The owner is friendly and helpful, as are his (local) staff. It's a good place for them to work – many stay for years. Home-grown or locally sourced food is served in a central kitchen; there's also an observation room and another with television and books. Simple, elegant cabins, crafted from local wood and stone, are reached via stone pathways through the trees. From the balconies, you can watch humpback whales in the bay.

- Rainforest trails; snorkelling, kayaking, riding; tropical farm tours; tortilla-making
- Tree frogs, howler monkeys, hawksbill turtles, whales, dolphins & over 270 bird species
- Bahia Ballena Marine Park

rooms	11 cabins: 7 for 2-3 (2 double beds); 1 suite; 1 cabin for 1; 2 dorm-style cabins for 12.
price	US$118. Suite $140. Single $93. Dorm cabins $55 p.p. Plus taxes.
meals	Lunch & dinner US$12.50-$16.
closed	Never.
directions	200m south of Km166 on coastal h'way; 4.5km south of Uvita. On r'hand side of h'way. Bus from San Isidro del General to Uvita.

La Cusinga liaises closely with the National Park & has two foundations for community service work.

Eco lodge

	Geinier Guzmán
tel	+506 770 2549
fax	+506 770 4611
email	info@lacusingalodge.com
web	www.lacusingalodge.com

Danta Corcovado Lodge
83-8203 Puerto Jimenez

Sleep to the sound of night frogs, wake to the calls of monkeys. The only louder sound is Merlyn's laugh as he welcomes you into his family with an irresistible, intoxicating charm. This is an unpretentious, authentic, working farm mixed with Costa Rican flair and passion for the rainforest surroundings. Built of locally-grown teak, rooms have a cosy simplicity with charming artistic flourishes: hooks made from branches, decorative wooden windows, pebble borders, tree stump chairs. For complete privacy, choose one of the jungle-wrapped bungalows. Otherwise, it's open house. Browse a book in the sitting room, swing in one of the hammocks, join the family for meals – home-grown, often organic – in the open-air dining room. Merlyn's passion is inspiring. Forest regeneration, composting, recycling, a paper-making project and solar heating are underway or in the pipeline.

- Night jungle walks; kayaking through mangroves; birdwatching; hiking.
- Monkeys, sloths, anteaters, luminescent mushrooms, toucans, caimans
- Pristine rainforests of Corcovado National Park; Guaymi Indigenous Reserve

rooms	7: 3 doubles (2 with 4 bunks, sharing bathroom); 2 bungalows for 2.
price	US$30-$60. Singles $20.
meals	Breakfast US$6. Lunch & dinner $8.50
closed	Never.
directions	3km from La Palma. Danta hoof print signs indicate the way.

	Merlyn Oviedo & Jorge Mora
tel	+506 819 1860
mobile	+506 378 9188
email	info@dantacorcovado.net
web	www.dantacorcovado.net

The Lodge sources supplies, staff & guides from the local community & supports the local school.

Eco lodge

Lapa Rios

Mata Palo, Osa Peninsula

Half-close your eyes and you're asleep in the tree tops. Perched 350 feet above sea level, the teak and palm lodges capture cooling breezes – no air-con required – and you peer from your terrace over timeless greens and blues of trees and ocean. Simple but elegantly inviting, your airy home slips seamlessly into the rainforest. Floors are wooden, walls wide open, furniture bamboo, showers in the garden. Tropical flowers provide colour, sunshine heats the water. It's ten minutes to the beach or the 1,000-acre nature reserve with river and waterfalls. The main lodge, with its 50-foot high platform, has sensational views. Mealtimes, too, are distracting, though the food – made by newly skilled villagers – competes well: coconut crusted fish with mango-ginger salsa. Detailed information packs in the rooms ensure you needn't miss a trick. A treat for wealthy naturalists.

- Rainforest hikes, early-bird tours; surfing, kayaking, horse riding; yoga & massage
- Monkeys, ocelots, crocodiles, turtles & over 300 birds including toucans & eagles
- Corcovado National Park; jungle night camping

rooms	16 bungalows: 6 for 2, 10 for 2-3. Extra outside showers.
price	Full-board US$198-$319 p.p. sharing. Singles $308-$463. Children up to 10 half price.
meals	Full-board only.
closed	Never.
directions	Car, bus or flight to Puerto Jiménez. Transfer from Puerto Jiménez airport by taxi or car 20km south to Lapa Rios.

Guided walks support the reserve & the community.

Eco lodge

Reservations

tel	+506 735 5130
fax	+506 735 5179
email	info@laparios.com
web	www.laparios.com

Playa Nicuesa Rainforest Lodge
P.O Box 56, Golfito

The front garden is a powder blue ocean, the back yard is a tropical green rainforest. Access is by boat only. But who wants to go anywhere? This combination of adventure camp and chill-out retreat rubbing along happily with nature is totally seductive. Local woods, recycled plastic roof tiles, thatch roofs and solar energy are just the environmental starters. Wraparound louvre doors provide air conditioning and there are no TVs, radios or generator buzz. Just beautiful, relaxed surroundings of polished woods, colourful Guatemalan fabrics, jungle noises and spectacular ocean and forest views from private verandas. Retreat to a shady hammock or share jungle-adventure stories in the treetop bar. Local staff are a smiling presence while exuberant hosts Michael and Donna join guests for Latino-style meals. Fun, festive and under the stars. *Minimum stay two nights.*

- Guided rainforest hikes; snorkelling; horse riding, waterfalls, masages & kayaking in Piedras Blancas National Park
- Iguanas, monkeys (howler and whiteface), macaws, toucans, dolphins & tropical marine life

rooms	8: 4 twins/doubles, 3 cabins for 2, 1 cabin for 3-4.
price	Full-board US$280-$300. Singles $175-$195. Cabins $160-$180 p.p. sharing. Singles $195-$215. Children 6-12 $85. Includes pick-up.
meals	Full-board only.
closed	October-mid-November.
directions	Guests collected by boat at Puerto Jimenez (18km) or Golfito (15km).

Fruits, vegetables & breads are home-made or home-grown.

	Reservations
tel	+506 222 0704 or +506 735 5237
email	reservations@nicuesalodge.com
web	www.nicuesalodge.com

Eco lodge

D (Hello) 🍎 🍶

Albergue Cerro Escondido
Reserva Karen Mogensen, Nicoya Peninsula

It's a tough uphill hike to get here – pre-book a horse (cars, of course, are discouraged). Deep in the jungle, this modest lodge consists of a main house, some old farm buildings and four teak cabanas built in the traditional manner. Curved planks, carved patterns, screened windows, shared verandas – simple, yes, but perfect for this amazing setting, and, raised high in the forest canopy, with views. More bird-spotting from the dining room where the gentle, friendly couple who run the place serve wonderful home-cooked meals – using as much produce from the garden as the leafcutter ants allow. Ovens are wood-fuelled or solar and there's no washing machine or hot water; staying here is an eye-opener into just how labour intensive ecotourism can be. So it's (solar-powered) lights off after 8pm, and cold water for showers... in this humidity, just what you need. A retreat from the world – but be prepared to rough it! *$10 rate for volunteers. Activities must be pre-arranged.*

- Waterfall trails; guided birdwatching; boat trips to island
- Nearby orchid garden cultivated by a local woman

rooms	4 cabins: 1 double & bunk, 1 for 6, 2 quads. Student groups occasionally.
price	US$35. Triple $30. Singles $40. Students $25. Children 5-11 $15.
meals	Breakfast US$5. Lunch & dinner $8.
closed	Easter week.
directions	From Jicaral Asepaleco arrange transport: drive 16km to San Ramón de Rio Blanco, hike through jungle, cross rivers, up steep hill.

All profits go to the community and locals are taught about environmental issues, cookery and first-aid.

Eco lodge

	Luis Mena
tel	+506 650 0607
fax	+506 650 0201
email	asepalec@racsa.co.cr
web	www.asepaleco.com

Photo: Salamander Belize, entry 37

north
america

Photos left, this page top & middle www.alberta-canada.net
Photos this page bottom Toadhall Bed and Breakfast, entry 57

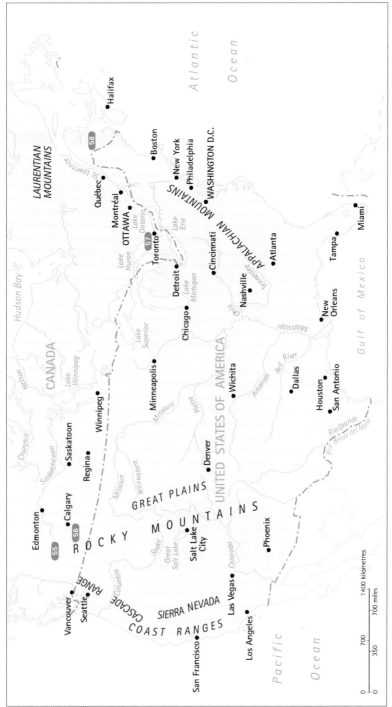

Halifax

58

Boston
New York
Philadelphia
WASHINGTON D.C.

LAURENTIAN
MOUNTAINS

St Lawrence

Québec
Montréal
OTTAWA

Lake
Ontario

57

Toronto

Lake
Erie

APPALACHIAN MOUNTAINS

Miami

Tampa

Atlanta

Cincinnati

Lake
Huron

Detroit

Lake
Michigan

Nashville

Tennessee

New
Orleans

Hudson Bay

Lake
Superior

Chicago

Ohio

Gulf of Mexico

Nelson

Lake
Winnipeg

CANADA

Mississippi

Churchill

Minneapolis

Missouri

Red River

UNITED STATES OF AMERICA

Wichita

Arkansas

Dallas

Houston
San Antonio

Saskatchewan

Winnipeg

Platte

Rio Grande
Rio Bravo del Norte

Saskatoon

Regina

Denver

Missouri

Yellowstone

GREAT PLAINS

Calgary

Edmonton

56

R O C K Y

M O U N T A I N S

55

Salt Lake
City

Great
Salt Lake

Snake

Phoenix

Colorado

Columbia

CASCADE

RANGE

Las Vegas

Vancouver
Seattle

SIERRA NEVADA

COAST RANGES

Los Angeles

Pacific

Ocean

San Francisco

Atlantic

Ocean

1400 kilometres

700 miles

700

350

0

0

Aurum Lodge
Cline River, P.O.Box 76, Nordegg, Alberta, T0M 2H0

A true wilderness retreat for nature lovers. In a natural clearing in the forest, overlooking the beautiful Abraham Lake and with the Canadian Rockies looming in the distance, this remote solar-powered lodge is the place to get away from it all. The emphasis is on low-impact living and there are no televisions or phones in the rooms; just wind whistling in the trees, water lapping at the lake's shore and a natural adventure playground on your doorstep. Madeleine and Alan like to join you for dinner – they have travelled the world over the last 40 years accumulating collectibles that are proudly on display; the living-dining area has an Asia theme while upstairs you're transported to the Middle East and Africa. Bright and airy rooms have recycled wood flooring, oriental rugs, with white walls, and large windows provide fantastic views. Clean and delightfully simple.

- Hiking, cycling, trail-riding, canoeing, climbing, glacier walking (summer only); snowshoeing, cross-country skiing, ice-climbing, dog-sledding
- Deer, elk, mountain sheep, coyote & bears
- Kootenay Plains Ecological Reserve; Lake Louise, Banff & Jasper National Parks

rooms	6 + 3: 4 doubles, 2 twins. 2 cottage units for 2, 1 apartment for 4.
price	CAN$110-$220. Self-catering units $130-$240.
meals	Dinner CAN$22 (for lodge guests only, by arrangement). Self-catering.
closed	Never.
directions	At Saskatchewan River Crossing in Banff National Park, leave Icefields Parkway (Hwy 93) & head east on Hwy 11 for 45km to Cline River.

The lodge has reduced its dependency on fossil fuels by 85% since 2000.

	Madeleine & Alan Ernst
tel	+1 403 721 2117
fax	+1 403 721 2118
email	info@aurumlodge.com
web	www.aurumlodge.com

B&B & Self-catering

Nipika Mountain Resort

RR #3, 4968 Timbervale Place, Invermere, British Columbia, V0A 1K3

Nipika smells like the wilderness. Pine forests, freshly cut firewood and gurgling mountain streams invigorate the senses even before you embark on one of the many low-impact outdoor activities. Lyle and Dianne double as tour guides in the summer and ski instructors in the winter. Lyle once coached the Canadian Olympic cross-country ski team but his motivation now comes from environmental stewardship at this wilderness haven (hunting and motorised activities are prohibited). The rustic-looking (though luxurious inside) hand-built log cabins and impressive split-level timber-framed main lodge are designed for comfort after a day's adventure. Showers only, but there are wood-burning stoves to snuggle up to, and a barbecue area from where you can enjoy views of the spectacular Rocky Mountains. Watch elk come up from the river at dusk. A dream for outdoor enthusiasts.

- Hiking, rafting (summer); cross-country skiing, snowshoeing, ice-skating (winter)
- Deer, elk, black bear, grizzly bear, wolves, coyote & 280 species of birds
- Kootenay & Banff National Parks; Columbia River Wetlands

rooms	2 cabins for 6; 4 cabins for 8; 1 lodge for 4-13.
price	CAN$170-$240 p.p.
meals	Self-catering.
closed	Never.
directions	From Calgary west on Highway 1 to junction of Hwy 93; south 86km to Settlers Rd; 14km to lodge. Bus to Radium Hot Springs for pick-up. Also on TransRockies Mountain Bike Route.

All their electricity is generated by solar or micro-hydro power.

Lyle Wilson

tel	+1 877 647 4525
fax	+1 250 342 0516
email	info@nipika.com
web	www.nipika.com

Self-catering

Toadhall Bed and Breakfast

225 Lakeland Crescent, Richmond Hill, Ontario, L4E 3A5

A treat for the greenest amphibian! A hop and a jump from suburbia, this most modern retreat provides expansive views across the lake's wide horizon. Wake to the sound of a loon as the morning sun strikes the blue walls of this queen-sized bedroom. The building's angular brutalist design creates a feeling of openness, while the minimalist décor soothes the senses. High-quality leather furniture and Seventies-style dining add to the overall modernist feel. Gloria is well-travelled, attentive but not fussy, and has a genuine passion for the environment that is reflected in her approach to every detail, from the energy-efficient shower head to the brick in the water tank. Bread and vegetables are sourced locally; breakfast includes ham crusted soufflé with roasted yams and green salad. In the late afternoon, enjoy a glass of wine and organic tapas on the back patio overlooking the garden – chances are you'll also spot a toad or two!

- Hiking, swimming, canoeing, windsurfing; cross-country skiing, skating, snowshoeing
- Lake Wilcox; Oak Ridges Moraine; McMichael Gallery

rooms	1 double & pull-out couch.
price	CAN$125. $175 for 3. Singles $95.
meals	Restaurants in Oak Ridges 1km; Aurora & Richmond Hill 5km.
closed	Never.
directions	From Toronto on Don Valley Parkway to Hwy 404 N; exit left at Stouffville Rd; right at Bayview Ave, left at North Lake Rd, left at Lakeland Cres. Or subway to Finch Station, then Viva blue bus to New Market; King Rd for pick-up.

Passive solar design ensures heat is circulated throughout the building.

	Gloria Marsh
tel	+1 905 773 4028
email	toadhall@aci.on.ca
web	www.225toadhall.ca

B&B

Chic-Chocs Mountain Lodge

Réserve faunique de Matane, Gaspé Peninisula, Québec

An exclusive winderness hideaway where you are privy to the great outdoors, country haute cuisine and the warmth of a wood fire in an atmosphere that resonates with the appreciation of nature. Alain Laflamme is the resident host, chef and sommelier and draws on 27 years experience of working in some of Eastern Canada's most illustrious kitchens. There's fresh bread, yogurt and desserts made on site and for all meals you're invited to dine with the other guests around one of the large dining tables where there are panoramic views of the mountains. The well-insulated building is designed to be energy-efficient and includes a hot-water heating system, a strict recycling policy and biodegradable detergents. The rooms have either two single beds or one king-size bed with chic, white bathrooms; downstairs there's a games room, sauna, outside spa, and a changing room with direct access to the surrounding wildlife reserve.

- Snowshoeing & ski touring (winter); hiking & mountain biking (summer)
- Moose, caribou & white-tailed deer
- Matane Wildlife Reserve: La Chute Hélène, Mount Matawees, Mount Coleman

rooms	18 twins/doubles.
price	Full-board CA$550. Singles $315. Includes guided activities, equipment & transfers.
meals	Full-board only.
closed	Mid-April-mid-June; mid-October-mid-December.
directions	Transport provided from Cap-Chat reception office.

Trails in the surrounding reserve are designed to leave no trace.

Reservations

tel	+1 418 890 6527
email	inforeservation@sepaq.com
web	www.chicchocs.com

Hotel

E   ♿   ✕   💬   🍶   🚲   👞

The Greenhouse
Bottom of the garden

Transparency, seeing through your hosts, stone-throwing – the puns tend to hover around this place like flies around jam. Please forgive this writer if one or two slip through. But the Greenhouse lends itself to slight ridicule, does it not? Like it or loathe it, the owners have chosen the easy way of capturing the sunlight – south, north, east and west. You cannot avoid it. It caresses you, pursues you, harasses you, chases you out of any comfortable corner you may have found. Then – and here is the rub – with all its warmth, it abandons you in the evening. At which point you have to seek solace in a sweater or under the duvet. Yes, you are among vines, perhaps among great ones, but you gain nothing from such neighbours. But your hosts try hard to please – they say they are committed to fighting global warming; perhaps so, but they appear equally committed to their own form of client-warming.

- Grape-tasting; talking to tomatoes; watering
- Worms, aphids and other greenfly

rooms	One open-plan space.
price	A pound of mulch.
meals	Help yourself.
closed	Never.
directions	Follow the signpost and then your nose.

They have saved on wood for the signpost.

	Mr & Mrs Compost
tel	+0 000 911 911
email	not_quite_kew@gardens.com
web	www.bottomofthegarden.com

europe

Hotel Hellnar
Brekkubær, Hellnar, 356 Snæfellsbær

A haven of warmth and well-being wedged between the wave-lashed Snæfellsnes coast and a wall of black basalt lava, at the foot of the brooding, ice-clad volcano Snæfellsjökull. Originally conceived as a spiritual retreat by owner Gudrun, the lodge is single-storey timber building where simplicity reigns. Shades of blue, yellow and white mirror the surrounding natural features of sea, light and ice. Bright and modern, each of the Scandinavian-style rooms has a compact shower and uninterrupted sea or glacier views. In the dining room, with its wide ocean views, expect the freshest of home-cooked fish and lamb, rounded off with exquisite bilberry pancakes. Stay up for the midnight sun as it illuminates the crater summit… sooner or later the lure of a fluffy duvet and soft cotton sheets will have you horizontal, lulled to sleep by the plaintive wail of restless kittiwakes.

- Hiking & horse riding; whale-watching (June–mid-August)
- Arctic fox, birds, Arctic tern, guillemots, Slavonian grebe, shovelers, white-tailed eagle, 130 species of Arctic flora
- Snæfellsjökull National Park (including Snæfellsjökull Glacier)

rooms	20 twins. Extra bed available.
price	IKR10,700-KR13,900. Singles KR8,400-KR10,900.
meals	Buffet lunch IKR1,990.
closed	October-April.
directions	From Reykjavik Rd 1 to Borgarnes; 2nd exit at r'bout onto Rd 54; to junction with Rd574 (1hr); left & drive for 19km, left to Hellnar; 1st left & drive past church.

It is the first hotel in Iceland to be certified by Green Globe 21.

	Gudrun Bergmann
tel	+354 (0)435 6820
fax	+354 (0)435 6801
email	hotel@hellnar.is
web	www.hellnar.is

Hotel

C

Ongajok Mountain Farm
Mathisdalen, 9518 Alta

It may be a long and bumpy road to get here, but the rushing waters of the many rivers you pass will have you lacing up your walking boots the second you arrive. The commitment to nature and the environment is as genuine as the welcome you will receive from the softly-spoken Espen. He's a chef by training, and has converted this remote traditional Norwegian farmhouse into a flourishing centre for outdoor activities where the delicious food is as reviving as the fresh arctic air. Mountains dominate the landscape while silence permeates the ambience. The pine rooms are very basic (include en suite compost toilets), but you can relax in the main building's cosy log-fired sitting room, and if you can brave the night air, there's an outside hot tub from where you can soothe your aching muscles, lie back and gaze at the galaxy in all its glory. Great for groups.

- Hiking, fishing (summer); cross country skiing, ice-fishing, snow mobile safaris (winter)
- Elk, reindeer, lynx, wolverine, eagle, owl
- Alta Rock Art Museum & Alta Canyon

rooms	16 for 1-2.
price	Half-board NOK1,790 p.p. Minimum 8 people.
meals	Half-board only.
closed	Never.
directions	Fly from Oslo (2 hrs) or Tromsø (30 mins) to Alta airport for (a bumpy!) 25km transfer by bus. Final 4km by 4x4 or horse & sleigh.

Stay a night in a lavoo (tipi) and learn from a local Sami about their traditional way of life.

	Espen Ottem
tel	+47 78 43 26 00
email	espen@ongajok.no
web	www.ongajok.no

Eco lodge

G 🧍 ⛄ 🔪 (Hello) 🍶

Westerås
6216 Geiranger

Wake up to one of the world's most awesome sights: the deep blue waters of Geiranger Fjord, surrounded by snow-covered mountain peaks and lush, green vegetation. The working farm is perched on the side of the fjord's entrance, overlooking the pretty village of Geiranger, and has been in the Westerås family since 1603. Iris and Arnfinn are the new generation diversifying into tourism and have sensitively built the cabins in keeping with the breathtaking landscape. The pine cabins have two double rooms, a living room with a sofabed and fireplace, and a simple kitchenette; the flats in the farmhouse have two double bedrooms, each with extra bunk beds, and similar amenities. Guides are available to take you to some of the abandoned old farms on the banks of the fjord as well as to many of the district's wonderful lakes and rivers. After a day's exploration, enjoy delicious jam scones and cream tea (and dinner) on the restaurant terrace overlooking the world-famous fjord.

- Shetland ponies & goats on the farm
- Storseterfossen (30m high waterfall); Vesteråsfjellet

rooms	Cabins: 4 for 5, 1 for 6. Flats: 1 for 6, 1 for 7.
price	Cabins NOK500-NOK750. Flats NOK450-NOK750. Final clean & bedlinen extra.
meals	Self-catering. Restaurant nearby, open June-August.
closed	October-April.
directions	4km from Gerainger.

Geiranger Fjord is a World Heritage Site.

	Arnfinn Westerås
tel	+47 70 26 32 14
fax	+47 (0)92 64 95 37
email	iwester@online.no
web	www.geiranger.no/westeras/

Self-catering

C 🐾 ✗ ♭ 🚜

Hagal Healing Farm
Coomleigh, Bantry, Co. Cork

Hagal is different, marvellously different. It always was: the farmhouse was built 150 years ago by one man in 40 days. You can now seek yourself or the truth in a leafy labyrinth, take lemon-balm tea under the huge old vine in the conservatory among candles, buddha chimes and lots of harmony, retreat from the pressures of modern life into a secluded corner of the beautiful wild garden, left natural like everything here, eat subtly-spiced organic vegetarian food – or learn to cook it yourself. Seating is low, ethnic and tempting; the yoga room at the top has breathtaking views of Bantry Bay, as does the chill-out room with its white sofas and angel cards. All is run by gentle Dutch eco-life crusaders – Fred the garden-lover, Janny the yoga teacher – residents for almost 30 years, among simple pine furniture, natural fabrics in unfrilly rooms, white walls, chunks of oak timber and the boundless natural energy of this land.

- Holistic therapies & courses in complementary therapies; walking & cycling
- Glengariff & Gougan Barra National Parks; Bantry House

rooms	4 doubles.
price	€60. Singles €55. Full-board €130. Singles €90.
meals	Lunch €15. Dinner €25. BYO.
closed	Rarely.
directions	From Bantry for Glengariff; right after Casey's petrol station at Donamark; 12km of winding road; left at Hagal Farm sign. Bus to Bantry. Owners will pick up.

	Janny & Fred Wieler
tel	+353 (0)27 66179
fax	+353 (0)27 66179
email	hagalhealingfarm@eircom.net
web	www.hagalhealingfarm.com

They are creating a reed bed sewage treatment system for the whole centre and a new treatment building that will be geothermally heated.

Guest house & B&B

Entry 63

Ballin Temple
Ardattin, Co. Carlow

The only tracks beaten here are those of generations of Butlers, the ghosts of the Templars who preceded them and eager fishers on their way to the Slaney. The family are intelligent, caring people. Tom and Canadian wife Pam took a radical turn from investment banking to develop the estate salvaged by Tom's parents. Sustainable thinkers, they run the estate as a nature sanctuary and have developed organic gardening, producing masses of delicious vegetables from artichokes to rhubarb. Chickens and ducks roam freely. The family also practices and teaches yoga, and designs and delivers holonic retreats in the Lodge — a new farmyard house on old walls, where good paintings vie with stunning views. Recently renovated, the two cosy cottages evoke memories of an Ireland of long ago. The wood for wood-burners is harvested on site to warm these open-hearted hideaway homes; the water comes from artesian wells. Stroll along the banks of the river in magical ancient woodlands, be enveloped by peace.

- Walking, cycling, archery, fishing; yoga & retreats
- Altamont Gardens; Kilkenny Castle & Cathedral

rooms	2 cottages for 3. B&B occasionally in the lodge.
price	Cottages from €500 p.w.
meals	Self-catering in cottages.
closed	Cottages available all year.
directions	From Carlow N80; R725 to Tullow; from Ardattin signed, 3km. Bus to Carlow & Tullow, taxi or cycle (Carlow 20km, Tullow 10km).

The family conserves 50 acres of ancient woodland that harbour rare plants & wild deer.

The Butler Family

tel	+353 (0)59 915 5037
fax	+353 (0)59 915 5038
email	manager@ballintemple.com
web	www.ballintemple.com

Guest house & B&B & Self-catering

C 👑 ✗ 💬 🐕 ⚲ 👟

Anna's House

Tullynagee, 35 Lisbarnett Road, Comber BT23 6AW, Newtownards, Co. Down

Steel and song is Ken, garden and guests is Anna. With her love for all that grows and his passion for music and metal, theirs is a house of contrasts and artistry. Creative energy streams into their green crusade. That field spread before the house is the geothermal source of its heating, using electricity only for the pump, and Ken has installed solar panels for the hot water. Anna's two-acre organic garden provides fruit and veg galore, flowers to lift your heart and a series of corners for contemplation – a pine wood with hammock, a secret lily pond – while wildlife flourishes in thick hedges. She uses organic paints and natural fabrics in simply pretty bedrooms, two (each with sitting room and balcony) just off the new musicians' gallery, Ken's soaring symphony of steel struts with a wall of glass to tip you into the serenity of the lake. Anna also loves cooking (all organic): one guest told of "breakfasts like wedding feasts". Rural bliss just 20 minutes from Belfast.

- Sir Peter Scott Wildfowl and Wetlands Trust (Castle Espie)
- Strangford Lough for migrating birds & closely fought sailing competitions

rooms	3: 2 doubles, 1 twin
price	£70-£85.
meals	Pub/restaurant 0.5 miles.
closed	Christmas & New Year.
directions	From Belfast A22 for Downpatrick; 3 miles after Comber, pass petrol station & pub on right; right Lisbarnett Rd 0.5 mile; right into private lane to end.

	Ken & Anna Johnson
tel	+44 (0)28 9754 1566
fax	+44 (0)28 9754 1566
email	anna@annashouse.com
web	www.annashouse.com

The only place to stay in Northern Ireland where the owners have signed up to the Soil Association's Catering Code of Practice.

B&B

Entry 65

Cornish Tipi Holidays

c/o Tregeare, Pendoggett, St Kew, Cornwall PL30 3HZ

A great idea, born of goodwill and a profound sense of what makes people happy. Working with the natural environment, Lizzie has created a magical world of sylvan beauty – 37 tipis of white canvas, lent great swathes of colour and atmosphere by their low-level linings. Floors are covered with Turkish rugs; there are bed rolls, North African lanterns, a powerful Camping Gaz light, a baby Belling cooker, kitchen box full of utensils, and all you need to start a camp fire outside. You walk to the lovely wooden shower blocks. In fact you walk everywhere once you have arrived; no cars are allowed after unloading. The site is in 16 acres of undulating woodland; streams and grass pathways meander through and there is a long, beautiful lake where you can swim and catch fish. No concrete, no nasty signs, no noise – just wildlife. There's a stream pool for toddlers in the meadow beside the 'big' tipi. Choose a site on your own or all together.

- Swimming, cycling, birdwatching, pony trekking, abseiling, surfing
- Over 50 species of birds & native British trees; whales & dolphins off the coast

rooms	37 tipis: for max. 3, max. 6 & max. 12; 3 shower blocks.
price	£315-£685 per week. Short breaks £225-£425.
meals	Self-catering.
closed	November-March.
directions	From A395, B3314 to Delabole; through Delabole; left at Port Gaverne x-road, 1.5 miles.

Hot water showers are powered from wind and solar technologies.

	Ms Elizabeth Tom
tel	+44 (0)1208 880781
fax	+44 (0)1208 880487
email	info@cornish-tipi-holidays.co.uk
web	www.cornish-tipi-holidays.co.uk

Tipi & Self-catering

A

Higher Lank Farm

St Breward, Bodmin, Cornwall PL30 4NB

Families rejoice: you can only come if you have a child under five! Celtic crosses in the garden and original panelling hint at the house's 500-year history; one bedroom is modern with new pine, the other two more traditional. Nursery teas begin at 5pm, grown-up suppers are later and Lucy will cheerfully babysit while the rest of you slink off to the pub. There are farm-themed playgrounds, new bikes for little ones, piglets, chicks, a pony to groom and eggs to collect. Oh, and leave the nappies at home – Lucy can lend you re-usable nappies free of charge for your baby's holiday; she promotes them to reduce the amount of waste sent to landfill sites. There's a laundry service, too. The new 'nursery rhyme' barns are being completed using the highest-spec insulation available, underfloor heating saves on oil consumption, woodburning stoves use logs from their woods and recycling is taken seriously.

* Borrow a backpack & net & carry your child to private stretch of river to look for minnows
* Trebarwith strand beach; Lappa Valley Steam Railway

rooms	3 family rooms.
price	From £85.
meals	Supper £16.25. Packed lunch £6.50. Nursery tea £4.75.
closed	November-Easter.
directions	From Launceston, A395, then A39 through Camelford. Left onto B3266 to Bodmin. After 4 miles, left signed Wenfordbridge Pottery; over bridge, past pottery & on brow of hill, left into lane; house at top.

Dream green holidays for
pre-school children.

	Lucy Finnemore
tel	+44 (0)1208 850716
email	higherlankfarm@waitrose.com
web	www.higherlankfarm.co.uk

Trelowarren

Trelowarren, Mawgan, Helston, Cornwall TR12 6AF

Cornwall without the crush. Deep in woodland, a mile from any road, thirteen eco-cottages sit in one of Europe's top five botanical sites in a mystical Celtic land of serene coves and sun-dappled creeks. The truly visionary Sir Ferrers is creating a natural paradise – one that not only his five young sons will be proud of but the wider community, too. His aim is self-sufficiency – in food and fuel – and he hopes to supply chef Greg Laskey with 70-80,000 tonnes of organic fruit and veg each year (reluctant self-caterers note: no need to cook *anything*!). Paints are organic and high-spec showers and baths are fed with reclaimed rainwater. But there is tangible comfort for the sybarite... Heals' tables, leather sofas, Conran crockery, ash floors, superb beds and cotton linen. Children can explore a vaulted chamber or go with the gamekeeper on a dusk wildlife walk. You'll be hard-pushed to find a more alluring choice for gatherings of family or friends.

- Boat & bike hire can be arranged; wildlife walks; pool & spa
- Iron Age fort, Neolithic vaulted chamber, 18th-century pleasure gardens & botanical garden

A vast woodchip Bison boiler heats ach cottage, the estate's water & the pebble-lined pool.

rooms	13 cottages: 8 for 6-8, 3 for 3-4, 1 for 4, 1 for 8-10.
price	From £425 per week for 2.
meals	Self-catering. Lunch £12.50. Dinner, 3 courses, £28.
closed	Never.
directions	From Helston, A3083 towards Culdrose; pass Culdrose & left on B3293 for about 1.5 miles. At top of hill 3rd exit (not Mawgan village), pass Garras school then left, signed.

Mrs Anne Coombes

tel	+44 (0)1326 221224
fax	+44 (0)1326 221440
email	info@trelowarren.com
web	www.trelowarren.com

Self-catering

Percy's Country Hotel

Coombeshead Estate, Virginstow, Okehampton, Devon EX21 5EA

Fresh air, restorative food, tranquillity. The Bricknell-Webbs don't fuss or boast, they just get on with looking after you – beautifully. Wherever you are on these 130 acres – organic conversion now complete – you can be sure that Tina and Tony have been working sympathetically with the land. A huge kitchen garden provides fresh herbs, salad leaves and vegetables all year round, a recently planted 60-acre woodland has a 'food from the forest' theme and a Bramley apple orchard. Game, lamb, pork and venison, goose, duck and chicken eggs come straight from the estate; wild mushrooms too. Once ingredients are harvested Tina works her magic in the kitchen; expect food that is worth travelling far for. Bedrooms in the converted granary are smart, with huge comfortable beds, chic leather sofas, flat screen TVs and harlequin-tiled spotless bathrooms (some with whirlpools). Grab a pair of wellies – and maybe a labrador or two – and discover one of England's loveliest spots.

- Walking; watersports on Cornish coast (30-minute drive)
- Dartmoor; RHS Gardens Rosemoor; Roadford Lake; Eden Project

rooms	8 twins/doubles.
price	£150–£210. Singles £155–£185. Half-board from £230.
meals	Lunch from £20. Dinner, 3 courses, £40.
closed	Never.
directions	From Okehampton, A3079 for Metherell Cross. After approx. 8.3 miles, left. On left after 6.5 miles.

Tina makes her terrines, brawn & sausages, & cures bacon and hams from their Large Blacks.

	Tina & Tony Bricknell-Webb
tel	+44 (0)1409 211236
fax	+44 (0)1409 211460
email	info@percys.co.uk
web	www.percys.co.uk

Hotel

Milden Hall

Milden, Lavenham, Suffolk CO10 9NY

When you find somewhere so alive with familial love, you've struck gold – and in this case green gold. Christopher farms the land as sustainably as possible; Juliet is a passionate conservationist, full of ideas for making the most of the surrounding countryside, on foot or by bicycle. Over five generations of Hawkins have also filled this seemingly grand 16th-century hall farmhouse with splendid period furniture and odds and ends that weave together in 'country' style. Bedrooms, ranging from big to vast, are old-fashioned and spared from the sometimes homogenising hand of interior design. Heating is by woodburner, the wood is coppiced from the hedgerows, waste is imaginatively recycled and local produce is promoted. Expect delicious home-grown bacon, sausages, bantam eggs or fruit compotes for breakfast.

- Circular walks & cycle routes; pond-dipping; boating down the Stour; tutor-led environmental activities
- Great-crested newts
- Courses at Assington & Flatford Mills, from dowsing to bee keeping

rooms	3: 2 twins, 1 family room, all sharing bathroom.
price	£60–£80. Singles from £40.
meals	Dinner, 2 courses, £20. Supper £15. BYO. Pubs/restaurants 2-3 miles.
closed	Rarely.
directions	From Lavenham, A1141 for Monks Eleigh. After 2 miles, right to Milden. At x-roads, right to Sudbury on B1115. Hall's long drive 0.25 miles on left.

Hosts provide pack of 7 car-free days of activities, & transport you to the start of walks.

	Juliet & Christopher Hawkins
tel	+44 (0)1787 247235
email	hawkins@thehall-milden.co.uk
web	www.thehall-milden.co.uk

B&B

Strattons

4 Ash Close, Swaffham, Norfolk PE37 7NH

Nowhere is perfect, but Strattons – one of the country's most eco-friendly hotels – comes close. Silky bantams strut on the lawn, funky classical interiors thrill – and green policies gently insinuate into the fabric of this bohemian country-house bolthole. Les and Vanessa met at art school and every square inch of their Queen Anne villa is crammed with mosaics and murals, marble busts, cow-hide rugs on stripped wood floors, art packed tight on the wall. Bedrooms are exquisite: a carved four-poster, a tented bathroom, Indian brocade and stained glass. Wonderful food in the candlelit restaurant (turn right by the chaise longue) is all organic and seasonal, perhaps pea ice cream, leg of lamb, then hazelnut parfait. Recycled iron and steel, and local artist Rachel Long, created the red deer stag standing proud in gardens thoughtfully sculpted for wildlife and relaxation – a splendid endorsement of the hotel's recycling philosophy and strict 'buy local' stance.

- Cycle tracks through The Brecks & Thetford forest; hand-picked series of walks
- Gooderstone Water Gardens; Castle Acre Priory; Ecotech Centre, Swaffham

rooms	8: 1 twin/double, 3 doubles, 4 suites.
price	£130–£140. Singles from £85. Suites from £200.
meals	Dinner, 4 courses, £40.
closed	Christmas.
directions	Ash Close runs off north end of market place between W H Brown estate agents & fish & chip restaurant.

	Vanessa & Les Scott
tel	+44 (0)1760 723845
fax	+44 (0)1760 720458
email	enquiries@strattonshotel.com
web	www.strattonshotel.com

There is a 10% reduction for anybody who arrives by public transport only.

Hotel

Ecocabin

Langdale Cottage, Obley, Bucknell, Shropshire SY7 0BZ

It looks like a vast, interesting garden shed. Within, there is an unassuming naturalness, with wooden floors, wooden doors and furniture at every turn. Splashes of colour (bright red sofas and armchairs, chunky blue checks on the bedcovers) set off white lime-plastered walls and ash floors. Tiles are hand-made, fabrics are natural and organic, toiletries biodegradable, the cooker 'slow'. The wood-pellet stove is a feature, with a reclaimed-slate surround. It is light, earthy, fun and refreshing. Your energy comes from the sun and you can be ferried to public transport. There is even an 'honesty' store for your shopping. Wild flowers are strewn in the garden, too; there are log 'planters' and a barbecue from a local blacksmith. The cabin is a remarkable, lone achievement by an unusual woman. Kate was a veterinary nurse but her baby transformed her attitude to the world around her. *Minimum stay two nights.*

- www.wheelywonderfulcycling.co.uk delivers bicycles for hire

The new building is constructed from wood, wool, reeds, lime & clay.

rooms	Cabin for 4–5 (1 double, 1 twin/double).
price	£90–£105. £420–£575 p.w.
meals	Self-catering. Shopping service available.
closed	Never.
directions	Train to Craven Arms, 9 miles from Ecocabin. Free collection. Shuttle bus during summer from Clunton, 3.5 miles.

Kate Grubb

tel	+44 (0)1547 530183
fax	+44 (0)1547 530183
email	kate@ecocabin.co.uk
web	www.ecocabin.co.uk

Self-catering

Trericket Mill Vegetarian Guesthouse
Erwood, Builth Wells, Powys LD2 3TQ

Part guest house, part bunk house, part campsite – all Grade II*-listed. The dining room has been created amid a jumble of corn-milling machinery: B&B guests, campers and bunkers pile in together to fill hungry bellies with Nicky and Alistair's delicious and plentiful veggie food – fair-trade, wholefood and free-range – from a chalkboard menu. Stoves throw out the heat in the flagstoned living rooms with their comfy chairs; the bedrooms are simple pine affairs; all is well insulated and efficiently lit. On an SSSI – Skithwen brook meanders through the property – the mill hosts a breeding colony of bats in the roof each summer, quite a sight at dusk. Wildlife is a joy in this conservation area – kingfishers, dippers, coots and swans play on the river Wye a 30-yard stroll away. Lovers of the outdoors looking for good value and a planet-friendly bias will be in heaven.

- Walking, cycling, kayaking & Canadian canoeing
- Red kites, buzzards, woodpeckers, kingfishers, tree-creepers, otters
- 5 miles from Brecon Beacons National Park; festivals in Brecon & Hay-on-Wye

rooms	3: 2 doubles, 1 twin.
price	£56. Singles £38.
meals	Simple supper £6.50. Dinner, 3 courses, £15.50. Pub/restaurant 2 miles.
closed	Rarely.
directions	12 miles north of Brecon on A470. Mill set slightly back from road, on left, between Llyswen & Erwood. Train to Llandrindod Wells; bus to Brecon every 2 hrs will drop at mill on request.

	Alistair & Nicky Legge
tel	+44 (0)1982 560312
email	mail@trericket.co.uk
web	www.trericket.co.uk

National Cycle Route 8 passes 50m from the mill.

Guest house

Entry 73

Penpont

Brecon, Powys, LD3 8EU

Penpont is in the heart of a National Park, and sustainability is at the heart of life at Penpont. The Hoggs live and breathe it – all within the bosom of a traditional and beautiful 'mini' stately home and bang beside the river Usk. It is run with a rare informality and warmth and has long been one of our most special places. The green aspects are impressive: a 150kw wood-chip heating system with a well-managed woodland supporting it. Sixty thousand trees have been planted, 60 tonnes a year of carbon emissions saved, an organic vegetable garden created and all these efforts put to the service of the local community. They have gone way beyond recycling and composting. Art and imagination are woven into the fabric of the place – in the maze, the fencing, the willow sheep on the lawn. The courtyard wing doesn't try to be spectacular, just cosy and human, well-decorated and generous. One of Wales's finest places to stay.

- Walking, cycling, mountain-boarding, fly-fishing, tennis, canoeing; residential yoga
- Red kites, otters, badgers, barn owls & sparrow hawks; arboretum of 200 species
- Brecon Beacons National Park; Fforest Fawr Geopark

rooms	House wing sleeps 15-17.
price	£1,200-£1,700 p.w. Ask about short breaks.
meals	Self-catering.
closed	Never.
directions	From Brecon, west on A40 through Llanspyddid. Pass 2nd telephone kiosk on left. Entrance to house on right. Approx. 4.5 miles from Brecon.

The farm is run as an organic demonstration project.

Davina & Gavin Hogg
tel   +44 (0)1874 636202
email   penpont@btconnect.com
web   www.penpont.com

Self-catering

Quinta do Rio Touro

Caminho do Rio Touro, Azóia, 2705-001 Sintra, Estremadura

The Reino family have planted over 5,000 trees on their farm in the Sintra-Cascais Natural Park. Lush organic gardens heave with fruit – peaches, bananas, grapefruit, oranges, apples, plums, strawberries and, above all, limes. Feel free to pick your own. Scented jasmine tumbles over the entrance to the manor house along with an eclectic collection of artefacts: Roman pots, Moroccan stone-carved tables, antique fans. Your hosts worked in the diplomatic field for many years and their library too reflects their many travels. Senhor Reino likes nothing more than to help you plan your own journeys. Choose a traditional Portuguese room with balcony and sea view or go for touch more privacy in the little house at the foot of the garden. The locally sourced organic breakfasts are outstanding: home-laid eggs, local pastries, fresh cheeses, their own honey, ginza jam and pumpkin chutney. *Minimum stay two nights.*

- Walking, cycling; swimming, surfing & sailing
- Bonnelli eagles, screech owl, salamander, horned viper & 901 species of native flora
- Roman ruins & Moorish castle in Sintra

rooms	6: 2 doubles, 4 suites for 2-4.
price	€120-€200. Singles from €110.
meals	Restaurants within walking distance. Dinner occasionally available.
closed	Rarely.
directions	Train to Cascais or Sintra then bus 403 to Azóia (30 mins). By car, A5 towards Cascais, junc. 12 for Malveira; right for 8km; left for Azoia, left again, signed, past 1st house.

	Senhor & Senhora Reino
tel	+351 21 929 2862
fax	+351 21 929 2360
email	info@quinta-riotouro.com
web	www.quinta-riotouro.com

The cultural landscape of Sintra is a World Heritage Site.

B&B

D 🛉 (Hello) 🗴 🚜

Cerro da Fontinha

Turismo da Natuereza Lda, Brejão, 7630-575 São Teótonio

Miguel has used locally sourced, natural materials in these inspiring self-catering cottages. The simple character of simple dwellings has been preserved, and funky, chunky touches added. And to reveal the fabric of the building Miguel has left visible areas of *taipa* so you can see the mix of soil and stones between lath and plaster. Everything is as natural as can be: showers have stone bases and terracotta surrounds, a bunk bed has a carved ladder and fat wooden legs. Pebbles embedded in walls create coat and towel hooks, thick cuts of wood become mantelpieces, stone sofas are cosily cushioned! There are alcoves for oil and vinegar, curving work surfaces and cheerful stripes and gingham. You have countryside on the doorstep, a eucalyptus wood for shade, good restaurants and Carvalhal beach nearby – hire mountain bikes to get there. There's also a little lake for swimming and fishing. Astonishing. *Minimum stay two nights. Casas Brancas member.*

- Horse riding, canoeing, guided nature trails, cycling, climbing; body & mind therapies run by local people
- Parque Natural da Costa Vicentina

Organic fruit & veg can be delivered to your door.

rooms	2 cottages for 4.
price	€90–€160 for 2 nights; €280–€560 per week.
meals	Self-catering. Restaurants nearby.
closed	Rarely
directions	From Faro A22 to Lagos, N120 though Aljezur for São Teótonio. 5km after crossing into Alentejo, left to Brejão, 1st left. House on right after lake. Train from Faro to Lagos, bus to Odeceixe.

Senhor Miguel Godinho

tel	+351 282 949083
fax	+351 282 949083
email	info@cerrodafontinha.com
web	www.cerrodafontinha.com

Self-catering

C 👞

Casa Grande da Fervenza

Ctra. Lugo-Páramo km11, O Corgo, 27163 Lugo, Galicia

The river Miño laps at the walls of this house and ancient, working mill. Girdled by 18 hectares of magnificent ancient woodland, the area is a UNESCO Biosphere Reserve. The Casa is named after the amazing rocky waterfall outside, and is both hotel *and* museum – a fascinating one, in perfect working order; ask for a guided tour. The restaurant with glorious open fireplace is in the oldest part and dates from the 17th century, and the menus are based on the sort of food that was around when the building was built... beef and wild boar stew with chestnuts, mushrooms in November. Wines are outstanding, the region's best. After a day on the river, return to quiet, simple, stylish bedrooms. Restoration has been meticulous in its respect for local tradition and lore, yet there's no stinting on creature comforts. Antiques have been beautifully restored, rugs woven on their looms, there are linen curtains, chestnut beams and floors and hand-painted sinks. Superb. *A Rusticae hotel.*

- Walking & cycling; canoeing in traditional wooden batuxo
- 300-year old oak trees; boar, roe deer, heron

rooms	9: 8 doubles, 1 suite.
price	€56–€70. Singles €39.20–€49. Suite €80–€100.
meals	Breakfast €5. Lunch/dinner €15; €15–€30 à la carte.
closed	Never.
directions	From Lugo, N-VI for Madrid. After 4km in Conturiz, right by Hotel Torre de Núñez for Páramo for 11km; right at sign for 1km to hotel.

The Casa is working towards organic status.

	Juan Pérez Sánchez-Orozco
tel	+34 982 150610
fax	+34 982 151610
email	info@fervenza.com
web	www.fervenza.com

Hotel

La Quintana de la Foncalada

Argüero, 33314 Villaviciosa, Asturias

Severino welcomes you with unaffected simplicity at this honeysuckle-clad farmhouse in the flat, coastal *mariña* area of Asturias. The shady, breezy front garden is a delight, while the inside of the house is light, bright and simple. Bedrooms have basic furniture and artistic splashes of colour; bathrooms are small with hot water from solar pnaels and flow-limiters on the taps; the stable apartment with open fire is the most atmospheric. Make yourself a hot drink in the big, rustic kitchen whenever you like; enjoy the games room – popular with families; find out about the area in the book-filled sitting room. Much here is home-produced: honey, cheese, juices, cider, jam. Your hosts encourage adults and children to try potting in their new workshop: every plate, lamp and tile in the house is homemade. You may also help with the Asturian ponies and the organic veg patch. Arrive by train or bus and you will be transported for free to the door.

- Walking, cycling routes, pony riding; traditional handicraft courses
- Delectable beaches; Jurassic coast (dinosaur footprints); Villaviciosa Nature Reserve

Severino has created a museum dedicated to the Asturian pony, the *asturcón*.

B&B & Self-catering

rooms	5 + 1: 5 twins/doubles. 1 apartment.
price	€45-€50. Apartment €600-€700 p.w.
meals	Breakfast €4. Dinner €15. Self-catering in apt.
closed	Rarely.
directions	A-8 Santander-Oviedo, at exit to Villaviciosa AS-256 for Gijón. Argüero 8km further. Train to Gijón; buses from Gijón & Villaviciosa to "Cuatro Caminos" stop, 2km from house.

Severino Garcia & Daniela Schmid

tel	+34 985 999001
fax	+34 985 876365
email	foncalada@asturcon-museo.com
web	www.asturcon-museo.com

L'Ayalga Posada Ecológica
La Pandiella s/n, 3357 Infiesto, Asturias

Abandon the car and take a train on the narrow-gauge railway to Infiesto. Or come by bus. Either way, if you let them know beforehand, Luis or Concepción will be there to meet you. They're a friendly, caring couple who've taken infinite pains in restoring their farmhouse to use only healthy, non-contaminating materials. Even the cleaning products are homemade from borax and essential oils. Outside, herbs scent the garden, a pair of Asturcon ponies graze quietly and green slopes lead the eye inexorably to dramatic mountain profiles. The rooms are attractively simple and unadorned, with white walls, golden wood and warm rust colours. Thanks to solar panels, the showers have constant hot water and the wooden beds, treated with natural oils, are fairly comfortable. Your hosts, who run the place without any help, will give 1% of the bill to charity. If you crave a massage, your children will be looked after — you might even find them harvesting watermelons for lunch...

- Therapeutic massages (Luis is an osteopath); tai chi & chi con
- Redes Natural Park (15km)

rooms	5: 2 twins, 3 doubles. Extra bed available.
price	€45–€50. Singles €39. Plus 7% tax.
meals	Vegetarian dinners (except in August) €10. Plus 7% tax.
closed	Christmas.
directions	AS245 Infiesto-Campo Caso. After 3km left to La Pandiella; guest house on right as you enter hamlet. FEVE train or ALSA bus to Infiesto for pick-up.

Sand is used as sound insulation
between floorboards & ceiling.

Luis Alberto Díaz González
& Concepción de la Iglesia Escalada
mobile   +34 616 897 638
email   layalga@terrae.net
web   www.terrae.net/layalga

Guest house

B 🏕 ✕ 💬 🍶 🍷 👟

Entry 79

El Correntiu

c/Sardalla 42, 33560 Ribadesella, Asturias

Near the mountains and the sea. And it must be the swishest grain silo in Spain. Set in nine acres, El Correntiu stands to one side of the Asturian farmhouse – a stunning renovation. It is stylishly simple: a crisp use of wood, ochre tones to impart warmth, discreet lighting to give character, lots of space. There are three apartments in all, each with its own kitchen garden. There is also an abundance of kiwi, avocado and citrus trees: in this micro-climate everything thrives. Inside, a feast for the eye – chunky rafters, chestnut floors, country furniture, bright cushions – and all you need: books, games, linen, towels. If you're a traditionalist you may prefer the little cottage nearby, just as beautifully equipped. A stream babbles by: *escorentia* means 'place that collects rain water'. Your hosts keep rare Xalda sheep. María Luisa, who speaks very good English, couldn't be nicer. An irresistible place.

- Long, steep walk down to the lovely fishing village of Ribadesella; magnificent beaches
- Picos de Europa National Park

Pick to your heart's content from the kitchen garden.

Self-catering

rooms	3: 2 apartments for 2; 1 cottage for 4.
price	Apartments €55-€70. Cottage €85-€110.
meals	Self-catering.
closed	Rarely.
directions	From Santander A-8/N-632. At Ribadesella N-632 for Gijón. Immediately after bridge, left for Cuevas & Sardalla. From here, 2km to El Correntiu.

María Luisa Bravo & Jose Luis Valdés

tel	+34 985 861436
mobile	+34 651 582 440
email	aldea@elcorrentiu.com
web	www.elcorrentiu.com

Hotel Posada del Valle

Collia, 33549 Arriondas, Asturias

After two years of searching the hills and valleys of Asturias, Nigel and Joann Burch found the home of their dreams – a century-old farmhouse just inland from the rugged north coast, with sensational views to mountain, hill and meadow. (Find a seat in the green, hillside garden and gaze.) Now they are nurturing new life from the soil, while running this small and beguiling hotel. The apple orchard has been planted, the flock graze the hillside, the menu celebrates the best of things local, and you will delight in this sensitive conversion. Bedrooms are seductive affairs with shutters and old beams, polished wooden floors, exposed stone, colourful modern fabrics and matching colour-washed walls. There's a stylishly uncluttered living room with an open brick fire, and a dining room with glorious views. You are close to some of the most exceptional wildlife in Europe and there's lots of information on the best local rambles available from your hosts. Great value.

- Walking; canoeing; canyoning; horse riding; biking
- Little-known sandy beaches of the Cantabrian coast; Picos de Europa National Park

rooms	12 twins/doubles.
price	€58-€80.
	Singles €46.40-€56.
meals	Breakfast €7.50.
	Dinner €20.50.
closed	November-March.
directions	N-634 Arriondas; AS-260 for Mirador del Fito. After 1km, right for Collia. Through village (don't turn to Ribadesella). Hotel 300m on left after village.

This is a fully-registered organic farm.

	Nigel & Joann Burch
tel	+34 985 841157
fax	+34 985 841559
email	hotel@posadadelvalle.com
web	www.posadadelvalle.com

Hotel

C ✗ Hello 🍷 🍶 🚜 ᗣᗣ 👟

Entry 81

Casa de Aldea La Valleja

Rieña, 33576 Ruenes, Asturias

If you fancy turning your hand to preserve-making, cheese-culturing or gathering berries in the mountain, then head here. Tending the livestock and pottering in the garden are also a must: Paula is passionate about rural tourism and loves guests to muck in. The house was built in 1927 and the original materials – bricks, tiles, stones and chestnut beams – maintain the rustic charm. Each bedroom, gaily coloured, has been named after wild berries; if yours feels sombre, throw open the shutters and drink in the views – sensational. La Valleja is a working homestead but there's comfort too, in orthopaedic mattresses, good heating and scrumptious food. After a rugged day's walk – don't miss the spectacular Cares gorge – you'll be well fortified: meals are hearty and the food organic and lovingly prepared. So whether you want to sit and enjoy the views, join in the chestnut harvest or birdwatch with binoculars, this is the place. Be sure to buy some of the jams and preserves to take home.

- Walking among the gentle slopes of the Sierra del Cuera or the rugged gorge of Cares
- Paisaje protegido de Sierra del Cuera; Picos de Europa National Park; Cares gorge

rooms	5 twins/doubles.
price	€49.
meals	Packed lunch €7. Dinner €12. Plus taxes.
closed	Christmas & January.
directions	N-634; at Unquera left for Panes. Here, right onto AS-114 for Cangas de Onís. 10km beyond, at Niserias, right to Ruenes. Through Alles & 800m after Pastorias right up a steep track to Rieña. Park at top.

All products used are organic; an excellent example of agrotourism.

Paula Valero Sáez

tel	+34 985 415895
mobile	+34 689 183625
fax	+34 985 415895
email	valleycas@yahoo.es

B&B

B ♿ 🐾 (Hello) 🍷 🥾

The Hoopoe Yurt Hotel

Apartado de Correos 23, Cortes de la Frontera, 29380 Málaga, Andalucia

Here, under the shade of cork and olive trees, these authentic Mongolian and Afghani yurts sit in splendid isolation in the tranquil Andalucian countryside. On raised wooden platforms, the felt-lined white circular tents are reinforced with arching roof poles that support a domed crown. Inside, wicker baskets, ethnic furniture and sheepskins on the floor create a rustic Central Asian theme, enriched with vibrant colours that decorate the walls and ceiling. The talented young owners Ed and Henrietta – she has a designer's eye – have made the yurts stylish while maintaining a 'back to nature' feel (there's a compost loo and hot shower in a small bamboo-walled bathroom outside). Wonderful views of the Grazalema mountain range are best enjoyed from a hammock slung between two cork trees or on a bamboo sun bed beside the freshwater pool. Feast on the delicious, local food (mostly organic) outside in the warm Mediterranean air.

- Yoga, reiki, massages, aromatherapy in local village; hill walking & riding nearby
- Mountain rock pools at Cuevo del Gato near Ronda

rooms	4: 3 yurts for 2, 1 children's yurt for 2 (under 12s), each with separate shower.
price	€85. Child €20.
meals	Lunch €15. Dinner, 3 courses, €30.
closed	November-March.
directions	From Ronda, into Cortes de la Frontera; sharp left after fountain; dirt track left before petrol station; left fork 1km; right track before white house. Buses Ronda-Cortes de F; train to Cortes de F.

The yurts run entirely on solar power.

	Ed & Henrietta Hunt
tel	+34 952 117055
mobile	+34 660 668 241/+34 696 668 388
email	yurthotel@terra.es
web	www.yurthotel.com

Yurt

Hotel Cerro de Híjar

Cerro de Híjar s/n, Tolox, 29109 Málaga, Andalucía

On a clear day you can see – well, if not forever, at least to the sea and the Sierra Nevada. It has a wonderful remote position, this hotel, on a bluff 2,000 feet above sea level, and an unrivalled view. From the ancient spa village of Tolox, follow the winding road up and up... The young hotel looks like a traditional hunting lodge and inside there is a terrific sense of light and space: creamy stucco walls, bright rugs and attractive furniture, a winter fire (known to get a bit smoky in the dining room!) and modern Andalucían paintings and prints on every wall. The bedrooms are large, comfortable, beautifully finished, dazzlingly clean. You'll eat and drink well for Martín's cooking is inspired – traditional Andalucían with a modern touch. No surprise to learn that he once worked in the area's only Michelin-starred restaurant... He, Guillermo and Eugenio all have excellent English and are most welcoming. Memorable.

- Magnificent walking and horse-riding in the Sierra Nevada National Park
- Medicinal spa in village of Tolox

rooms	18: 14 twins/doubles, 4 suites.
price	€66–€92. Singles €59–€71. Suites €92–€104.
meals	Breakfast €8. Lunch/dinner, à la carte, around €35.
closed	Never.
directions	From Málaga, on Cártama. Filter right to Coín, then onto A-366 for Ronda. Left to Tolox, through village to Balneario (spa); right up hill for 2.5km to hotel.

Every guest is given a tree to plant nearby.

Hotel

	Guillermo Gonzalez
tel	+34 952 112111
fax	+34 952 119745
email	cerro@cerrodehijar.com
web	www.cerrodehijar.com

Los Piedaos
Apartado 13, Orgiva, 18400 Granada, Andalucía

At the end of the long winding track, on a tree-covered ridge beneath the soaring Sierra Nevada, the multi-levelled farmstead has been renovated by its architect owner with shade, privacy and huge views in mind. Each white *casita* promises old tiles and timbers, recycled shutters and doors and a colourful melée of terraces and furnishings: convivial dining tables, throws over sofas, plenty of novels. The owners – discreet but welcoming – are passionate about the organic growth of the Orgiva area and are aiming for carbon neutrality. Roofs are painted white to reflect sunlight, grey water is channelled into pretty gardens, hot water comes from solar panels, the pools are cleansed by copper/silver purification, and air conditioning (extreme temperatures only) is low energy. Trails lead to quiet spots, swallows swoop above ancient olives and a 40-minute walk brings you to delightful Orgiva.

- Yoga, tai chi & healing courses in market town Orgiva – the 'spiritual' centre of Spain
- Sierra Nevada National Park, for sports & protected mountain flora

rooms	4 cottages: 3 for 4, 1 for 2-3.
price	Cottages for 4, £345-£625 p.w. For 2-3 £275-£475 p.w.
meals	Self-catering. Restaurants in Orgiva (3.4km).
closed	Never.
directions	On C333 leaving Lanjaron 6km towards Orgiva, right on to track at Km14 opp. white & orange walled store. Bus from Granada, ask for Buena Vista stop then 5-min walk.

	David & Shujata Dry
tel	+34 958 784470
email	holidays@lospiedaos.com
web	holidays-in-southern-spain.com/

The farm maintains the olive & orange groves organically & employs Wwoofers to help on the land.

Self-catering

Can Marti Agroturismo

07810 Sant Joan de Labritja, Ibiza

Only the tinkling of bells from the neighbour's sheep, or the occasional bray from one of Can Marti's two donkeys, breaks the silence in this tranquil wooded valley. A far cry indeed from the crowds of holiday Ibiza. Peter and Isabelle have breathed organic life back into the gently sloping terraced land. Olive, fig, almond and carob trees have been revived, fruit and vegetables planted and the old stone farmhouse has been lime-washed and transformed into rustic but immaculate guest apartments. Simple, colourful rooms are designed in the traditional Ibicencan way with a touch of the contemporary: juniper-beamed ceilings, thick walls; broadband internet connections and thoughtfully equipped kitchens. The Brantschens' passion for travel informs the different cultural themes: Morroccan mirrors, an antique Indian staircase, a French sink, Mexican pots. Delicious organic breakfasts, with homemade breads and jams and fresh orange juice in season, may be brought to your terrace each morning.

- Walking, cycling, pretty beaches & local picturesque village a 1km walk
- Rare wild orchids in spring

They conserve water by filtering through reedbeds & collecting rainwater.

rooms	3 studio/apartments for 2. Extra bed available. 1 cottage for 4.
price	€110. Cottage €180-€210.
meals	Breakfast €9. Farm shop. 10min walk to restaurants & village shops.
closed	15 October-March.
directions	27km from airport, 20km from Ibiza town. On Km21 Ibiza-Sant Joan road, right turn to Can Marti, signed; house 900m up track. Bus from Ibiza to Sant Joan twice a day for pick-up.

Peter & Isabelle Brantschen

tel	+34 971 333500
mobile	+34 607 600 051
email	info@canmarti.com
web	www.canmarti.com

B&B & Self-catering

Canvaschic

Milles Etoiles, Camping du Mas de Serret, 07150 Labastide de Virac

Yurts are in! And here is one of the first multi-yurt camps. Lodewijk and Ruth started with just three yurts at their old site in Languedoc but (with two young children) have moved up in scale and location to the top of the beautiful Gorge d'Ardèche. At an old camping ground within a nature reserve, the new camp retains the air of communal living – there is a shared toilet and shower block, and breakfast (fresh and local) is provided in the main building. Raised on wooden platforms, the yurts are scattered sparingly among leafy oak trees. Inside, they are about as chic as tents can be: a large four-poster bed, dressing table, and two bedside lanterns provide a soft evening glow to these extraordinarily durable cocoons of comfort. The campsite is named 'milles étoiles' – and the sensitive use of solar lanterns at night helps you count every single one of them.

- Walking, riding, canoeing; private yoga lessons
- Woodpecker, kingfisher, Bonneli eagle
- Ardèche Gorge, Pont du Gard, Valon Pont d'Arc

rooms	12 yurts: 9 for up to 4 (2 on camp beds), 3 for 2. Shared showers.
price	B&B from £255 for 3 nights. From £595 for 1 week.
meals	Dinner, 3 courses with wine, €27 (available twice a week).
closed	November-April.
directions	4km from Labastide de Virac, rd to Orgnac; left to Hameau des Crottes; signed Milles Etoiles to track, camp 200m on left. TGV Paris-Avignon; bus to Vagnas for pick-up.

	Ruth Lawson
tel	+33 (0)4 75 38 42 77 (camp site)
mobile	+33 (0)4 66 24 21 81 (out of season)
email	info@canvaschic.com
web	www.canvaschic.com

You're provided with a solar powered lantern to guide you to your yurt at night.

Yurt & B&B

Entry 87

Whitepod
1871 Les Cerniers

Tucked up in your well-insulated pod in the silent majesty of the Alps, you are as snug as a winter bunny. Through the icy outer canvas zip you enter a surprisingly airy geodesic dome: a wood stove glows (with additional light from Tilley lamps, torches and the moon); an i-pod entertains; organic throws soften recycled furniture; a washstand and gloriously warm, sheepskin-covered bed face a huge window – a room in nature with a breathtaking view. Yards from the 12 pods, two of which have a mezzanine level and in-pod bathrooms, is the hub of the camp: the restored chalet, charming with library, log fire, bar, dining area, and five double showers. Run on a generator – on for a few hours a day – there's (just) enough electricity and hot water for all. Chef Beate uses an abundance of local and organic produce and it is all masterminded by youthful Swiss entrepreneur Sofia, whose eco-philosophy is inspirational. *Minimum stay two nights.*

- Guided back-country skiing, snowshoeing, ice-climbing, dog-sledging, yoga
- Chamois, deer, golden eagle, lynx

The pods are dismantled at the end of the season without leaving a trace.

rooms	12 pods for 2 (2 with baths). Shared showers. Glass relaxation & spa pods in 2008.
price	CHF325-CHF525 per pod. Plus 17.5% VAT
meals	Half-board. In-pod dining in 2 pods.
closed	May and November.
directions	Train to Aigle. Transfers to Whitepod reception chalet. From there, guests are guided to the camp on foot (15-min walk).

Sofia de Meyer
mobile +41 (0)79 744 62 19
email reservations@whitepod.com
web www.whitepod.com

Under canvas

Casa del Grivò

Borgo Canal del Ferro 19, 33040 Faédis, Udine

This is the house that Toni built – or, rather, lovingly revived from ruin. The smallholding sits in a hamlet on the edge of a plain; behind, wonderful, high-wooded hills extend to the Slovenian border. Your lovely hosts have three young children. Simplicity, rusticity and a green approach are the keynotes here, from the traditional wool-and-vegetable-fibre-filled mattresses to the solar-heated pool. Beds are comfy and blanketed, some with wonderful quilts. Your children will adore all the open spaces, the animals and the little pool that's been created by diverting a stream. Maps are laid out at breakfast, and there are heaps of books on the region; the walking is wonderful, there's a castle to visit and a river to picnic by. Paola cooks fine dinners using old recipes and their own organic produce. There's a lovely open fire for cooking, and you dine by candlelight. *Minimum stay two nights, five in summer.*

- Hill walking, mountain biking & hang-gliding in the upper Torre valley, one of Friuli's most unspoilt corners
- The charming medieval towns of Venzone & Cividale del Friuli

rooms	4: 1 double, 2 family rooms sharing 2 bathrooms; 1 family room with separate bathroom.
price	€55. Half-board €45 p.p.
meals	Dinner from €25. Lunch in summer only. Picnic on request.
closed	December.
directions	From Faédis, via dei Castelli for Canébola. After 1.5km right, over bridge; 2nd house on left.

	Toni & Paola Costalunga
tel	+39 0432 728638
fax	+39 0432 728638
email	casadelgrivo@libero.it
web	www.grivo.has.it

They have an organic certificate (IMC) for bread, pasta, fruit, veg, pigs, poultry & wine.

B&B

Entry 89

Tenuta Le Sorgive - Le Volpi

via Piridello 6, 46040 Solferino, Mantova

Although one cannot deny the beauty of Lake Garda, it's a relief to escape to the open and unpopulated land of Lombardy. This 19th-century *cascina* with ochre-washed façade and green shutters has been in the Serenelli family for two generations. The exterior, crowned with pierced dovecote and flanked by a carriage house and stables with wide open arches, remains impressive, even if a little character has been lost during restoration. Le Sorgive is a working 28-hectare family farm with vines, cereal crops and livestock; the big rooms, with wooden rafters, are a mix of old and new. Some have attractive, metalwork beds; two have a mezzanine with beds for the children. All are crisp and clean. There's also a large gym and a pool. Vittorio's sister runs the *cascina* Le Volpi just near the stables where you can sample gnocchi, Mantovan sausages and mouthwatering fruit tarts.

- Horse riding, archery & mountain biking from the farm; go-karting nearby.
- 10km to Lake Garda for hiking & swimming

You can buy some of the farm's lovely organic produce at Le Volpi.

B&B & Self-catering

rooms	8 + 2: 8 twins/doubles. 2 apts for 4.
price	€85-€105.
	Apartments €516-€845 p.w.
meals	Dinner with wine €15-€23.
	Restaurant closed Jan & Mon/Tues.
	Self-catering in apartments.
closed	Rarely.
directions	Exit A4 Milano-Venezia at Desenzano for Castiglione delle Stiviere; left at traffic lights ; left after 20m to Solferino. At x-roads turn left. Signed.

Signor Vittorio Serenelli

tel	+39 0376 854252
fax	+39 0376 855256
email	info@lesorgive.it
web	www.lesorgive.it

Locanda della Valle Nuova

Locanda della Valle Nuova, La Cappella 14, 61033 Sagrata di Fermignano, Pesaro e Urbino

In gentle hills surrounded by ancient, protected oaks and within sight of glorious walled Urbino, this 185-acre farm produces fine organic meat, vegetables and wine – and schools horses. An unexpectedly modern conversion has given La Locanda the feel of a discreet modern hotel, where perfectly turned sheets lie on perfect beds, as crisp and as clean as new pins. Signora Savini, a force to be reckoned with, and daughter Giulia, create delicious meals from their own and local produce; all the breads, pastas and jams are homemade. Water is purified; heating is solar or from wood stoves, supplied by the prunings from the farm woods where truffles are gathered in autumn. The riding school has two outdoor arenas. And there is a lovely pool. If you arrive in the area after dark, Giulia kindly meets you to guide you back. *Children over 12 welcome. Minimum stay three nights.*

- Cycling, walking, riding; weekend basket-weaving courses; truffle-hunting in October
- Golden eagle, sparrowhawk, peregrine, Montagu's harrier, wolves, porcupines, polecats
- Numerous art treasures in medieval walled Urbino, World Heritage Site (12km)

rooms	6 + 2: 5 doubles, 1 twin. 2 self-catering units to be added in 2007.
price	€100. Half-board €75 p.p.
meals	Dinner €30.
closed	Mid-November-May.
directions	Exit Fano-Rome motorway at Acqualagna & Piobbico. Head towards Piobbico as far as Pole; right for Castellaro; signed. Bus from Pesaro or Fano to Fermignano, owners will pick up.

Over 70% of the food served is from the Savini's organic farm.

	Giulia Savini
tel	+39 0722 330303
fax	+39 0722 330303
email	info@vallenuova.it
web	www.vallenuova.it

B&B & Self-catering

Il Tufiello

SS 399 Km 6, 83045 Calitri, Avellino

Sunflowers alternate with wheat and oats in the rolling acres that surround the farm. Tomatoes dry in wicker baskets in the sun, others are bottled with basil; there are chestnuts and honey and vegetables in abundance – all organic. The Zampaglione family have farmed here for generations; wholly committed to ecological principles, they are proud to show guests around the place – and delighted if you help out in the vegetable garden! A white house standing four-square in the fields is the family home, but it is the old, single-storey farmhouse, and Grandfather's House, that have been made over to house guests. The old stable, with its huge fireplace, high rafters, excellent sofas and little library full of local information, serves as a general gathering place. Borrow a bike and set off for a nearby farm to buy fresh ricotta and pecorino, book in for a cookery course, bake bread in a wood oven. *Minimum stay two nights.*

- Horse riding; mountain biking; paragliding; fishing
- The steeply terraced town of Calitri, known for its ceramics & 12th-century castle

The family make organic pasta from their own flour, milled on the premises.

B&B & Self-catering

rooms	4 + 2: 4 doubles. 2 apartments: 1 for 2-4, 1 for 4.
price	€60. Apartment €80–€120.
meals	Breakfast €3. Packed lunch €6. Restaurants 6km. Self-catering in apartments.
closed	November-Easter. Open at Christmas.
directions	A16 Naples-Bari exit Lacedonia towards Calitri. Il Tufiello midway between Bisaccia & Calitri.

Pierluigi & Nerina Zampaglione

tel	+39 0827 38851/081 5757604
fax	+39 081 5757604
email	info@iltufiello.it
web	www.iltufiello.it

Trulli Country House

Contrada Figazzano 3, 72014 Cisternino, Brindisi

An ultra-fashionable trulli tower in Puglia? But wait till you get inside. This is a rare and inspired fusion of the rustic and the minimalist, utterly sympathetic to its origins, lovingly restored by local artisans. Bedrooms have polished cement floors and whitewashed walls, distressed cupboards, sweet raffia, natural hessian. Niches glow with antique lanterns or fresh flowers, a bedstead has been constructed from an olive-tree ladder, spotless shower rooms are arched and curved. Artistic, hospitable Caroline is a mother and photographer whose fine prints decorate the house. On cooler days, she serves breakfast at her kitchen table, charmingly fashioned out of two rustic doors. The young garden is dotted with olive trees and the jacuzzi is perfect for unwinding. The setting, too, is special: negotiate the external staircase to the rooftop for timeless views of olive groves and the distant Murgia hills. *Minimum stay two nights.*

- Massage & yoga courses; guided visits to old masserias
- Egnazia Archaeological Park & Museum; Valle d'Itria Festival of Opera & Music (July/August)

rooms	5 + 1: 3 doubles; 1 double, 1 twin sharing bath. 1 studio for 2.
price	€75-€85. Studio €75-€140.
meals	Dinner with wine €20. Restaurants 2-3km. Self-catering studio.
closed	Generally closed in winter.
directions	From N379 Bari-Brindisi, exit Ostuni, signs to Cisternino; there, SP134 to Locorotondo; at blue boundary signs of Bari & Brindisi, left into Contrada Figazzano; immed. right; house 2nd on left.

	Caroline Groszer
mobile	+39 335 6094647
email	carolinegroszer@tre.it
web	www.trullicountryhouse.com

They support the Natural Reserve of Torre Guaceto: a stretch of crystal clear waters & important wetland habitat.

B&B & Self-catering

Entry 93

Hotel Bourazani

Bourazani, Konitsa, Ioannina – Zagori

Tucked into Greece's northwest corner surrounded by the mountains of Albania sits this totally unexpected hotel on the shady banks of the turquoise Aoös river. At first sight it's a bit blocky and Balkan; inside, a pine-clad dining room with a hundred deers' heads recalls an Austrian hunting lodge. But this place is unique. Lanky Giorgos, a vet with a touch of the Basil Fawlty, spent thirty years reintroducing threatened animals like mouflon, wild boar and red deer into a 200-hectare, oak-covered reserve which guests can now visit by minibus. Meanwhile, British botanists have ascertained that there's a higher density of butterflies and flowers (notably orchids) here than anywhere else in Greece; Giorgos can give you field books, or even an illustrated lecture. Almond and judas blossom rings out in spring. Rooms are clean, simple, balconied; suites are huge; food, including venison moussaka, is local and full of taste.

- Walking; butterfly spotting; kayaking
- Traditional flour mill & carpet-washer upstream; frescoed Byzantine monastery downstream

rooms	23: 18 twins/doubles, 2 suites for 2-4. Annexe (pictured): 3 twins/doubles.
price	€60-€70. Suites €100-€120.
meals	Breakfast €6. Lunch/dinner from €10.
closed	Rarely.
directions	From Ioannina, E90 to Konitsa; after 45km left (signed) towards Basiliko; 14km, on left. From Konitsa, through Mazi, Aetopetra, across bridge, right. On left.

Otters swim in the crystal-clean river Aoös.

Hotel

	Giorgos Tassos
tel	+30 26550 61283/61320
fax	+30 26550 61321
email	burazani@otenet.gr
web	www.bourazani.gr

Ionian Eco Villagers

Gerakas, c/o PO BOX 6051, Weymouth, Dorset DT4 4AH, UK

In green and sunny Zante, under pine-scented hills, a mere stroll from miles of sand, this collection of brightly coloured villas, apartments and stone cottages splashes over ancient olive groves in lush gardens of citrus and bougainvillea. But it is the warmth of the Yannis's and Maddy's welcome and their commitment to conservation that really stand out. The Gerakas peninsula, now part of the marine park, is one of the last nesting sites of the loggerhead sea turtle. And Yannis has battled impressively to keep mass tourism at bay. Comfortable homes, many solar-powered, have sea views, timbered ceilings, cool tiled floors, simple kitchens, open showers, a family ornament here, a touch of kitsch there. The cracking sound of the locals taking pot shots at the birds might puncture the tranquillity but you are in rural Greece. Come in spring or autumn for meadows of wild flowers and venture out with volunteers in a summer's dawn for the unforgettable sight of hatchlings on the beach.

- Catamarans to turtle habitats; snorkelling in secluded coves; mountain biking & nature walks.
- Loggerhead sea turtles, monk seals & conservation work

rooms	1 cottage for 5, 1 farmhouse for 6, 3 villas for 5, 3 studios for 3, 4 apts for 3, 4 apts for 4.
price	£363–£480 p.w. for 2.
meals	Basic breakfast included. Restaurants in Gerakas Village.
closed	October–April.
directions	14km from Zakynthos town signed Vassilikos & Gerakas. Follow final sign for Gerakas 1km from site. Bus from Zakynthos.

	Madeleine Doggett & Yannis Vardakastanis
tel	+44 (0)871 7115 065
mobile	+30 697 9934746
email	maddy@relaxing-holidays.com
web	www.relaxing-holidays.com

£10 from every booking is donated to the Earth Sea & Sky conservation centre in Gerakas.

B&B & Self-catering

Agroktima Boukouvala

Vathi, 23200 Gythion, Laconia

This 80-hectare fruit farm spills onto Vathi's sheltered beach – blissfully peaceful, yet within reach of lovely Gythion. Children are in heaven: warm shallow seas, huge safe gardens, pet rabbits, impromptu barbecues and theatre games. Families return year after year. There are three harvests (orange, olive, fig); three generations of hosts (charming Stella and Iannis, his parents, their kids); three buildings spaced among the citrus groves. The oldest lies on the sand: prime position, though its rooms are simple (bare walls, pine beds, functional kitchenettes, no air-con). Most are triple bedded (one double, one single). Inland, alongside the owners' house, are two newer buildings with family apartments. We liked the stone-clad ones: an earthy, open-plan bedsit downstairs, a wooden loft in the eaves. Sit outside to inhale orange blossom and mountain views. You can buy their fruit, walk to Vathi's mini-market and taverna, or drive to Gythion for ouzo and octopus.

- Explore rugged Mani
- Mount Taygetos (highest in Peloponnese, snow-covered for six months of the year)

You may take part in the harvesting of oranges & figs.

rooms	8 studios for 3; 11 apartments for 2-4.
price	Studios €40-€55 for 2-3. Apartments €55-€95 for 4.
meals	Self-catering. Taverna & shop walking distance; more 1-2km.
closed	Rarely.
directions	From Gythion, start towards Areopolis, left after 9km to Vathi. Just past 'Belle Helene' (signed), towards sea.

Iannis & Stella Boukouvalas

tel	+30 27330 25060/93524
fax	+30 27330 29055
email	bukubala@otenet.gr
web	www.boukouvala-apartments.com

Self-catering

Milia Traditional Settlement

73012 Vlatos, Chania, Crete

Organic farm, hikers' hostel or Cretan mountain village? Milia is all three.
A tiny settlement in a fold of the White Mountains, it was abandoned after a
cholera outbreak, briefly sheltered guerillas in WW2, before being resurrected
by two local lads in the 1980s. Stone houses were reroofed, spring water piped in,
terraces replanted, livestock introduced, a generator installed. Fourteen cottages
now dot the plane-shaded valley: some isolated, others spilling onto neighbours'
roofs. All are pure rusticity: iron beds, woodburning stoves (logs supplied),
flagged floors, tiny windows in crude walls. Bathrooms are basic, but the greatest
luxuries – fine air, food and company – are in endless supply. Giorgos cuts back
ancient paths through chestnut and arbutus groves; Tassos brings cooking courses
and mountain bikes to this peaceful spot. Bean-stews, chestnuts, dandelions, pork
are all home-grown; raki and herbal brews flow. A bold, unique project.

* Hiking to the Sirikari gorge
* The timeless cave-chapel of Ayia Sophia; the sandy crescent of Elafonisos beach

rooms	14: 3 doubles, 2 twins, 3 triples, 4 family rooms, 2 suites for 2-4.
price	€60-€65. Singles €55. Triples/suites €80. Family rooms €90.
meals	Lunch/dinner €13-€17.
closed	Never.
directions	From Chania E65 west. Just before Kastelli (Kissamos), left onto old road & south for Elafonisos. After Topolia gorge, right to Vlatos; right again (sign) along track to Milia. Park outside hamlet, walk down.

All food is home-grown &
organically produced.

	Mr Tassos Gourgouras
tel	+30 28220 51569/46774
fax	+30 28220 51569
email	milia@cha.forthnet.gr
web	www.milia.gr

Eco lodge

B 🍴 💬 🍷 🚜 🚲 👟

Entry 97

africa & middle east

Photo left José Navarro
Photo this page Vumbura Plains, entry 116

RABAT 98
MOROCCO
ATLAS MOUNTAINS
99
100 101

S A H A R A

Niger
S A H E L
Lake Chad

Niger Benue
Lake
Volta

Congo

South

Atlantic

Ocean

NAMIBIA
114
115
WINDHOEK

Orange

0   600   1200 kilometres
0   300   600 miles

CAPE TOWN

Mediterranean Sea

AMMAN

JORDAN
122,123

CAIRO

EGYPT
102

Nile

Lake
Nasser

Red Sea

ARABIAN
PENINSULA

Gulf of Aden

White Nile

Blue Nile

ETHIOPIAN
HIGHLANDS

Ubangi

Congo

Lake Albert

GREAT RIFT VALLEY

Lake
Turkana

KENYA

103   104

NAIROBI

105

Lake
Victoria

106

CONGO
BASIN

Lulobo

Kasai

TANZANIA

DODOMA

107

Lake
Tanganyika

111

110   MALAWI

108   Lake
Nyasa   113   112

ZAMBIA

LUSAKA

Zambezi

LILONGWE

MOZAMBIQUE

109

Mozambique Channel

116

BOTSWANA

117

GABORONE

Limpopo

119   118

KALAHARI
DESERT   PRETORIA   MAPUTO

120

SOUTH
AFRICA

121

Indian

Ocean

©Maidenhead Cartographic, 2005

Berbari

Dchar Ghanem, Cercle de Tnine Sidi El Yamani, Asilah

Out in the country, in the middle of the village, three hefty pillars bend under the weight of the years and the iron roofs so typical of this region. You find storks rest on their scruffy great nests, the widest starriest skies in the north (Berbari uses candles or dim bulbs so as not to compete), a grand piano with a few good old armchairs under the sweeping tataoui salon roof and a splendidly light-hearted approach to décor, all items resuscitated from other lives and full of soul (quirky plumbing, too). Beamed, lime-washed rooms are all different in their simplicity of bright local fabrics against rough white walls, the Moroccan salon with its comfortably cushioned benches and uncluttered style is much favoured and your private space, be it sitting area or piece of garden, is a delight. Discover genuine rural Morocco, the neolithic village, the braying, praying dawn chorus. In summer, you can rent one of their beach huts and sleep in splendid isolation.

- Visits to village markets; talks on local Berber history
- Lixus; M'zoura Cromlech; Tomb of the Giant Antéus; Asilah

Their well provides the local school with water.

Guest house

rooms	7: 4 doubles, 3 suites, each with salon or garden.
price	300Dh-700Dh. Beach huts 250Dh, book ahead.
meals	Snacks 60Dh. Lunch & dinner 120Dh-200Dh. By arrangement.
closed	Never.
directions	If you have no 4x4 vehicle, in winter ring from Asilah for escort last 4km. Bus to Asilah.

	Louis Soubrier & Rachida Youdra
tel	+212 (0)62 58 80 13
email	contact@berbari.com, louis.soubrier@caramail.com
web	www.berbari.com

Kasbah du Toubkal

BP 31, Imlil, Asni

Below North Africa's highest peak the Imlil valley soars away on wings of fertile terraces and red villages. This exceptional mountain retreat is a Berber-European union born of the desire to share Jbel Toubkal's splendours with like-minded visitors without destroying them. Painstakingly rebuilt by entrepreneur Mike McHugo and tireless Hajj Maurice, their 'Berber Hospitality Centre' provides two-budget sleeping: Berber salons (cushioned sitting/sleeping benches round double-height rooms), or good double rooms with bathrooms plus one superb cliff-hanging apartment. Hospitality is a Berber talent: big open smiles, intelligent local knowledge, deep respect for people and animals, and wonderful tagine! Enjoy fascinating glimpses of their culture while walking and mule-trekking; and soothe aching limbs in the hammam. Only 90 minutes from Marrakech, it's another world. *Sole occupancy possible.*

- Rambles around Berber villages; guided ascent of Jbel Toubkal (crampons & ice-picks in winter); ski mountaineering

rooms	14: 11 doubles; 1 apartment for 6; 3 Berber salons for 3-10, sharing bathrooms.
price	€140-€400. Apt €700. Salons €110-€140 for 3-4.
meals	Lunch €15. Dinner €20. BYO.
closed	Rarely.
directions	From Marrakech for Asni then Imlil (65km). Park in village (guarded); 500m walk or mule ride.

	Hajj Maurice
tel	+212 (0)24 485611
fax	+212 (0)24 485636
email	kasbah@discover.ltd.uk
web	www.kasbahdutoubkal.com

5% is added to your bill to help fund local community projects.

Hotel

Dar Raha
Hay Amezrou, BP 142, 45900 Zagora

The real riches of Morocco are here: these thoughtful, creative, committed owners have made Dar Raha ('house of rest') into a place for encounters. Under their guidance, discover local history, architecture and culture, meet craftsmen and families, glimpse their gentle, traditional lifestyle, take mountain, valley or desert treks with seriously knowledgeable guides in partnership with a local association. In the heart of dusty red Amezrou where the flourishing palm grove keeps the desert at bay, their big old family house sits proud and cool beneath a protecting kasbah. Sober pisé architecture, minimal decoration, simple comforts. Rooms have their own or shared terraces, colourful Moroccan fabrics to match their spice labels, ingenious 'clothes ladders', shared washrooms. From the terrace, way up above, you can watch 5,000 years of history melting into the palm grove as earth bricks give way to cement. Your interest can help save some of it.

- Walking, camel riding & making local crafts at artisan workshops
- Qsar (fortified village) of Amezrou; Mount Zagora; holy town of Tamgrout

rooms	9: 7 doubles, 1 triple, 1 single, all sharing 5 showers, 5 wcs.
price	375Dh. Half-board 500Dh for 2.
meals	Half-board.
closed	Mid-June–mid-August.
directions	From Zagora centre for M'Hamid; over bridge 500m to Amezrou entrance; right at Maison Toudra & follow signs.

A variety of traditional homemade foods are provided according to season.

Josiane Morillon & Antoine Bouillon
tel	+212 (0)24 84 69 93
fax	+212 (0)24 84 61 80
email	darraha_zagora@yahoo.fr
web	darraha.free.fr/

Guest house

Kasbah Mohayut

Ksar Hassi Labiad, 52202 Merzouga

What makes this dune-side inn so special? The people, ten times over. Moha took a degree in English; then, realising that tourism had become the only source of livelihood for his friends and relatives here, returned to turn his family house into a delightful place to stay. He has natural charm, exceptional integrity and puts all his energy into making your stay unforgettable. Indeed, the whole family works together with welcoming smiles and caring attention. After all the dryness outside, you find two cool garden courtyards with flourishes of greenery and fountains. In the rambling traditional earth building palm and eucalyptus beams hold the roof, old Berber doors are carved with ancient symbols, walls are encrusted with lettering. It has warm inviting bedrooms, good little shower rooms, wrought-iron furniture standing on Berber carpets. Lovely people, great value.

* Trekking & camel excursions into the desert
* Erg Chebbi & the oasis

rooms	14: 6 doubles, 2 twins, 2 triples, 4 suites.
price	Half-board 400Dh–600Dh.
meals	Lunch/dinner 90Dh. Picnic 40Dh. By arrangement. BYO.
closed	Never.
directions	From Rissani for Merzouga, after 33km left at sign then 2.5km of track.

Moha supports a local crafts cooperative.

	Mohammed Oubadi
tel	+212 (0)66 03 91 85
fax	+212 (0)35 57 78 61
email	mohamezan@yahoo.fr
web	www.mohayut.com

Hotel

B 🚶 🍴 🍲 🛏 🧍 👞

Desert Lodge
Al Qasr

Though so much part of the landscape that it could have been here for centuries, Desert Lodge is new. And it has been meticulously planned to minimise its impact on the ancient environment. Traditional mud-brick construction has been carried out by local craftsmen using local materials, waste is minimised and plastic banned! The position, high on a ridge overlooking the oasis and Al Qasr (once a Roman settlement), is spectacular, invigorating and blissfully quiet. Airy, high-ceilinged, stone-floored rooms have a traditional, minimalist feel, with whitewashed walls and brightly striped bed covers. As well as an artists' workshop, internet café and sitting areas, there's a little library; the restaurant serves good, simple, local food. Vegetables are grown organically alongside cacti in the big garden encircling the lodge buildings. Staff are courteous, friendly and quietly efficient.

* Guided walks with trained Bedouin staff; cycling & camel rides; workshops for artists
* Birds, gazelle & desert plants in the sculpted sand dunes
* Mosque, museum, market & local craft outlets in Al Qasr (500m)

rooms	32: 10 doubles, 21 twins, 1 triple. Extra beds available.
price	Half-board $50-$80 p.p. Singles $70-$95.
meals	Lunch $12. Packed lunch $8.
closed	Never.
directions	500m from Al Qasr village. Buses from Cairo-Dakhla Oasis, 2 daily. Weekly flight Cairo-Kharga (neighbouring Oasis) on charter basis.

The Lodge staff regularly clean the village with the help of the local school children.

Eco lodge

	Ahmed Moussa
tel	+20 (0)2690 5240
fax	+20 (0)2690 5250
email	info@desertlodge.net
web	www.desertlodge.net

Basecamp Masai Mara

c/o Basecamp Travel, PO Box 433 69, Nairobi

Wrapped protectively by the river Talek on the northern perimeter of the Masai Mara National Park is a community of luxury eco-huts forming the perfect base for safaris across the immense African savannah. Looped around a luscious green lawn where monkeys play and solar panels are proudly displayed, the tented huts come with riverside terrace, hammocks and private open-air showers. Simple furniture is made on site from local natural materials and crisp linen sheets line comfortable beds. Sip a fresh juice in the cool restaurant; spy on the great annual migration that saunters past the shared tree house; listen to Maasai anecdotes. Precious rainwater is caught in a huge tank and shared with local families. Let the convivial atmosphere of Basecamp inspire group game drives and shared dinners – both here and in the authentic restaurants of Talek village.

- Walking safaris, cultural activities
- Lion, cheetah, leopard, elephant, buffalo, zebra, hippo, rhino, 300 bird species, (one resident crocodile!)
- Spectacular migration of wildebeest through park July-October

rooms	16: 15 tents for 2, 1 family tent for 4.
price	Full-board US$200 p.p. Family $140 p.p.
meals	Full-board only.
closed	Never.
directions	Drive in via Sekenani Gate; signed for Basecamp; pass Talek Gate & Talek Centre staying right; continue for 2km. Direct bus booked by Basecamp.

Maasai *Mamas* make and sell traditional beads at on-site workshop.

	Reservations
tel	+254 (0)20 38 77 490/91/92
mobile	+254 733 333 909
email	info@basecampexplorer.co.ke
web	www.basecampexplorer.com

Safari camp & Eco lodge

E ﴾ ﴿ Hello ﴾ ﴿

Entry 103

Il N'gwesi Lodge
P.O. Box 763, Timau

Shrouded by acacia trees and raised above a vast forested plateau, an eco lodge proudly owned by the Il N'gwesi tribe. Colour your dreams with the breathtaking views of the sacred mountains that flank these acres of wildlife-rich flatlands; watch in awe as elephants stop at the neighbouring watering hole for their daily drink. The *bandas* on stilts are luxuriously simple – and spacious; the pool is exquisite. Spy antelope scuffling from the privacy of the loo; see the tawny eagle glide whilst soaking under the heavenly solar-heated shower; drop off to sleep under the stars to distant lion roar. The utopia of Il N'gwesi ('people of wildlife') is a wonder to behold: each of the 448 tribal households owns an equal share of the lodge and joint decisions are made. Schools have been built, mobile clinics reach the needy, wildlife is protected. Indulge in the wisdom and energy of tribal 'elder', Kip, who delights in recounting the story of the tribe. Inspirational.

- Guided bush walks & visits to 'cultural village': experience Maasai blood tapping and traditional dancing
- Lions, elephants, rhinos, leopards, buffalo

Fruits & vegetables are kept in refrigerators of coal and water.

Eco lodge

rooms	6 bandas: 1 double, 5 rooms for 2-3.
price	Full-board US$240 p.p. & $20 conservation fee.
meals	Full-board only.
closed	Never.
directions	Fly from Nairobi Wilson Airport to Lewa or Il N'gwesi airstrip, pick-up. Bus from Nairobi to Isiolo (change Nanyuki). Staff pick up from Matunda gate. Game-drive through Lewa conservancy to Il N'gwesi.

Jonathan Kipkorir Nteere

tel	+254 (0)64 31405
fax	+254 (0)64 31405
email	ilngwesi@lewa.org
web	www.laikipia.org/hotel_ilngwesi.htm

E

Lewa House

c/o Lewa Wildlife Conservancy, Lewa Wildlife Conservancy, 00100 Nairobi

With stunning views of the rolling grasslands and the distant, jagged and snow-capped peak of Mount Kenya, Lewa House is intended for exclusive use – a (lavish) home from home. The bedrooms are divided among the three stone cottages that have a hint of colonial indulgence: there are sheep-skin rugs, four-posters and open fires, and the bathrooms are spotless. The fantastic open-aired reception/dining room, furnished with African relics, faces Kenya's highest peak and is a cool place to escape the midday sun before a dip in the pool or a round of tennis – all elegantly positioned above the natural habitat of ambling giraffe and zebra. Lewa House is an influential member of the Lewa Conservancy: relax in the knowledge that your stay contributes to the protection and preservation of land and animals or take a more active part in conservation orientated activities.

- Game drives, guided bush walks, horse and camel safaris
- Endangered Grevy zebra; white & black rhinos; lions, cheetahs, leopards, elephants
- Mount Kenya; Lewa Wildlife Conservancy; Mathews range & sacred mountain of the Samburu, Ol Lolokwe

rooms	Sleeps 6-12: 1 twin, 1 double in each of 3 cottages.
price	US$840. Conservancy fees: adult $50, child under 12 $25, per day.
meals	Full-board US$120 extra p.p.
closed	April and November for rains.
directions	Bus from Nairobi bus station, change at Nakuki for Isiolo; pick-up from Lewa Conservancy gate or from Lewa airstrip.

Talks provide information about the Conservancy and related issues.

	Clare Moller
tel/ fax	+254 (0)643 1405
mobile	+254 (0)722 203 562
email	bookings@lewa.org
web	www.lewa.org/lewa_house.php

Guesthouse

Kahawa Shamba

Kahawa Shamba, KNCU Fair Tourism Project, PO Box 3032, Moshi

On the edge of a rushing river gorge, where salmon dance to a chorus of birdsong beneath the mighty Kilimanjaro, bustles a little village belonging to the Wachagga people. Coffee-makers by trade, the historically hospitable tribe have dotted their village with some traditional but luxurious huts (*chaggas*) for visitors to glimpse Africa's highest peak and at the same time contribute to the protection of local homes. Vines from the forest and stones from the river are masterfully sculpted under a dried banana-leaf roof; locally woven mats sit under firm beds; spicey soap, made by the deft hands of local women, scents the spotless bathroom. Breakfast is an abundance of fresh fruit served in a communal dining-hut overlooking the gorge. Crickets sing in harmony as colobus monkeys swing in tune to a bush baby solo. Acclimatise with gentle guided walks before you take on the majesty of the mountain.

- Horse riding; visits to local homes for traditional dinner (all contributions go to the families, the coffee farms & banana beer brewers)
- Mount Kilimanjaro

rooms	4 huts for 2.
price	Full-board US$196. Singles $110.
meals	Full-board only.
closed	Never.
directions	30km from Moshi. Bus from Moshi to Lyamungo village, walk 2km to Kahawa Shamba-Kibera.

A project set up by Tribes Travel, Twin, Cafédirect & DFIO.

Emilson Malisa

tel	+255 (0)27 2750464/2785
fax	+255 (0)27 2754204
email	kncutourism@kilinet.co.tz
web	www.kirurumu.com/kahawa

Homestay

Chumbe Island
Zanzibar

Take a moment to gaze wholly upon this small island clothed by forest and white sand and you'll feel like Robinson Crusoe reviewing years of hard work. Two-tiered eco bungalows, crafted from mangrove poles and coconut leaves, with their own solar panels and compost toilets, capture freshwater from the heavens through their innovative roof design. Zanzibari spices sing their sweet aroma near the comfortable bed and a removeable side wall allows for natural air conditioning and sumptuous views of palm trees and turquoise waters. From your capacious hammock take a short stroll to the water's edge where the crystal clear Indian Ocean washes over the sand. Staff are friendly islanders and will take you on a snorkelling tour of the protected coral reef, or for an educational walk through the forest. Climb to the top of the resident lighthouse and peer down at paradise. Perhaps, with luck, you will be happily stranded.

- Snorkelling; nature trails.
- The endangered Ader's duiker and coconut crab, 64 bird species (roseate terns, fish eagles), hawksbill turtles & 423 species of fish (incl. batfish & potato grouper)

rooms	7 bungalows for 2.
price	Full-board US$150-$200 p.p. Includes transfers & activities.
meals	Full-board only.
closed	April 9-June 11.
directions	From Zanzibar Mbweni Ruins Hotel in Stonetown, 45-min boat trip to Chumbe Island.

No plastics are brought to the island.

	Helen Peeks
tel	+255 (0)242 231 040
fax	+225 (0)242 231 040
email	info@chumbeisland.com
web	www.chumbeisland.com

Eco lodge

F 🍴 Hello 🐚 🕯

Robin Pope Safaris Nkwali Camp

Robin Pope Safaris Nkwali Camp, P.O.Box 80, Mfuwe, South Luangwa

Baboons chatter from nearby ebony trees while you tuck into a delicious outdoor buffet lunch of asparagus quiche, chicken and salad at this relaxed upmarket camp on the banks of the Luangwa River. Robin and his wife Jo run a comfortable camp with six bamboo and thatch chalets, each with netted beds and private open-air bathroom, dotted around the park-like grounds. There's also the two-bedroom Robin's House, set above a favourite hippos' bathing spot on the river bank (grunting hippos may wake you up!), and the spectacular, four-bedroom Luangwa House, with its private dining deck under an ebony tree in the middle of a plain packed with game. But visitors are encouraged to swap this luxury for a night in a mud hut at nearby Kawaza village, where many camp staff come from. You will help with cooking, share *nsima* (the local maize dish), and visit the local school.

- Walking & photographic safaris; game drives
- Big game include lions, hippos, elephants, leopards, wild dogs & the Thornicroft giraffe
- Kawaza village; South Luangwa National Park

RPS supports 18 schoolteachers through guest donations and fundraising.

rooms	6 chalets: 5 for 2, 1 for 4; 2 houses: 1 for 5, 1 for 8.
price	Full-board, US$500-$1,000 per chalet/house.
meals	Full-board only.
closed	Never.
directions	Fly from Lusaka to Mfuwe Airport (transfers arranged). Drive 4x4 from Chipata, take Mfuwe road, after 110km of dirt rd right at T-junc., tar road for 20km, left past BP garage, follow signs.

Reservations

tel	+260 (0)6 246090-2
email	info@robinpopesafaris.net
web	www.robinpopesafaris.net

Safari camp

Tongabezi Lodge
Private Bag 31, Livingstone

Don't set the alarm clock – awake to the light with a noisy pod of hippos! High on the riverbank, each of the four (different) houses has one side missing, liberating the view to a sweep of the Zambezi River. Some, like the Tree House, are split-level, with tree-trunks (still growing) around the billowing mosquito net of the king-size bed. Stairs to a deck below reveal the open-air toilet and sunken bath. The airy cottages (slightly smaller than the houses) stand beside the water's edge, their claw-footed baths looking out through picture windows. Amidst the riverbank's vegetation, Tongabezi's open layout feels very natural – from the waterfall tumbling into the small splash-pool to the floating deck where efficient local staff serve breakfast. Tongabezi sets the pace for African lodge design and is notable for employing and training Zambian managers – surprisingly uncommon in the safari industry.

- Boating, birdwatching & white-water rafting
- Crocodiles, hippos & occasional elephants
- The Victoria Falls; Livingstone

rooms	15: 5 river cottages for 2, 5 chalets, 1 garden cottage, 4 houses for 2.
price	Full-board US$750-$1,060 for 2.
meals	Full-board only.
closed	Never.
directions	Take the Kazangula road from town towards Botswana. Exit park & take next left (500m) after lay-by. Follow dirt road for 3km to Tongabezi.

Tongabezi supports a programme for the schooling of local children.

	Honour Schram de Jong
tel	+260 (0)3 324450
fax	+260 (0)3 324483
email	reservations@tongabezi.com
web	www.tongabezi.co.za

Safari camp

G

Shiwa Ng'andu Manor House

P.O. Box 1, Shiwa Ng'andu, Mpika

Indulge your aristocratic fantasies at this Tuscan-style manor house carved from Zambia's bush by Edwardian eccentric Sir Stewart Gore-Browne. His grandson Charlie and wife Jo are passionate about conservation and also manage an NGO that runs a hospital and schools, helping the lives of thousands of local indigenous people living below the poverty line. Their family history is almost tangible: take tea in the drawing room surrounded by original portraits; browse the library's archives; explore the family chapel. Soak in your original ball-and-claw bath before sundowners on the terrace above sculpted gardens, or beside the lake after which Shiwa N'gandu is named. Exquisite rugs and silver candelabra adorn the dining room, where you feast on traditional English dishes made from estate produce, before sleeping it all off in a vast four-poster bed. A benevolent alternative world.

- Walking, birdwatching, fishing, horse riding, game drives
- 24 mammal species (including the rare blue duiker), crocodiles, birds
- Kapishya hot springs; North Luangwa National Park

rooms	5: 2 doubles, 2 twins; children's room for 2, with separate bathroom.
price	Full-board US$440 p.p.
meals	Full-board only.
closed	Never.
directions	Air charter from Lusaka/Mfuwe.

Income from guests funds the estate's social & conservation projects.

tel	+44 (0)208 232 9777
fax	+44 (0)208 758 4718
email	info@expertafrica.com
web	www.expertafrica.com

c/o Expert Africa

Guest house

Entry 110

Vamizi Island

Quirimbas Archipelago, c/o Maluane, Cabo Delgado Biodiversity & Tourism, Limitada

Samango monkeys cavort in the trees, hermit crabs scuttle over the sand, a fishing dhow glides through the waters. Watch from the privacy of your room, ten metres from the beach and not a building in sight. Scattered amongst casuarinas, the traditionally built beach houses are cool with space and elegant with furnishings – wafts of muslin, marbled bathrooms, jewel-bright cushions, carved wooden screens – locally sourced and crafted. If you can stir from your sofa-strewn veranda, there are coral reefs to explore, trails to walk, birds to spot or you can help with conservation surveys. Vamizi Lodge is part of the project, encouraging locals to protect and sustain their island. They've gained new skills, a clinic and school room. Solar panels and rainwater collection are future plans. Staying here is no hardship – you dine amidst white napery and soft lights – just unhurried and sensitive.

- Turtle monitoring; game fishing (tag and release); diving, snorkelling, dhow sailing, ocean kayaking; guided bird walks
- Humpback whales (seasonal), dolphins (3 species), dugong, 132 bird species

rooms	10 beach houses: 8 for 2, 2 for 4.
price	Full-board US$560-$740 p.p. (discounts for children). Includes guided activities.
meals	Full-board only.
closed	Never.
directions	From Dar es Salaam (Tanzania) or Jo'burg (South Africa) flight to Pemba (Mozambique); then 1 hr 10 mins transfer to Vamizi's airstrip.

The Lodge provides a boat for islanders to patrol the waters for illegal foreign fishing.

	Reservations
tel	+258 (0)27 221 299
fax	+258 (0)27 221 274
email	reservations@maluane.com
web	www.vamizi.com

Eco lodge

Quilálea
Quilálea Island, Província de Cabo Delgado

In bed, in the shower, in the restaurant, there's no escaping those dancing ocean views. Tiny Quilálea island (an hour and you've walked the shoreline) sits in a marine sanctuary in the Quirimbas National Park. The only buildings are the villas scattered amongst undisturbed coastal forest – baobabs and paperbark trees – overlooking escapist-pure beaches. Before opening in 2002, only fishermen camped here. There's every chance you'll discover a new plant species. Built in 'Creole Muani' style, with local stone and thatch roofs, villas have a simple luxury: cool stone floors, white walls, hand-crafted teak and mahogany furniture and super-size beds draped in muslin. It's comfort but with serious intent. Water is desalinated, the waste waters the plants, produce is local – as are the smiling staff – and boats are traditional dhows, perfect for that sunset drink. *No children under 16.*

- Diving, snorkelling, fishing, dhow sailing, kayaking
- Forts, villas & crafts on Ibo Island; mangroves & sea birds on Sencar Island
- Flamingos, fish eagles, dolphins, turtles, humpback whales & 375 species of fish

rooms	9 twin/double villas.
price	Full-board US$425-$475p.p. Includes diving.
meals	Full-board only.
closed	5 villas available from 15 November-6 December; 24 January-15 February.
directions	Helicopter transfer from Pemba.

Local fishermen have new-found skills as waiters, cooks & guides.

Beach hut

Marjolaine Hewlett
tel	+258 (0)272 21808
mobile	+258 82 326 3900 (Reservations)
email	info@quilalea.com
web	www.quilalea.com

Guludo Beach Lodge
Quirimbas National Park

The greatest luxury Guludo has to provide is space. Here, where the African bush meets the Indian Ocean, the white coral sand beach seem to last forever and thatched *bandas* camouflage rustic exclusivity. Rooms are basic yet spacious, large double bed, writing table and chairs are all locally made, and a bamboo screen surrounds a solar-powered shower in the marbled bathroom. Meals are exotic but unpretentious; kingfish, tuna, prawn or lobster cooked by local chefs. Youthful Amy and her partner Neal came here in 2004 with the aim of using tourism "to sustainably reduce poverty and promote biodiversity". Their work in progress is already impressive: a Social & Environmental Regeneration Fund facilitates reef and humpback whale projects and they work with local fishing communities to promote sustainable fishing techniques. The location and ethos are hard to beat.

- Walking; local community visits; sunset dhow trips; snorkelling; archery
- Yellow-billed stork, African fish-eagle, coral, turtles, sharks, humpback whales
- Ibo Island; Quirimbas National Park; fringing reef

rooms	9 tents: 3 doubles, 6 twins. Some wcs shared.
price	Full-board US$185-$235 pp.
meals	Full-board only.
closed	Never.
directions	4hr drive from Pemba. Main road north to Macomia, right towards Mocojo on dirt road (4x4 essential) for 50km then right towards Naunda. On through Guludo village to left fork, lodge at road end.

	Reservations
tel	+44 (0)1323 766 655
email	contact@bespokeexperience.com
web	www.guludo.com

Dive courses teach guests about reef conservation & their socio-economic importance for local communities.

Tented camp

Damaraland
Torra Conservancy

Expect a real Namibian welcome from the Damara community-run Torra Conservancy, here in the heart of the red basalt and sandstone-coloured desert. Your first encounter as you step into the open-plan dining room is with your host – the smiling and indomitable Lena Florry, or Mama Namibia. Lena prides herself on her introductions to each course of a delicious dinner round the *boma* under the stars – and points out that there is one problem: there is no word for pudding in the Damara click language! The comfortable walk-in tents – with flowers by their bedsides – are solar powered at night and the views all around are sensational, especially when you go down the valley with the Huab river in the distance and its outline of green Ana trees; it acts as desert motorway for the wildlife of this region. The light is especially radiant at sunset, with the changing colours of reds, golds and coppers casting dark shadows off the hills and cliffs in the distance. *Children over 8 welcome.*

- Tracking, walking & game drives
- Desert elephant, oryx, ostrich, springbok, cheetah, giraffe, kudu & black rhinos

rooms	10 tents: 2 doubles, 7 twins, 1 family.
price	Half-board NA$1,170-$1,680 p.p. Full-board $2,140-$2,815 p.p. Includes activities. Discounts for children 8-12.
meals	Half- or full-board only. Packed lunch NA$85.
closed	Never.
directions	From Khorixas 118km (1.5 hrs) drive to Camp (DC) on 2620/C39.

The camp has ensured the survival of one of Namibia's first wildlife conservancies.

Reservations
email   enquiry@wilderness.co.za
web   www.wilderness-safaris.com

Tented camp

Wolwedans

NamibRand Safaris (Pty) Ltd., PO Box 5048, Windhoek

Desert doves take flight and young ostriches dart along the road. Among the striking sands of one of the largest nature conservation areas in Africa, beneath eternally blue skies, 'Where the Wolves Dance' is 80 miles from the nearest petrol station… a place to lose (or perhaps find) yourself. The rustic-luxurious chalets, built along the ridge of a sandy plateau, thrill to 180-degree views of towering natural edifices, their decks perfect for dune- or star-gazing. Be glad of down duvets, hot showers, solar lights, canvas blinds, wildlife magazines. The double tents, perched on wooden platforms, are equally appealing. In the main lodge is an *Out of Africa* feel: sepia photographs, classic wooden furnishings, sundowner decks; more voguish is the open-plan kitchen. Chat to the chef as he prepares his fabulous pan-African cuisine: every one of Wolwedans' custodians is delightful.

- Safari drives, hiking, nature walks; hot-air ballooning, accompanied by experienced guides
- Antelope, red-hartebeast, zebra, spotted hyena, jackal, kudu, baboon, leopard
- Giant dunes at Sossusvlei, 70km

rooms	Dunes Lodge: 9 doubles, 1 suite. Dune Camp: 6 tents for 2. Private Camp: 2 tents for 2.
price	Full-board Dunes Lodge from NA$2,650 p.p. Singles $3,710. Camps from $1,750 p.p. Includes activities. Park fees $135 p.p. per day.
meals	Full-board only.
closed	Never. Dune Camp: December-February.
directions	Directions on booking.

Stephan Brueckner

tel	+264 (0)61 230 616
fax	+264 (0)61 220 102
email	reservations@wolwedans.com.na
web	www.wolwedans.com

The Namib Rand is entirely free of tour buses and self-drive 4x4s.

Safari camp

G (Hello) 🍴 🍷 🏊

Vumbura Plains
Okavango Delta

Delight in the eco-chic of this luxury camp in the extreme north of the magnificent Okavango Delta. The suites span two camps, linked by raised boardwalks (to minimise environmental impact), each with their own splash pool, dining area and outside lounge deck where there are extraordinary views of the vast attractive floodplain of the Kwedi concession. Enjoy it all from the stylish, spacious bedrooms where there are floor-to-ceiling sliding screens and diaphanous curtains on runners that billow in the afternoon breeze. Shower in the oversized indoor platform (built for two) or outside under the stars and enjoy fabulous dinners beneath a canopy of shady, indigenous trees. The region is known for the wonderful variety of habitats and large diversity of wildlife. True to Wilderness Safari's ethos, the land is leased from the local community, many of whom are employed and provided with skills training. *Children over 8 welcome.*

- Game drives; birdwatching safaris; dugout canoe trips
- Elephant, hippopotamus, crocodile, lion, cheetah, leopard, baboon, zebra, giraffe, warthog, red lechwe, antelope & sable

rooms	14: 2 camps of 7 suites
price	Full-board US$600-$1,095 p.p. sharing. Single supplement $185.
meals	Full-board only.
closed	Never.
directions	By air to Vumbura's airstrip 45-min drive from camp: from Maun 38 mins; from Kasane 1 hr 15 mins. Kasane to Victoria Falls 20 mins. If waters high in winter, access by mekeros or boat.

The entire lodge is built from sustainable pine.

	Reservations
email	enquiry@wilderness.co.za
web	www.wilderness-safaris.com

Safari camp

G

Makulu Makete Wildlife Reserve
PO Box 227, Alldays 0909, Limpopo Valley

A flash of cheetah, an inquisitive baboon, sunset-firing baobab trees – every day brings new experiences, shared over evening drinks round the camp fire. Makulu Makete gets you upfront and personal with life in the South African veld. Wander amongst the danger-free 4,500-hectare reserve currently being restored to wild savannah. Camp by the river, do your own thing (stone and thatch lodges where monkeys watch you frolic in the pool) or take it easy in safari tents. Comfortable rather than grand, with simple wooden furniture and colourful bedspreads, the tents' balconies overlook waterholes. The dawn drinking chorus is the only alarm clock you need. After a day outdoors, stroll lantern-lit paths to the large, thatched lodge for another of the chef's gut-busting meals. Peter and Jane, and their team of locals, have a quiet, friendly dedication. Relaxing and inspiring.

- Game drives; cheetah tracking; guided walks; birdwatching; ecology lectures
- Over 270 birds & 40 mammals include giraffes, zebras, oryx, wildebeest
- The archaeology of Mapungubwe National Park – a World Heritage Site

rooms	Main lodge: 6 tents for 2. Madia Pala Camp: 3 units for 2. Lulu's Camp: 5 sites for tent/caravan.
price	Main lodge: full-board R1,140 p.p. Includes activities. Madia Pala: R1,000 (whole camp). Lulu's: R200 site for 2, R300 site for 3-4.
meals	Full-board only in main lodge. Self-catering in campsite.
closed	15 December-4 January.
directions	Fly from Jo'burg to Polokwane. Minibus pick-up, 2.5 hr drive.

Re-introduced grasses help conserve water & prevent invasive bush & shrubs from taking root.

	Jane Chidgey
tel	+27 (0)82 903 8697
mobile	+27 82 903 8697
email	pgr@worldonline.co.za
web	www.makulumakete.com

Safari camp & Self-catering

Umlani Bushcamp

P.O. Box 11604, Maroelana 0161, Kruger

You're so close to nature, you might feel tempted to swish your tail. Screeches, squawks, grunts and grumbles are the only sounds you'll hear. There is no electricity – so no TV, no radio, no generator hum. In a remote part of the 10,000 hectare Timbavati Nature Reserve, this camp blends adventure with comfort. Tribal-style, reed and thatch 'rondavels' are lit with candles and oil-lamps and have crisp white linen, comfy beds and elegant wood furnishings. And there's plentiful (wood-fuelled) hot water for the open-air showers. When you're not tracking game, swing in a hammock by the free-form, rock pool, watch wildlife from the deck of the bar or take a cool-box and blankets to the private tree house. Umlani's meals are legendary, at their best when eaten under inky skies in the light of flares and cauldron fires. Staff are smiling, caring and proud to share their knowledge.

- Twice-daily game drives; bush walks; village cultural trips; elephant research trips; horse riding; white water rafting
- 'Big Five' animals & 350 bird species including eagles, orioles, spoonbills, storks

rooms	8 cabins: 5 for 2, 1 for 3, 2 for 4.
price	Full-board R1,500-R2,100 p.p.
meals	Full-board only.
closed	Never.
directions	Bus to Hoedspruit, then 1hr transfer (arrange on booking). By car, 5 hrs from Gauteng: 4.5 hrs from Pretoria or 5 hrs from Jo'burg.

The camp is certified by Fair Trade in Tourism South Africa.

Umlani Reservations

tel	+27 (0)12 346 4028
fax	+27 (0)12 346 4023
email	info@umlani.com
web	www.umlani.com

Safari camp

Djuma Bush Lodge

PO Box 338, Hluvukani, 1363, Mpumalanga

Cool off in the pool while elephants do it their inimitable way in a nearby watering hole. It's hard to tell where the camp ends and the game reserve begins. Part of the Sabi Sand complex, this is classic game reserve country – big, wild, uncrowded – but with a social conscience. Staff, including guides, are local; many helped design the lodges, and it's not long before you're invited to meet their families. The three lodges have breathtaking savannah views but individual styles. Galago, traditional and colonial, is for friends and families who want flexibility. The Bush Camp's thatched-roof chalets, simply furnished, sit in their own gardens while Vuyatela, with its minimalist furniture and modern art, is a fabulous, modern take on South African building styles. Think Coke-bottle chandeliers and outdoor showers. No TV, no radios, just bags of fresh air and dining under the brilliant Milky Way.

- Morning & evening game drives; guided bush walks; on-site spa; village trips
- Classic game reserve animals plus 200 species of bird
- Kruger National Park; Moholoholo Wildlife Rehabilitation Centre

rooms	Bush Camp: 8 chalets for 2. Vuyatela: 8 chalets for 2. Galago: self-catering lodge for 10.
price	Full-board R1,950-R2,950 p.p. Includes 2 daily safaris, guided walks & tourism levy. Self-catering R6,500 for whole camp per night.
meals	Full-board or self-catering.
closed	Never.
directions	Flights from Jo'burg. Air shuttle from KMIA, Nelspruit & Hoedspruit. Also road shuttle.

The camp supports two village crèches & sponsors further education, HIV talks & sports events.

	Charmian Cooke
tel	+27 (0)13 7355118
fax	+27 (0)13 7355070
email	djuma@djuma.co.za
web	www.djuma.com

Eco lodge & Self-catering

Photo: © CC Africa

Phinda Private Game Reserve
Private Bag X27, Benmore 2010

See dawn rise over Africa – and nothing but miles and miles of green trees. Rock Lodge, the most intimate of the five places to stay at this luxurious game reserve, is built into the side of a rocky hill on which leopards are often seen. The living area feels like a chic African home, with welcoming hosts, a drinks tray and roaring fire awaiting. Each detached suite has its own plunge pool, wooden deck, living area, baths, indoor and outdoor showers, Getti House has an 'interactive' kitchen and its own infinity pool, and the whole place invites hours of delicious solitude. Walls are roughly plastered in pale ochre; heavy wooden furniture, local rugs and art add colour; bathrooms are sensuous and food not too far from gourmet, with treats like pumpkin and cinnamon soup, springbok pancetta and mint sorbet. The service is so friendly that guests return just to see the staff.

- Walking safaris & game drives; turtle watching; horse riding; Zulu culture
- Africa's 'Big Five' game, suni antelope, 378 species of bird (Rudd's apali, Neergaard's sunbird, pink-throated twinspot) & 80 species of butterfly
- Greater St Lucia Wetland Park, Mkuze Game Reserve

rooms	46 + 1: Rock: 6 suites; Forest: 16 suites; Mountain: 20 suites; Vlei: 6 suites; 4 cottages for 2-4. Getti House for 8.
price	Full-board R2,605-R4,795 per suite. Cottages R15,340 (one party). House R28,000.
meals	Full-board or self-catering.
closed	Never.
directions	6hr drive from Jo'burg; 3 hrs Durban; 1.5 hrs Richards Bay. Daily flights to Phinda & Richards Bay.

Most staff are from neighbouring villages supported by The Africa Foundation.

Eco lodge & Self-catering

Suzanne Henderson

tel	+27 (0)11 809 4313
fax	+27 (0)11 809 4524
email	suzanne.henderson@ccafrica.com
web	www.phinda.com

G 🏕 Hello 🍷 🥾

Hog Hollow Country Lodge
PO Box 503, Plettenberg Bay, 6600, Western Cape

Built on a regenerated wattle plantation on the edge of the Matjies river gorge on the Garden Route the lodge and luxury suites survey a kingdom of century-old indigenous forest and the Tsitsikamma mountain range. Staff are attentive to the smallest detail, there are gingerbread men and hot milk at children's bedtime and the food is superb and sensitive to all family diets. You're encouraged to take part in the Hog Hollow ritual of being introduced around the dinner table by a different member of staff. Share tales of the day's elephant rides and nature trails around the *boma* (fire); you'll feel as though you're among old friends. The pool setting is blissfully relaxing and the suites are beautifully designed and furnished, each with a private veranda and uninterrupted view of the valley and mountains. Watch out for the monkeys at breakfast – they're big fans of toast and marmalade, but great entertainment for children.

- Hiking; canoeing, kayaking; horse riding; treetops canopy walk; whale watching
- Birds, monkeys, baboons, bushpigs, bucks, porcupines
- Tsitsikamma National Park; Monkeyland Primate Sanctuary

rooms	18: 15 suites, 3 family suites.
price	R1,920-R2,112. Singles R1,550. R467 per child including dinner.
meals	Lunch R35-R75. Dinner R180-R280.
closed	June.
directions	18km east of Plettenberg Bay. Take N2 towards Port Elizabeth. At Hog Hollow/Barnyard sign, right onto Askop Rd. 1.3km further on left.

	Jo Melton-Butler
tel	+27 (0)44 534 88 79
fax	+27 (0)44 534 88 79
email	info@hog-hollow.com
web	www.hog-hollow.com

All the lodge staff have been trained & recruited from the nearby villages of Kurland & Kwanokathula.

Eco lodge

Entry 121

Feynan Eco Lodge

Dana Nature Reserve, west side, near Griegra, South Jordan

Solar-powered, majestic and modern Arabesque. Amid the arid mountains of the southern Rift Valley, flanked by sloping ridges, the low flapping Bedouin tents of old have been replaced by this impressive, solid, adobe-walled retreat. Your hosts are local Bedouin whose hospitality is world-renowned, and mountains of food are served in the enormous dining room where you dine at long tables on benches; expect bread and houmous with everything, as well as lentils, vegetables and beans, but no meat. Rooms are simple but stylish. The lodge is a cool escape in the heat of the day, while at night, it takes on a monastic, shadowy feel as 250 goat-skin shaded candles illuminate the high walls against the purple sky. Slip under Egyptian cotton sheets and drift off listening to the sound of a thousand years of silence. You are in one of the most archeologically important and spectacular wilderness regions in the Middle East.

- Walking, birdwatching, camping
- Griffon vulture, Bonelli's eagle, Sinai rosefinch, Tristram's grackle, fan-tailed raven
- Dana Nature Reserve; Roman copper mines

rooms	26 rooms for 2-4. Extra mattresses available.
price	JOD44. Singles JOD35. Triples JOD54. Quads JOD60.
meals	Dinner JOD6.
closed	July & August.
directions	From Amman (3.5 hours), follow Dead Sea highway to 5th army checkpoint; cont. to Greigra; then from Al Rashaydeh village with Bedouin shuttle to lodge .

Bedouin run the lodge using solar power.

Eco lodge

	RSCN Reservations
tel	+962 (0)6461 6523
fax	+962 (0)6461 6483
email	tourism@rscn.org.jo
web	www.rscn.org.jo

Dana Guesthouse

Dana Village, Dana Nature Reserve, near Quadissiyya, South Jordan

Here, at the edge of the Jordan Rift Valley, the ancient history of the Middle East lies before you. Strategically perched on the mountainside with dramatic views of the Wadi Dana gorge and Dana Nature Reserve, the guest house is a simple but comfortable place to explore this fascinating region, which has been occupied since 4000 BC. It has the feel of an upmarket dormitory: camp beds (actually more comfortable than they sound; we slept deeply!), bare walls and a private terrace with spectacular views, especially early morning when the sun rises over the mountains behind the lodge and reveals the canyon in all its glory. All but one of the bathrooms are shared and guests eat together in the spacious dining room. Both guest house and reserve are managed by Jordan's Royal Society for the Conservation of Nature whose slogan is 'helping nature helping people' through linking conservation and ecotourism.

- Griffon vulture, Bonelli's eagle, Sinai rosefinch, Tristram's grackle, fan-tailed Raven
- Dana Nature Reserve; Roman copper mines

rooms	9: 1 double; 4 doubles, 2 triple, 2 quads, all sharing bathrooms.
price	JOD43. Triples JOD53. Quads JOD57. Singles JOD34.
meals	Breakfast included. Lunch JOD6, Dinner JOD6.
closed	Never.
directions	Desert highway (airport road) south from Amman as far as Al-Husayniya Village; exit on right to Dana Wildlife Reserve (2.5 hours from Amman.)

Guests' income helps fund the Dana Nature Reserve.

	RSCN Reservations
tel	+962 (0)6461 6523
fax	+962 (0)6461 6483
email	tourism@rscn.org.jo
web	www.rscn.org.jo

Guest house

indian
ocean

0 20 40 kilometres
0 10 20 miles

125

INNER ISLANDS

Praslin

See Inset

126

SEYCHELLES

●VICTORIA 127

Mahé

SEYCHELLES

Indian

Ocean

0 200 400 kilometres
0 100 200 miles

0 150 kilometres
0 75 miles

●Antsirañana

Mozambique Channel

124

●Mahajanga

Mahajanba

128
●MALE

●Toamasina

●ANTANANARIVO

MADAGASCAR

Arabian Sea

●Fianarantsoa

Indian

Mangoky

Toliara ●

Ocean

MALDIVES

0 200 400 kilometres
0 100 200 miles

●Gan

Anjajavy Hotel and Reserve
Nr Majunga

French flair and panache in splendid isolation. Secluded bays, sandy beaches, deciduous forest and mangroves are the backdrop for a collection of beautiful villas sympathetically placed behind the beach and all with sea views. Villas are spacious oases of tranquillity, with comfortable beds, crisp sheets and lovely bathrooms, supplied with water filtered from the sea. The pool and main dining area are the focus, together with the gardens that attract wildlife. Lie on the beach in front of your villa listening to the soothing wash of the Mozambique Channel and look up to see a coquerel's sifaka – one of Madagascar's most beautiful and engaging lemurs – feeding nonchalantly above you. By night, outdoor candlelit dining is both romantic and sumptuous. Food is simple and inventive, wonderful fish dishes, and fresh ingredients are supplied by the nearby eponymous village where most of the staff live.

- Walking; watersports; sea-fishing; mountain biking; bird & wildlife watching
- Coquerel's sifaka, brown lemurs, nocturnal lemurs, flying foxes & Madagascar fish eagles

rooms	25 duplex villas for up to 4.
price	Full-board €149–€260 p.p.
meals	Full-board only.
closed	Never.
directions	Fly from Antananarivo or Nosy Be. Charter flights & yacht charter on request.

Agence l'Hotel

tel	+33 1 44 69 15 03
email	contact@anjajavy.com
web	www.anjajavy.com

The hotel operates a micro-credit scheme for local fisherman and farmers.

Hotel

Bird Island Lodge
PO Box 1419, Victoria

Simplicity is style on this remote island, as far away from the creature comforts of multi-starred over-pampering as you are from city lights and crowded beaches. There are no telephones, televisions or air conditioning in the naturally ventilated chalets (solar-powered hot water), and each has a large bed, large shower room and spacious veranda that overlook the gardens – and the white sands and Indian Ocean just beyond. Owned, staffed and managed by resident Seychellois, the chalets line either side of the main reception and informal dining area where the fabulously laid-back local hospitality includes the best in Creole cuisine, including red snapper and fresh vegetables from the island. The eponymous island is a haven for thousands of birds which nest to the north (their squawking is distracting at first but you soon get used to it); a living testament to a remarkable conservation success story.

- Swimming, snorkelling, fishing, kayaking; nature walks & boat tours
- Over ten bird species, incl. the white-tailed tropic bird; green & hawksbill turtles; & Esmeralda, aged 235, reputedly the largest giant tortoise in the world

rooms	24 chalets for 2-3.
price	Full-board €430 for 2. €625 for 3. Singles €325. Chidren 2-11 €115.
meals	Full-board only.
closed	1-21 December.
directions	30min flight from Mahé.

Income from tourism provides nesting ground for over one million sooty terns.

Joanna & Nicholas Savy
tel   +248 (0)248 323 322
fax   +248 (0)248 323 335
email   thelodge@birdislandseychelles.com
web   www.birdislandseychelles.com

Eco lodge

Cousine Island

PO Box 977, Victoria, Mahe

Luxury and conservation really do go hand in hand. A former coconut plantation, the private island has been rehabilitated as an upmarket tropical hideaway while maintaining conservation as its raison d'etre. Some 30 metres apart, the quiet, elegant villas are plush, spacious, French-colonial style with all the creature comforts that you'd expect, including a sunken jacuzzi and double shower. The wide-decked terrace provides convenient access via a short path to the beach and round to the main pavilion's pool, bar, library and lounge. Dine on the veranda with wonderful views of the pounding surf and beyond to the sister island and nature reserve, Cousin. The friendly and discreet young South African managers Jock and Janine are on hand to make sure you get the most out of your stay, and resident conservationists Dylan and Frankie will inform about the island's conservation work.

- Guided nature walk, snorkelling & swimming
- Hawksbill & green turtles, giant tortoise, fruit bats, magpie robin, lesser noddy
- Cousin Island bird reserve: turtles breed September–April

rooms	4 villas for 2.
price	Full-board €1,400.
meals	Full-board only.
closed	Never.
directions	15 mins by helicopter from Mahe.

	Janine Samuel
tel	+248 (0)321 107
mobile	+248 713 420
email	cousine@seychelles.net
web	www.cousineisland.com

There are currently no fewer than 40 conservation projects running on the island.

Hotel

Frégate Island

c/o Worldwide Reservations, Schwalbenstrasse 15, 63263 Neu-Isenburg, Germany

White sandy beaches, crystal clear water, exotic wildlife and first-class cuisine and spa: everything you could possibly wish from a secluded tropical island. There are even rumours of buried treasure hidden in the interior's lush vegetation. Sea-facing villas dot the rugged coastline, camouflaged by wild, scented flora and indigenous trees. The vaulted ceiling of bamboo thatching and merbou timber provide the structure to each villa, with its living room, large bedroom and two bathrooms. African chamfuta teak wooden boards frame cream-coloured, polished Botticino marble floors, while natural linen, Thai silk and Egyptian cotton provide soft comfort for cushions, pillows and drapery. Steve, the Conservation and Ecology Manager, will be delighted to show you how they are trying to create a 'Noah's Ark' of rare species. Pure Swiss Family Robinson. *Minimum stay three nights.*

- Guided nature walk; scuba diving, sailing
- Magpie robin, Seychelles blue pigeon, Seychelles fody, Aldabra giant tortoise
- 'Mont Signal', a 125m-high granite rock

rooms	16 villas for 2.
price	Full-board €1,900. Plus 15% tax. Special rates for children.
meals	Full-board only.
closed	Never.
directions	20-min flight from Mahé by helicopter or twin-otter.

60,000 native trees have been planted on the island.

Reservations

tel	+49 (0)6102 50 13 21
fax	+49 (0)6102 50 13 22
email	reservations@fregate.com
web	www.fregate.com

Hotel

Banyan Tree Maldives Vabbinfaru
Vabbinfaru Island

On the North Malé Atoll, there's some stiff competition for the title of best place to sling a hammock. Though for castaways with a conscience, here is the definitive paradise island. Villas squat on sand around the rim of the island, some with their own stretch of sugar white beach and views of the gin-clear waters. Every villa gets a jet pool; those facing west get the sunsets. Drag yourself from the sumptuous four-poster bed and prop majestically on the silk scatter cushions that fill the window seat as sheer drapes flutter in the breeze. Here, insense and oils and his and hers toiletries; in the spa, inspired by Asian health and beauty remedies, natural and fresh ingredients. Go barefoot to your private table on the sandbank, where you tuck into grilled Maldivian lobster by a sea that shines like mercury in the moonlight. A perfectly-run place. *Guests are invited to give US$2 per room per night to Green Imperative Fund for reef conservation.*

- Snorkelling; diving; dolphin-watching; island-hopping; wind-surfing; catamaran sailing
- Coral, dolphins, green turtle, reef sharks

rooms	48 villas.
price	Half-board US$650–$1,700 per villa.
meals	Half-board only. Lunch à la carte.
closed	Never.
directions	20 mins by speedboat from airport & Malé.

	Banyan Tree Maldives Vabbinfaru
tel	+960 (0)664 3147
fax	+960 (0)664 3843
email	reservations@banyantree.com
web	www.banyantree.com

Banyan supports a marine biology laboratory for reef & fish conservation.

Hotel

G 🗨 Hello

south asia

THAR DESERT

Delhi
NEW DELHI
133

Jaipur

Kanpur

Arabian

Sea

Narmada
134

INDIA

Nagpur

DECCAN
135
Godavari

Hyderabad

Krishna
EASTERN GHATS

136
137

Indian

Ocean

WESTERN GHATS

Bangalore
Chennai

138

139

SRI
LANKA
141

COLOMBO
142
144

143

131

Indus

132

Indus

| 0 | 300 | 600 kilometres |
| 0 | 150 | 300 miles |

Tiger Mountain Pokhara Lodge

GPO Box 242, Gongabu, Kathmandu

Framed at the centre of the doorway are the astonishing peaks of the Annapurna, Dhaulagiri and Manaslu, and the 'fishtail' summit of Machhapuchhare. Many of the rooms have similar views from their own verandas. Each has been built from hand-cut stone and is designed to blend, chameleon-like, into the local landscape. Floors are wooden, furnishings are simple, and there's handmade soap sourced from Kathmandu in the stone bathrooms. Hot water is available for just two periods a day. In the main lodge, the charismatic English-born manager Marcus Cotton greets guests by the open hearth, offering a special Tiger Mountain cocktail and tasty pre-dinner snacks. Many of the herbs and salads are grown organically in the lodge's own gardens and produce is bought from local farmers when available. Homemade jams and honey from the Tiger Mountain's own jungle bees are available every day. Breakfast has both western and Nepali fare, including a Masala Rumble Tumble: spicy scrambled eggs!

- Guided jungle & village walks, micro-light flying, paragliding
- Over 200 species of bird & 120 species of butterfly

rooms	13 bungalows: 5 doubles, 2 twins, 2 triples, 9 family.
price	Full-board US$200 p.p. Singles $300. Plus taxes.
meals	Full-board only.
closed	15 June-15 September.
directions	40min drive from Pokhara. Flights & road transfers arranged on reservation with Tiger Mountains office in Katmandhu. Quote Sawdays.

The lodge was built by local people, now employed as its staff.

Marcus Cotton

tel	+977 (0)1 436 1500
fax	+977 (0)1 436 1600
email	info@tigermountain.com
web	www.tigermountain.com/pokhara

Eco lodge

E

Tiger Tops Jungle Lodge
PO Box 242, Tiger Mountain

The adventure begins as courteous staff meet you by jeep and deliver you to a rustic but comfortable billet (good beds, copper sinks). Tiger Tops comprises two raised houses, one bungalow and a big domed dining hall with logs warming its middle. Meal times are pure pleasure: rice, vegetables, pork, honey and eggs flow freely from two organic farms and menus are Nepalese or western. Pans are heated by rice husk briguette, waste is recycled, ceiling fans solar-powered, laundry washed by hand. But you're here for the thrill of the chase: crashing through jungle on elephant-back in search of leopard and tiger, spotting crocodiles and one-horned rhino, catching the cry of the jackal at dusk. The Tiger Tops phenomenon started in 1965 before Chitwan became a National Park. Now tigers are back in impressive numbers, thanks to Nepal's anti-poaching campaign.

- Jeep, boat & elephant safaris – some guides have over 30 years' experience
- Tigers, leopards, one-horned rhino, gaur, monkeys, crocodiles, deer & 450 species of bird
- Royal Chitwan National Park, Tiger Mountain Farms

rooms	28 doubles.
price	US$350p.p. Plus taxes
meals	Full-board only.
closed	June-August.
directions	Nearest town is Narayanghad. From Kathmandu, by air or bus to Meghauli airport; pick-up in jeep.

Honey, vegetables, salads & meat come from its own organic farms.

	Reservations
tel	+977 (0)5652 1488
fax	+977 (0)1436 1600
email	info@tigermountain.com
web	www.tigermountain.com

Eco lodge & Treehouse

Entry 130

Himalayan Homestays

c/o Snow Leopard Conservancy, IBEX Hotel Complex, Leh, 194 101 Ladakh

Here is the real high life. As authentic a place as you'll find, where the traditional life of Ladakhi working farms survives in the stunning remote environment of the world's highest mountain range. The views are worth the trip alone, but at 5,000 metres the altitude as well as the scenery will take your breath away (only the healthy and acclimatised should consider the journey). Homestays invite guests on a rotational basis so that income is shared around. The rooms couldn't be more basic (that's the charm): a mattress on the floor, a hole in the ground. Meals are taken in the kitchen with the family – delicious curries from local ingredients. Herders tell of encounters with the snow leopard; it's unlikely you'll see one, but watch for signs of these elusive creatures in the village. The warmth and generosity of your hosts makes you feel closely connected to the ecotourism ideal.

- Acclimatise in the cultural city of Leh; mountain walking (summer); snow leopard trekking led by local guides (winter)
- Snow leopard, wolves, lynx, marmots, blue sheep, wild ass, eagles, lammergeier

rooms	1 room for 4-5, sharing bath.
price	Half-board US$10 p.p.
meals	Half-board only.
closed	Never.
directions	6hr drive from Leh in Ladakh. The Himalayan Homestay Office arranges car transfer from Leh to nearest village & directs guests for final 1km walk up track.

10% of proceeds is given to snow leopard conservation while remainder of income is distributed among village community.

Homestay

Reservations

tel	+91 (0)1982 250 953
fax	+91 (0)1982 252 735
email	slcindia@sancharnet.in
web	www.himalayan-homestays.com

Kalmatia Sangam Himalaya Resort

Kalimat Estate (near Kasar Devi), Post Bag 002, Almora, 263 601 Uttaranchal

Snow on the Himalaya blinks down at slate-roofed houses and carved painted doors in the valleys below. The terraces produce wheat and vegetables; buffalos graze with goats; the women wear startling colours. Almora is close – with a good market (woollens and jewellery). Geeta inherited this hilltop estate and after living in Germany she and Dieter took a deep plunge to create an Indo-European hotel. Geeta bubbles with enthusiasm, the staff are impeccable, the furniture is imaginative (modern, wrought-iron, Scandinavian, dhurries on the floor), the food delicious – a fusion of Indian and European. You can light a fire in your bedroom and sleep in a cottage of your own; they are scattered among pine trees, each with big beds and duvets, stone walls, good bathrooms. The Reebs have a strong eco-policy: take a walk among the trees they have planted and collect herbs and mushrooms in season.

- Trekking in valleys; yoga, reflexology & meditation on a special terrace
- Langur, pine marten, flying fox, leopard; cedar, cypress, mimosa
- Kumaon Hills; Binsar Wildlife Sanctuary; temples, waterfalls, lakes & local villages

rooms	9 cottages: 7 for 2, 2 for 1-2.
price	US$84-$163. Singles $60.50-$111.50. Plus 5% tax.
meals	Breakfast US$6.75. Lunch $11.25. Dinner $13.50.
closed	Never.
directions	Upper Binsar road towards Kasar Devi temple. Resort 1km before temple, on right. Airport: Delhi (380km). Train: Kathagodam (2.5 hours). Pick-up possible.

The kitchen uses organic vegetables from local villages.

	Dieter & Geeta Reeb
tel	+91 (0)5962 233 625
fax	+91 (0)5962 231 572
email	info@kalmatia-sangam.com
web	www.kalmatia-sangam.com

Hotel

D 🏃 🌳 👟

Apani Dhani Eco-Lodge

Jhunjhunu Road, Nawalgarh, 333 042 Rajasthan

Here you and your conscience can be at peace. The principles are 'eco' and 'low impact', rooted in Ramesh's concern for the disappearing local heritage and the damaging effects that tourism can have. Pioneer Ramesh, delightful and well-travelled, lives here with his extended family, the sounds of their lives providing the backdrop to this beautiful, tranquil setting. The rooms are a cluster of traditional huts with mud-rubbed walls and thatched roofs. Wooden furniture and intriguing *objets* in russet-toned alcoves create a minimalist feel. Bathrooms are all gleaming white tiles and polished chrome but travellers are gently encouraged to conserve water so buckets and mugs are also provided. Everything you need is here: solar panels give light and hot water – and the cafetière coffee is superb – though luxuries are few. Seasonal food is dished out on leaf plates under a pagoda of bougainvillea in the circular courtyard. Harmonious living indeed.

- Walks; handicraft workshops with the local community; cookery classes, yoga
- The wonderful wall paintings of the Shekhawati region

rooms	8: 4 doubles, 4 twins.
price	Rs750–Rs950.
meals	Lunch/dinner from Rs150.
closed	Rarely.
directions	Near Kisan Chatrawas off Nawalgarh bypass, on road from Sikar to Jhunjhunu. Train & bus from Delhi & Jaipur & bus also from Bikaner & Jodphur, to Nawlgarh station (r'way 1km, bus 500m from lodge).

5% of Apani's turnover from rent goes to local social projects: schools for the disabled & finance for studies.

Eco lodge

	Mr Ramesh C Jangid
tel	+91 (0)1594 222 239
fax	+91 (0)1594 224 061
email	enquiries@apanidhani.com
web	www.apanidhani.com

Shergarh Tented Camp

Village Bahmini, Post Kareli, Tehsil Baihar, Kanha Tiger Reserve, 481 111

If you come across a small child climbing through nascent bamboo and swimming in rock pools, you might think you had found a real-life Mogli on the edge of Kanha. It's easy to get caught up in the exhilaration of Katie and naturalist husband Jehan who both have a deeply ecological vision for Shergarh. No more than six tents will be pitched here, so the impact is hardly apparent and the feel wonderfully natural. Zip open stone bathrooms and find constant hot water supplied by clean-burning LPG units. After a day's safari, everyone tucks into superb grub on the lodge veranda or under the stars by the lake; the food is fresh from the garden – even the hens. No waste here either for Katie is queen of composts. Light pollution is kept to a minimum to encourage wildlife and all is quiet on the less-busy Mukki side of the park. It would be hard to imagine a more magical environment to bring up Kai, their infant son, whose growth will be a reflection of Shergarh's own.

- Tiger viewing from elephant's back; safaris in Kanha National Park with naturalists
- Tigers, gaur (Indian bison), leopard, Barasingha deer, sloth bear, wild dog

rooms	6 tents for 2.
price	Full-board Rs16,000. Singles Rs10,000. Includes safaris.
meals	Full-board only.
closed	Mid-May–mid-October.
directions	Located at Mukki Gate. Bus from Jabalpur to Kisli; 4x4 to Shergarh. Train: Gondia (140km, 3 hrs). Airport: Nagpur (280km, 5.5 hrs).

	Jehan & Katie Bhujwala
tel	+91 (0)7637 226 086/215
mobile	+91 (0)9324 331 583
email	enquiries@shergarh.com
web	www.shergarh.com

Katie and Jehan are gaining local support for park protection by demonstrating its economic & social benefits.

Safari camp

The Orchid Hotel

70-C Nehru Road, Vile Parle (East), Mumbai, 400 099

A large, corporate hotel, not pretty, but we were impressed with its soft green underbelly. From dual flush toilets to an anti-plastic campaign to a systemic recycling programme, there's an extraordinary environmental passion and an attention to detail and energy efficiency that underpins the business. A welcome guest pack provides information on the hotel's efforts to 'Reduce, Reuse and Recycle' (waste water is treated and reused for air conditioning and gardening), and includes tips for guests on how to be energy efficient, especially with regard to limiting the use of water. Smart, comfortable rooms are what you'd expect for an airport hotel (wall-to-wall carpeting and interactive TV), but noise from outside is reduced thanks to triple glazing. Press the 'eco button' and you'll increase the thermostat of the air conditioner by two degrees. A 'green team' carries out environmental audits and works with local charities and schools. Enormous it may be, but we salute its eco effort.

* Fitness centre, rooftop swimming pool & business centre

rooms	250 twins, doubles, suites.
price	US$200-$800.
meals	Breakfast Rs425. Lunch Rs590. Dinner from Rs690.
closed	Never.
directions	By Mumbai Airport. 1hr drive from city centre.

Bathroom taps contain special aerators which save up to 50% of water.

Reservations

tel	+91 (0)22 2616 4040
fax	+91 (0)22 2616 4141
web	www.orchidhotel.com

Hotel

Yogamagic Canvas Ecotel
1586/1 Grand Chinvar, Close to Bobby Bar, Anjuna, 403509 North Goa

Spot the tents and flags from a distance – splashes of colour amid the palms, paddy fields and strolling buffalo. British Phil and Juliette greet you warmly – both are passionate about their natural retreat. In the bamboo, rammed-earth and palm-leafed restaurant, relax on soft cushions and watch the hummingbirds. Floating flowers, water candles, a Buddha statue, soft Indian music and delicious treats are here – from perfect eggs florentine to generous vegetarian buffets. Be inspired by the use of local wood and cotton, solar-power, recycling, and organic fruit and veg. The peaceful and luxurious suite is inside, while the Rajastani hunting tents, each lined with a different colour to represent one of the *chakras*, reveal comfy beds, wardrobes, a sink and a composting loo. Flower-filled gardens and outside showers are a short stroll. There's yoga by day (should you choose it) and a pool; fires and musical performances by night. A small piece of paradise.

* yoga; tai chi, massage & meditation in & around Ajuna
* Buffalo, wild birds, parakeets, owls, hummingbirds, kingfishers, kites, bee eaters.

rooms	9: 7 tents for 2 sharing showers; 1 suite; 1 eco pyramid.
price	Tents & pyramid from £50. Suite from £65. Plus tax 3%-10%.
meals	Dinner £4.50.
closed	April-October.
directions	Train: Thivim (16km, 20 mins). Airport: Dabolim, Goa (48km, 1 hr).

	Phil Dane
tel	+91 (0)832 562 3796
mobile	+91 9370 565 717
email	info@yogamagic.net
web	www.yogamagic.net

Phil is working to grow jetropha for making bio-diesel to run the Yoga Magic jeep naturally.

Under canvas & Eco lodge

Wildernest Nature Resort

At Swapnagandha, Off Sankhali, Chorla Ghats, Goa

Wild grass sways in the wind, long-billed vultures nest in the dense forest, and distant waterfalls (spectacular in the monsoon) tumble down the lush mountainside. Perched on the edge of a ridge (with breathtaking views of the valley), the infinity pool is surrounded by plants (some medicinal) and trees; you'll feel as if you're swimming in a jungle glade. Conservation of the land is paramount to the ethos; Captain Nitin Dhond bought the 450-acre site in 2004 to protect the area from mining and create a corridor for large mammals between two wildlife sanctuaries. Goa is close and offers many things, but here you're shown the traditions of the hinterland. Photographers, writers, artists come, many just to sit by the pool and relax with the reassuring sounds of nature. The log cabins are made from local materials, such as bamboo, mud, laterite stone, hay, and even a reclaimed railway sleeper. All food is organic with recipes from the local village. Remote and magical.

- Walking, birdwatching, yoga
- Indian gaur, barking deer, slender loris; 4 resident leopards; over 240 bird species

rooms	16 cabins for 2.
price	Full-board per room. Forest view US$70-$155. Valley view $95-$190. Singles 80% of price.
meals	Full-board only.
closed	Never.
directions	From Panjim to Sankhali to Keri Village. 16km up the Chorla Ghats after Anjunem Dam.

Complies with a 'carrying capacity' study to limit the number of guests to this protected area.

Eco lodge

	Nitin Dhond
tel	+91 (0)831 4207954
mobile	+91 9341112721
email	reservations@wildernest-goa.com
web	www.wildernest-goa.com

Cardamom House

Athoor Village, Dindigul District, 624701 Tamil Nadu

Chris is a foodie, a traveller, a gentleman and a comic. A retired British doctor, he has poured energy into creating his utopia. His humour and zest infuse the place, the staff wear the broadest smiles and the whole place sweeps you into a warm embrace. The house stands at the foot of a steep hill, huddled in a horseshoe of scrub hills with views from the pretty garden across the lake to the Western Ghats. Divided between three buildings, the bedrooms are a picture of taste and restraint – tiled floors, crisp white linen, solar-powered showers, fresh flowers on beds. Verandas crouch beneath bougainvillea cascading in every colour, creating hidden spots in which to escape into a book; the rooftop terrace sits beneath a nocturnal frenzy of Indian stars. Chris is passionate about the environment and social responsibility; his staff are in charge of the developing organic vegetable garden.

- Hiking, birdwatching; children can visit goatherd & see cows being milked
- Water buffalo, sunbirds, flower-peckers, bee-eaters, painted storks, peacocks
- Trips to Athoor village & colourful markets in Dindigul

rooms	8: 7 doubles, 1 suite.
price	Rs3,600. Suite Rs4,400. Peak season: December–March.
meals	Breakfast Rs150. Lunch Rs250. Dinner Rs350.
closed	Rarely.
directions	2km after Sembatti x-roads, on Madurai-Coimbatore rd, left for Athoor, follow signs for house. Airport: Madurai (70km, 2 hrs). Train: Dindigul (27km, 45 mins).

Guided trips to the village support the local community.

	Dr Christopher Lucas
tel	+91 (0)451 2556 765/66
mobile	+91 (0)9360 691 793 or (0)9842 156 765
email	cardamomhouse@yahoo.com;
web	www.cardamomhouse.com

Eco lodge

Friday's Place

Poovar Island Resort, Pozhiyoor P.O., Trivandrum, Kerala

Quirky wooden eco-cottages in quiet Keralan backwaters. From the moment you are greeted at the jetty with jasmine garlands and melon juice you know you are going to be looked after well. Mark and his Sri Lankan wife Sujeewa, a teacher in alternative healing, and their local staff do their utmost to make sure you have a memorable stay. The beautifully crafted, palm-thatched, solar-powered cottages are raised on granite steddle stones and surrounded by coconut palms. Cotton sheets drape over generous beds and sturdy kaya/rubber mattresses (excellent for the back!); ayurvedic soap is provided in the (blissful!) rainwater shower in the detached communal bathroom. Sujeewa uses traditional, southern Indian recipes for fresh fish and river crabs. Dine with other guests in the main dining area, which doubles up as a yoga sanctuary, or on your own veranda listening to the sounds of exotic rainforest birds. *Minimum stay three nights.*

- Punting on the river; fishing; yoga; ayurvedic treatments & massages
- Black-necked storks, kingfishers, kites, honey buzzards, woodpeckers
- Rubber tapping; Sivanandra Ashram in the foothills; Travancore palace

rooms	4 cottages for 2.
price	Full-board £100-£150. Singles £50.
meals	Full-board only.
closed	April-mid October.
directions	Boat transfer at Poovar Island Resort Welcome Area near Poovar Excise check post. 30km from Trivandrum airport.

Their refrigeration system runs on coconut oil.

Eco lodge

	Mark Reynolds
tel	+91 (0)471 2133292
fax	+44 (0)1428741510 (Apr-Oct)
email	amphibious_robinson_crusoe@hotmail.com
web	www.fridaysplace.biz

Barefoot at Havelock

Beach No 7, Radhanagar Village, Havelock Island, Andaman Islands

Here is a remote retreat that sustains the unwritten rule that the best places are the hardest to reach. Listen to forest-bird ballad in eight acres of gardens and mahua trees minutes from a long, white and curvaceous beach and stunning sunsets over the Andaman Sea. These beautifully designed, conically thatched cottages are locally made from bamboo, wood and palm leaves, and draw their water from the camp's own spring. The slightly more luxurious hardwood villas have floor-to-ceiling windows on three sides, shady balconies and opaque jungle-shower roofs to pull light in from the forest canopy. Relax by candlelight and cool jazz in the oriental living area before your next meal; the fusion food is local, organic, delicious and they cook your own catch. Susheel, a native islander who built the resort with the help of local friends, now oversees it all with Samit — who arrived as a backpacker and has never left. Easy to see why.

* Swimming with elephants; trekking; scuba diving, fishing & boat trips; iyengar yoga
* Elephants, crab-eating macaque, Andaman wild pig, turtles, dolphins
  & 250 bird species

rooms	18 cottages & villas for 2-4.
price	US$75-$145.
	Singles deduct $10 per room.
meals	Breakfast included. Lunch & dinner fixed menus & à la carte.
closed	Never.
directions	Fly to Port Blair Airport. Ask for details of boat transfers when booking.

Elephant dung is used as garden fertilizer.

	Samit Sawhny
tel	+91 (0)3192 236008
mobile	+91 94342 60321
email	reservations@barefootindia.com
web	www.barefootindia.com

Eco lodge

Hunas Falls Hotel
Elkaduwa, Kandy

Watch kites (live ones) wheel as you dine on vegetable tempura in a restaurant overlooking two thundering waterfalls and a lake. In this truly wild corner of Sri Lanka – untouched by detritus and poverty, free of hawkers and touts – the overwhelming impression from Hunas Falls is of utter, breathtaking beauty. Made up of two somewhat characterless wings – one residential, the other recreational – this swish hotel is set in 100 acres of landscaped lushness: a working tea estate, a man-made lake, a dragonfly sanctuary, and bamboo and fern gardens where monkeys gambol in avocado trees and butterflies flutter. The ecosystem is a montane cloud forest, so expect sunshine one day, mist and drizzle the next. Young staff are committed and courteous, and two naturalists take guests on mountain and valley walks. After which deep sleep is assured – in smart bedrooms with perfect beds, potted orchids, no mosquitoes and heavenly views.

- Swimming, tennis, golf; playroom for children
- Wild boar, ruddy mongoose, jungle cats, hawk eagles, tree swifts, whistling lizards
- Tour to a local village unfettered by modernisation & to a working tea factory

rooms	31: 28 doubles, 3 suites.
price	US$83–$100. Suites $180.
meals	Lunch US$10. Dinner $12.
closed	Never.
directions	45-min mountainous drive from Kandy (26km). Train from Wattegama (11km). Bus from Elkaduwa (3km).

Staff are knowledgeable about biodiversity & reforestation; the hotel motto is 'Reduce, Reuse, Recycle'.

Hotel

	Gamunu Sri lal
tel	+94 (0)812 476402/3
fax	+94 (0)812 470044
email	hunasfalls@sltnet.lk
web	www.jetwinghotels.com

Galapita Eco Lodge

c/o Isle of Paradise Resort Hotels (Pvt) Ltd., 62, Havelock Road, Colombo 05

The journey here is an adventure: tuk-tuk from Buttala, then a footbridge 40 feet above torrents. And what do you find? Four huts and a reception area perched on top of large rocks by a pool and a waterfall on the banks of the Menik Ganga. In the rainy season, when the natural 'jacuzzi' overflows, the rapids transport you in a tube downriver to the village of Demodara; it is a trip teeming with exotic birds and butterflies. You return, via jeep, to a cooling infusion of herbal flowers and a delectable meal cooked in clay pots on log fires. Garden lanterns glow, insects chirrup, solar-powered music plays. Then up a ladder to a bedroom-on-stilts under the stars: just bamboo half-walls, a romantic futon-style bed, a Buddhist ornament or two, a large power shower, a net to deter creepy-crawlies. Bring pencils and paints, batteries for your i-pod, notes for the novel you may finally write. Bliss for upmarket backpackers in search of a jungle haven off-the-beaten-track!

* Panning for sapphires in the riverbed – tools & know-how provided
* Elephants, peacocks, deer, flying squirrels, birds

rooms	4 huts for 2-3.
price	Full-board US$80 pp. Children under 6 free. Min. party of 6. Additional $200 if fewer.
meals	Full-board only.
closed	Never.
directions	Bus from Colombo, Nuwara Eliya or Galle to Kataragama, local bus (2 daily) 1 hr (30km north) to Buttala, 3-wheeler to Galapita. Car 6-7 hrs from Colombo; turn towards river opp. Km31 post.

No fridge (just solar power) means that all food is picked, plucked or netted that day.

	David/Ivor (Colombo office)
tel	+94 (0)1 597137/587110
fax	+94 (0)1 580507/583696
email	agasti@slt.lk
web	www.galapita.com

Eco lodge

D 🍲 ☕

Lighthouse Hotel and Spa
Colombo Road, Dadella, Galle

This Bawa-designed hotel is built from concrete blocks but don't let that put you off: it provides a minimal, modern structure from which an exquisitely stylish interior spreads out. From the sweeping foyer stair with spiralling bronze sculpture to the veranda'd dining room with ocean views, it's stunning. Landscape and building merge, and each room (and pool) connect to nature outside: a swathe of coconut forest behind, the Indian Ocean crashing below. Lotus flowers float in stone basins; bedrooms – the quietest away from the road – have waxed wooden floors, aquamarine shutters and frangipani blossom; smiling staff attend to every whim. The naturalists can spot a hermit crab at 20 paces and the area is an ornithologist's paradise. After a delectable meal – Jetwing pay local farmers to grow organic produce – succumb to an ayurveda massage in the spa. If your backpacking days are over but you crave luxury *and* the wild, come here.

* Rainforest treks & boat safaris down the Mahamodara river
* The reef is full of sea anemones, turtles, parrot fish, herons, shimbrel
* Yala National Park, a 3hr drive (elephants & leopards)

rooms	63: 60 twins/doubles, 3 suites.
price	US$250-$474. Suites $400-$624.
meals	Breakfast $15. Lunch $16. Dinner $20.
closed	Never.
directions	Hotel 2km from Galle, at Mahamudalimawatha junction. Taxi & tuk-tuk drivers know hotel. Train: Express Colombo-Galle. Bus: direct from Colombo. Sea-plane: Colombo-Koggala airport then taxi.

All waste is recycled & funds raised go to a post-tsunami staff welfare fund.

Hotel

	Chamin Wickrama singhe
tel	+94 (0)91 22 24017/20
fax	+94 (0)91 22 24021
email	chamin@lighthouse.lk
web	www.lighthousehotelandspa.com

Tree Tops Jungle Lodge
Weliara Road, Illukpitiya, Buttala

Slip out of your comfort zone and into the wild. And make sure you arrive by mid afternoon – you don't want to bump into an elephant on the drive. At full moon you can spot them from the open-air dining table; in dry periods (June to September) they gather at a nearby waterhole. The philosophy here is that peaceful coexistence with wild elephants is possible – if humans allow it – while the eco-vision is to live close to nature with just enough for comfort but no more. That means no electricity, no showers and mud when it rains. Adventurous nature lovers will love it: the jungle treks (at cooler times of the day), the birds, the dawn dips at the freshwater well, the untamed landscape of scrub jungle and trees. Drink pure jungle water, organic highland coffee or beer, dine on exotic fruits, spicy soups and flat breads baked on an open fire, sleep in huts of wood, thatch and clay. Come for at least three days. *Children over 15 welcome.*

- Guided jungle treks; camping in the wilderness; visiting forest monastery
- Elephant, sambur, spotted deer, leopard, sloth bear; over 160 bird species, incl. grey hornbill & Sri Lankan hanging parrot

rooms	4 clay huts & tree huts for 2. Bucket showers & wcs. Tents also.
price	Full-board Jungle Experience US$160 p.p. for 2 nights, $225 p.p. for 3 nights. Includes walks.
meals	Full-board only.
closed	10 days a month to balance tourism & wildlife
directions	Bus or car from Kataragarma (45km) or Wellaway (11km) to Buttala. Directions with bookings. Arrive before 3.30pm.

Environmental activism creates alternatives for locals to illegal hunting and logging.

	Lars Sorenson
tel	+94 (0)777 036 554
mobile	+94 777 036 554
email	treetopsjunglelodge@yahoo.com
web	www.treetopsjunglelodge.com

Eco lodge

central
asia

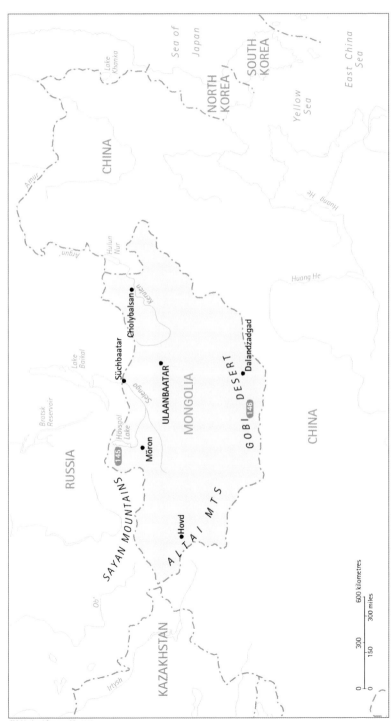

Toilogt Ger Camp

Toilogt Lake, West shore of Hovsgol Lake, Khatgal village, Hovsgol province

Let your spirit roam free in a land that has no fences. Gers are the traditional nomadic dwelling of Mongolians, designed to be both comfortable on the ground and portable on the back of a yak cart. Their design has proved the test of 2,000 years – south-facing, framed by collapsible cedar walls, covered by sheep wool felt and strapped together by horse mane. The delightful collection of trunks, stools, tea table and single beds fit to perfection, and a small stove warms the soul while the open roof circulates fresh air to gently remind you of the wild outdoors. The yurts are lit by solar power, though Mongolia's clear skies will help you find your way to the bathroom by the light of a full moon. Mongolian born and bred, the dedicated camp staff share a deep love of their country. Feast on grilled lamb and beef dumplings, while folk melodies and Hoomi throat-singing entertain. Close to Hovsgol Lake, the camp is clean and unspoilt. You'll be enchanted by a noble tradition.

- Elk, maral, reindeeer, argali sheep, ibex, red wolf, roe deer, musk deer.
- Hovsgol Lake (deepest lake in Central Asia); Khoridol Sardag Mountain

rooms	23 yurts for 1-4, 8 cabins for 2-4.
price	Full-board US$35-45 p.p.
meals	Full-board only.
closed	October-April.
directions	Fly from Buyant-Ukhaa airport (at Ulaanbaatar) to Khatgal or Moron (1 hr 20 mins) then by car follow main road towards Khatgal village to camp.

The camp is owned, managed & run by Mongolians.

Yurt

	Purevdorj
tel	+976 (0)11 460368
fax	+976 (0)11 460367
email	hovsgol_travel@mongol.net
web	www.hovsgoltravel.com

Three Camel Lodge
The Gobi

In the shimmering heat white gers rise from the wild heart of the Gobi desert in the lee of a red volcanic outcrop. But this is no mirage: here the traditional meets the sophisticatied – with community support. Draw open your own nomad's tent, hand-made from latticed Siberian larch covered with felt – to reveal a beautifully painted bed, pristine sheets, incredibly comfortable mattress and colourful artefacts. Pastoral scenes – passing nomads bring livestock to the nearby well – stretch over miles of steppe to the breathtaking Gobi Altai mountains. Sun and wind are harnessed to provide evening light and constant hot water; animal dung fuels stoves. Generous, friendly staff hail largely from the local Bulgan village. Camel trek in vast dunes and sup like a Khan on locally sourced Mongolian dishes under a brilliant dome of stars. A silk-route dream for the nomadic soul.

- Camel trekking; hiking; palaeontological digs; birdwatching; botanical trips
- White- & black-tailed gazelles, wild-mountain sheep, snow leopards, steppe eagles
- Flamming Cliffs & Togrogryn Shee: dinosaur remains; Khongoryn Els: vast sand dune

rooms	46 gers: 11 doubles, 5 twins; 30 twins sharing bathrooms in diner house.
price	US$120. Singles $90. Standard $70. Singles $50.
meals	Breakfast $8. Lunch $12. Dinner $15.
closed	Never.
directions	Fly from Ulaanbaatar to Bulagtai (35km) or Dalanzadgad (70km). Drive from Ulaanbaatar (610km) to Bulgan village; 30km to lodge.

	Reservations
tel	+976 (0)11 313 396
fax	+976 (0)11 320 311
email	info@threecamellodge.com
web	www.threecamels.com

"If you conserve every drop of water, that becomes an ocean."
Mongolian instruction.

Yurt

Entry 146

south east asia

Sukau Rainforest Lodge
Kinabatangan, Sabah

You're in the hands of an expert. An accomplished photographer, owner Albert Teo is also the author of *Saving Paradise*, a book that charts the years of effort that have gone into creating this fabulous community-based eco lodge. Secluded in one of the last remaining corridors of Borneo's jungle, the rustic dining room, library and lounge area are set on stilts above the silted river and open to the heaving pulses of jungle life. Here nature takes precedence. Geckos chirp in agreement with conversations, and the staff knock on the table in acknowledgement of local custom. The Malaysian longhouse-inspired rooms are basic but personal. Sarongs are left on the bed for guests to wear for the buffet dinner – all local food, naturally – which is heralded by a gong. Come here for inspiration, for this locally run rainforest retreat has defined ecotourism in south-east Asia.

- Wildlife spotting river cruises; guided jungle walks; ecotourism presentations
- One of only two places in the world where there are ten species of primate, including orang-utans & proboscis monkeys. Also over 200 species of bird

rooms	20 twins.
price	RM 400. Full-board for 2 nights RM 1,031. Includes transfers from Sandakan & river safari. RM 200 surcharge p.p. in Jul-Aug.
meals	Breakfast RM15. Lunch RM 20. Dinner RM 25.
closed	Never.
directions	Fly from Kota Kinabalu to Sandakan; 2.5hr by boat to lodge. Or bus from Sandakan fish market to Sukau village; 10-mins by boat to lodge.

Electric river boats minimise the disturbance to jungle wildlife.

	Reservations
tel	+60 (0)88 438300
fax	+60 (0)88 438307
email	info@sukau.com
web	www.sukau.com

Eco lodge

Villa Sebali
Sebali, Keliki, Tegallalang Gianyar, Bali

When Oliver and Sue decided to build their dream eco-house, they made a commitment to be as green as they could, both in the building and by adopting local customs. So the house, with its views of typical rice terraces and distant mountains, has been blessed at the appropriate times in its construction, and a village lady comes daily to make the house offerings. The overall impression is of light and air: the huge living area — with terracotta coloured floor, antique and modern furniture and many local Balinese art works — is open to the garden, and three of the bathrooms are partly open to the skies. The garden is exuberantly planted   fragrant frangipani everywhere! — and a cascade of lotus ponds leads down to the organic orchard of tropical fruits. Experiment with goodies from Ubud market in the kitchen before retiring from the heat of the day in the pretty thatched pavilion by the pool, where the staff happily bring drinks out to you.

- Walking; cycling; table tennis; painting; yoga & massage
- Gamelan & dancing performances; monkey forest & bird park; temples & ceremonies

rooms	House for 8-12 (4 suites).
price	US$260 per night. $1,800 p.w.
meals	Breakfast included. Self-catering.
closed	Never.
directions	15 mins drive from the centre of Ubud.

House solar-powered & built entirely from local materials.

Sue & Oliver Gillie
tel   +62 361 (0)81 2383 6227
email   info@villasebali-bali.com
web   www.villasebali-bali.com

B&B & Self-catering

Udayana Eco Lodge
PO Box 3704, 80001 Denpasar, Bali

Your holiday should get off to a flying start – just ask, and gentle staff will organise the rest of it. On the university campus, minutes from the airport, but in dense tropical gardens, this L-shaped lodge-hotel is an oasis of peace. In the distance a child laughs, a cockerel crows, a horn sounds; up here, birds sing and butterflies shimmer. The design reflects traditional Balinese style – carved door surrounds, wide staircases, breezy terraces – while natural materials are used throughout, from ikat bedspreads and mosquito nets (no chemicals) to wicker laundry baskets. Shower rooms planted with ferns open to the elements. The feel is one of elegant simplicity and, when the clouds part, the view from upstairs' dining room/lounge is stunning. After a delectable meal (local, organic), there's a library of DVDs and books to enjoy. Avoid the rainy season – humidity reaches 98%!

* Swimming here, massage, yoga and surfing throughout Bali
* Over 50 species of butterfly & bird in hotel gardens
* Ubud craft & cultural village; Uluwatu temple with Kecak dancing every night

rooms	12 doubles. Also 2 villas for 8.
price	US$60. Singles $55.
meals	Lunch & dinner US$20.
closed	Never.
directions	On Jimbaran Heights. Pick-up from Ngurah Rai airport (10 mins).

Alan Wilson

tel	+62 (0)361 7474204
fax	+62 (0)361 701098
email	lodge@ecolodgesindonesia.com
web	www.ecolodgesindonesia.com

The lodge is part of Foundation that works to reduce the impact of tourism and preserve local culture.

Eco lodge

Photo: © Nihiwatu resort – Indonesia

Nihiwatu
Sumba Island

You're spoilt for choice among the 17,000 islands of the Indonesian archipelago, but this is the place to come to spoil yourself. Sip champagne in the outdoor spa bath as the sun sets over the pounding surf. Exotic villas are sculpted onto the cliff's edge using thatch, bamboo and wood. Large rooms display tribal artefacts and ikat weavings, and you can relax into rattan chairs outside on the sea-facing balconies. Decadent dining could not be simpler: exquisite three-course lunches and dinners are served on communal wooden tables in the outdoor pavilions overlooking the pristine jungle-lined bay. Luxury is the lure, but there's a truly remarkable humanitarian story at work here. Claude and Petra camped on one of Sumba's isolated beaches for years with no electricity or running water while developing friendships with local people and gradually building a luxury resort that has done wonders for the health and education of the island's local communities.

- Surfing, diving, beach horse riding; yoga; visits to villages; aid volunteering
- Over 300 bird species, incl. hornbill, fruit dove, button quail & paradise flycatcher

rooms	7 bungalows for 2; 2 family villas for 4; 1 private compound for 4-6 (villa & bungalow).
price	Full-board US$390 for 2. $840 for 4. Compound $1,150-$1,500. Plus 21% tax & service charge.
meals	Full-board only.
closed	January-February.
directions	On Sumba island, 400km from Bali. Flights and transfers pre-arranged by Bali office.

Funded by voluntary donations, The Sumba Foundation has more than halved the prevalence of malaria in the surrounding area.

Hotel

Claude & Petra Graves

tel	+62 (0)361 757149
fax	+62 (0)361 755259
email	info@nihiwatu.com
web	www.nihiwatu.com

australasia &
south pacific

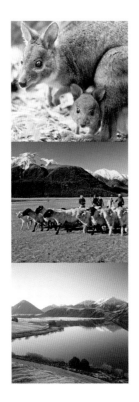

Photo left Lake Moeraki Wilderness Lodge, entry 163
Photo this page, top O'Reilly's Rainforest Guesthouse, entry 151
Photos middle & bottom Wilderness Lodge Arthur's Pass, entry 164

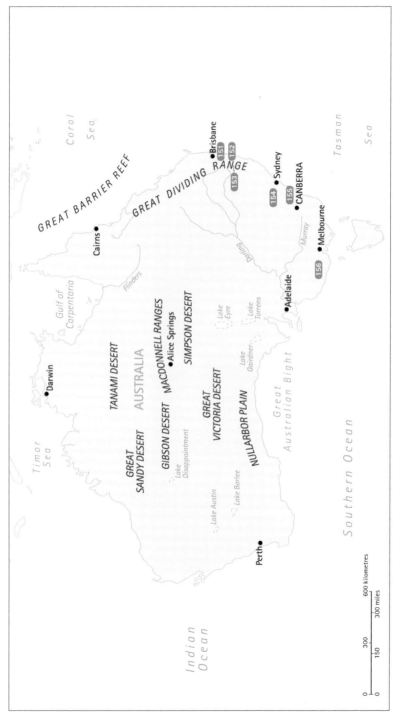

GREAT BARRIER REEF
GREAT DIVIDING RANGE

Coral Sea
Tasman Sea

Brisbane
151
152
153
Sydney
154
155 CANBERRA
Melbourne
156
Adelaide

Cairns

Darwin

Timor Sea

Gulf of Carpentaria

Flinders

TANAMI DESERT
MACDONNELL RANGES
Alice Springs
SIMPSON DESERT
AUSTRALIA
GIBSON DESERT
GREAT VICTORIA DESERT
NULLARBOR PLAIN
GREAT SANDY DESERT
Lake Disappointment
Lake Austin
Lake Barlee

Lake Eyre
Lake Torrens
Lake Gairdner

Darling
Murray

Great Australian Bight

Southern Ocean

Indian Ocean

Perth

0   300   600 kilometres
0   150   300 miles

©Maidenhead Cartographic, 2005

0 150 300 kilometres
0 75 150 miles

●Whangarei

Auckland● 157
●Manukau
Bay of
Plenty
Hamilton● ●Tauranga

Tasman

Lake
Taupo
Gisborne
159

158 NORTH ISLAND
Sea
Hawke
Napier ● Bay

NEW ZEALAND

160
Cook Strait
161
162 ●WELLINGTON

Clarence

Greymouth● SOUTH
ISLAND
163 Pacific
164
Lake
Tekapo ●Christchurch Ocean

165
Lake
Wanaka Waitaki

●Queenstown
Lake
LakeTe Wakatipu
Anau Clutha
●Dunedin

●Invercargill

0 100 kilometres
0 50 miles

●Labasa
Bua●

166
●Rakiraki
Koro Sea

●Nadi ●Lamiti
SUVA Tubou●
FIJI

●Vunisea

Pacific Ocean

O'Reilly's Rainforest Retreat
Lamington National Park Road, Via Canungra, Queensland 4275

A third generation, relatively large resort in the heart of virgin rainforest. Developed sensitively by the O'Reilly family since they settled on the mountain in 1911, there are wonderful views over the canopy and covered ridges towards the McPherson ranges – you wouldn't believe that this area south of Brisbane is actually well built up. The recycled timber lodges in four accommodation blocks are made from old sheep-huts brought over from Adelaide, and the neat and uniform rooms (all with rainforest-patterned bed covers) are well equipped with Queensland maple furniture. Documentaries are screened in the cosy rainforest bar, and the library has a baby grand piano and old leather chairs. Buffet lunch and a la carte dinners in the large dining area. The facilities are first class (it's hard not to be cajouled into some sort of activity), and although day visitors can make the resort feel overcrowded, once they've left, little will disturb the magical peace of the rainforest.

- Canopy treetop walk, guided nature walks, flying fox zip wire, glow-worm tour
- Lamington Nature Park (World Heritage site)

rooms	64: 39 Mountain View, 6 Garden View for 2; 6 family rooms, 8 singles, 5 suites; 48 villas for 4-6 from June 2007.
price	AU$250-$290. Singles $145. Suites $450-$650.
meals	Half-board AU$69. Full-board $84. Breakfast $26. Dinner $47.
closed	Never.
directions	Scenic 2hr drive from Brisbane. Daily coach from Brisbane & Gold Coast hotels & airports.

Commited to environmental sensitivity by publishing Environmental Management Plan.

Eco lodge

	Bernie Cochran
tel	+61 (0)7 55024911
fax	+61 (0)7 55020988
email	reservations@oreillys.com.au
web	www.oreillys.com.au

Eternity Springs Art Farm

483 Tuntable Creek Road, The Channon, New South Wales 2480

It's remote but not hard to find: a 1920s farmhouse in 20 acres with two pretty cabins in the trees and its own spring water. Vibrant, bohemian, hospitable Amanda was born in England but has lived here for years, looking after her horses and hens, clearing the hillside of scrub, being actively involved with the community and organising creative breaks. Guest rooms are divided between the house – original teak floors, red cedar walls, papier mâché art – and the light, airy Lotus and Cubby cabins, perfect for small groups. Lotus has living space and music; at the house there's the homely sitting room to share. Breakfast on poached eggs and garden fruits at the long table on the veranda: birds trill, dragonflies skim, the air is pure, the green hills beckon. Everything is recycled, from bottles to water to wood, there's a big platform on stilts for yoga and full-moon drumming, and a blissful rock shower for some uninhibited communing with nature.

- Art workshops celebrate nature & the environment
- Spot eight varieties of frog by torchlight at night

rooms	7: 1 double, 1 double & 2 'sleep-out' beds, 1 cabin for 2-3; 2 cabins for 4, sharing bath. Camping also.
price	AU$100. Singles $60. Cabins for 2 $80-$160. Extra person $25. Camping $15.
meals	Lunch & dinner, on request, AU$10-$20. Café & pub 5km.
closed	Never.
directions	5km from The Channon to Nimbin; on left, signed. Train to Byron Bay. Shuttle bus to Nimbin.

Deep commitment to developing economic & environmental sustainability within the community.

	Amanda Furze
tel	+61 (0)2 66 886 385
email	amanda@eternitysprings.com
web	www.eternitysprings.com

B&B

Binna Burra Mountain Lodge

Binna Burra, Binna Burra Road, via Beechmont, Queensland 4211

Come not for luxury but for walks, wildlife and crisp mountain air. And simple, communal living; this is a place where you arrive alone and leave with friends. Created in the 1930s for the lodging and conservation education of hikers to the Lamington National Park – the largest area of rainforest in Queensland – it is very well established and the setting extremely lovely. Shareholder-owned, today's lodge maybe lacks the personal touch – but friendly, local staff work closely with the National Park (maintaining walkways and signage, minimising tourist impact) and are full of enthusiasm. A big living room encourages reading, meeting and activity-planning and a bell summons you to meals in a clifftop canteen where glass walls open to a breathtaking panorama. Bedrooms have patterned quilts and basic showers; ask for an Acacia Cabin with a balcony and view. An unpretentious place with an earthy feel.

- Abseiling, mountain biking, bird weekends & free guided interpretive walks
- Snakes, spiders, wallabies, marsupials, frogs & birds
- Hire a car & drive to the pastures of Upper Beechmont

rooms	35 cabins: 16 doubles, 11 triples, 8 family. Some shared bathrooms.
price	AU$178-$296. Triples $267-$434. Children 5-16 $27. Includes some activities.
meals	Full-board option. Café meals.
closed	Never.
directions	From Brisbane exit 71 on M1 at Nerang, 36km winding rds signed. Airtrain from Brisbane city & airport to Nerang. Transfers from Gold Coast airport & Nerang.

Evening lectures provide information on the local rain forest & National Park.

Jennie Fitzgerald

tel	+61 (0)7 5533 3622
fax	+61 (0)7 5533 3747
email	res@binaburralodge.com.au
web	www.binaburralodge.com.au

Eco lodge

Kanimbla View Clifftop Retreat

113 Shipley Road, Blackheath, New South Wales 2785

If you ever had doubts, Kanimbla will convince you that eco lodges don't have to sacrifice comfort. Don't be worried by its easy accessibility, either – once you're here, it feels satisfyingly remote. It's on a mountain escarpment surrounded by bush and Hilary and her husband have channelled their environmental know-how into creating quirkily attractive accommodation. As well as the bungalow (here when they arrived), they've converted an old tin shed and built two cottages, using natural and recycled materials. The sunken living areas are cosy and well lit, with wood-burning fires and plenty of books and information on the retreat's impressive ecological features; kitchens are small, open-plan and well-equipped. There's even a tennis court, while an old greenhouse has been turned into an outdoor spa. Wander down the valley and you'll reach a stunning look-out point. There are restaurants and cafés in Blackheath. *Minimum stay two nights.*

- Trekking, abseiling, cycling, rock climbing, birdwatching, guided bushwalks, yoga
- Birds, lizards & frogs of the Australian bush
- Blue Mountains National Park

rooms	2 cottages for 6; 1 bungalow for 4-6; 1 studio for 2-4.
price	Cottage AU$210–$375 (up to 4). Bungalow $175–$225. Studio $135–$175. Entire retreat $1,100–$1,500.
meals	Self-catering.
closed	Never.
directions	2 hrs from Sydney onto F4 until Blackheath. Left across r'way tracks at lights, sharp left again. Right onto Shipley Rd 2km on RHS.

All the imported exotic plants on the site have been replaced with native bush species.

	Hilary Hughes
tel	+61 (0)2 4787 8985
mobile	+61 41 445 6452
email	inquiries@kanimbla.com
web	www.kanimbla.com

Self-catering

C 🏃 ⛷ 🦵 (Hello) 👢

Photo: © Paperbark Camp – Jervis Bay, Mike Gebicki

Paperbark Camp

571 Woollamia Road, Huskisson, on Jervis Bay, New South Wales 2054

Pack clothes for adventuring – and for dinner. This may be camping but it's camping in style. At the end of a long drive shrouded by elegant gum trees are 12 safari tents grouped around a handsome restaurant on stilts. This has sofas and a woodburner for winter, gliding glass walls for summer and a parrot's eye view of the forest, and the food is native produce cooked in inventive fusion style. As dusk falls, ring-tailed possums observe your every (delectable) mouthful and sugar gliders fly down from their roosts. Then follow solar-marked pathways to your elevated mosquito-mesh tent, its shower room through zippered back doors, its solar lights augmented by candle lanterns. You get a fabulous bed with a wool duvet, a bathrobe, a wind-up torch, ear plugs if you don't fancy the dawn chorus. Paddle the creek upstream through forest, or downstream (one hour) to Jervis Bay and its snow-white sands. Friendly, stylish, fun. *Minimum two-night stay at weekends.*

- Swimming (Nov-May), diving & snorkelling in Jervis Bay; learn to surf at Caves Beach
- King parrots; kangaroos at dawn; penguins off the bay; migrating whales (Jun or Nov)

rooms	12 tents for 2-3 (some with extra sofabeds).
price	Half-board AU$550. Third adult $145. Singles $310. Child 6-12 $80, 13-16 $120.
meals	Half-board only. Picnic basket AU$25 p.p.
closed	July & August.
directions	200km south of Sydney. 13km south of Nowra, left on Jervis Bay Rd; 1st left into Woolamia Rd; 6km on left past Goodland Rd.

The bush was cleared by hand, not machine, so as not to disturb the pristine environment, & the wood used to hand-craft furniture.

Tented camp

	Irena & Jeremy Hutchings
tel	+61 (0)2 4441 6066
fax	+61 (0)2 4441 7299.
email	info@paperbarkcamp.com.au
web	www.paperbarkcamp.com.au

Aquila Eco Lodges
Victoria Valley Road, Dunkeld, Victoria 3294

Gaze out of the huge windows framing the bush landscape and you may well see some of Australia's iconic animals venturing onto the terrace below. It's superbly quiet and isolated on this 100-acre site, which is a designated 'trust for nature'. The water tank is supplied by rain and seasonal creek flow. Built of recycled, sustainable material, the lodges (treehouses and lofthouses) are spaced well apart and angled to maximise winter (and minimise summer) sun; the rooms are stylish, subtle and minimalist. For those not wishing to cook, breakfast hampers can be provided and there are restaurants in Dunkeld. The site is dotted with sculptures and an amphitheatre hosts concerts and lectures. Barb and Madi care intensely about the eco way of life (they work hard at promoting legislative change), and are happy to give a guided walk or a torchlight tour.

- Bush walking; sheep shearings; spot-lit animal tours; cycling & rock climbing
- Kangaroos, echidnas, emus, birds, insects galore & some highly venomous snakes
- Grampians National Park; Sculpture in the Bush (biannual event); Dunkeld races; local wineries

rooms	2 lofthouses for 6, 2 treehouses for 4.
price	Lofthouse AU$220 for 2. Treehouse $250 for 2. Children 3 & under free.
meals	Breakfast AU$20-$30 for 2. Hampers available.
closed	Never.
directions	7km from Dunkeld. Along Glenelg-Ballarat h'way, right at service station & continue until Aquila sign.

64 varieties of native terrestrial orchids have been discovered on the land.

Eco lodge

	Barbara Bejerking
tel	+61 (0)35 577 25 82
fax	+61 (0)35 577 25 82
email	ecolodges@ozemail.com.au
web	www.ecolodges.com.au

C 👤 🐾 💬 🚜 🚲

Wairua Creative Retreat

PO Box 186, Whitianga, Coromandel Peninsula

Blessed by the chief of the local Iwi tribe, 'Wairua', meaning 'spirit' and 'water,' comes from the Maori legend of healing by water. For reasons of inspiration, guests on Creative Retreat are given a journal on arrival; useful too if you wish to jot down the directions back through rainforest dirt track! The guest house of plywood and corrugated iron separates into four simple cabins, brightened by the artistic efforts of the retreats, illuminated by a French window view of lawns, trampoline, fruit trees, a rockery and a small ford. Beneath the star-roof, peruse Kiwi literature from the library, before meditating on all you've learnt under heaven and glass. Homemade breakfasts, young children and creative temperaments make for the rough-homely feel nurtured by Louise, a graphic designer, and Hamish, husband and permanent artist in residence, who promises clean water for clean thoughts.

- Creative retreats; tramping; glow-worm tours; yoga, massage; kayaking, fishing & scuba diving
- Coromandel Peninsula; rainforest; Whitianga – Cook's first landing point

Maori principles have been revived that see water in particular as the source of creative healing.

Self-catering & Guest house

rooms	5: 3 doubles, 2 twins/doubles. Whole place for rent (min. 5 days).
price	NZ$200-$300 & on request.
meals	Lunch NZ$35. Dinner, 3 courses, NZ$50. By arrangement. Self-catering available.
closed	Never.
directions	12km from Whitianga; left onto 309; 4km, into Old Coach Rd; 1.6km, 3rd on left; cross ford. Bus from Auckland airport. Ferry Auckland-Coromandel; pick-up.

Louise McRae

tel	+64 (0)7866 0304
fax	+64 (0)7866 2304
email	info@wairuaretreat.co.nz
web	www.wairuaretreat.co.nz

Eco Inn

671 Kent Rd, New Plymouth, Taranaki

Sustainable living is a much bandied term these days, but here's the real deal. Few places can claim to be unconnected to the National Grid, but, by the elemental powers of sun, wind and water, Eco Inn powers three lodges and a workshop as daily models of complete self-sufficiency. Views from the hot tub out to the ocean and Mount Taranaki are enough for some, but sinking into solar warmth introduces another dimension of eco-bliss. Built from untreated, rot-resistant Macrocarpa, the lodges are unsurprisingly simple yet inviting too – and you'll happily spend time inside cooking up an organic feast of foods, fresh and complimentary from the greenhouse. Make sure you give scraps to the hens and compost. Michael appears reticent, but once he starts talking about what he loves, it becomes evident that he is an authority on renewable energy: he gives public lectures and there are monthly Open Days that offer a tour, a tea and a chat. All included in a stay.

- Bush-walking; gardening; canoeing; rock-climbing; mountain-biking
- Egmont National Park; Mt Taranaki; Maori middens

rooms	2 cabins: 1 for 4, 1 for 8.
price	NZ$110-$160 ($400-$700 p.w.) Individual rooms from $25 p.p.
meals	Self-catering.
closed	Never.
directions	From New Plymouth, h'way 3 to Egmont Village; right into Kent Road; 3km to Egmont Village; 6.7km along Kent Rd. Or bus from New Plymouth. Cycling possible.

Michael works with indigenous people who either cannot afford or have no access to renewable energy sources.

	Michael & Linda Lawley
tel	+64 (0)6752 2765
fax	+64 (0)6752 2768
email	enquiry@ecoinn.co.nz
web	www.ecoinn.co.nz

Eco lodge

Entry 158

Knapdale Eco Lodge
114 Snowsill Rd, Waihirere, Gisborne RD1

Placed to receive the 'first light' of the world each day, a sunrise over Knapdale is not to be missed. Captain Cook made sure he didn't in 1769 when he sighted nearby Te Kuri a Paoa and his first glimpse of New Zealand. As well as basking in tranquillity, guests are encouraged to interact with all around them, from harvesting garden-fresh produce to tree-planting, handling Highland cattle and keeping an eye on Kitty the deer and Oscar the sheep. Adobe-styled buildings ensure minimum impact on their surroundings and are kept warm in winter by log fires. Interiors display an artist's touch, but the real Maker's best work is outside, with stunning forest views from the Romance Room – if you can spare the time to gaze. Dedicated owners, Kees and Kay recently took home the equivalent of an eco-Oscar and more than likely you'll be sitting down to one of Kay's tasty creations in the stylish dining room and sampling one or two award-winning wines.

- Gardening; animal handling; guided forest tours; sunset celebrations
- Knapdale Forest; Te Kuri a Paoa; Gisborne

rooms	3: 2 doubles, 1 twin sharing bathroom.
price	NZ$275-$330. Singles $250-$330.
meals	Lunch by arrangement. Dinner, 4 courses, NZ$65.
closed	Never.
directions	8km from Gisborne and airport. Bus from Auckland to Back Ormond/Snowsill Rd junc, 400m from driveway to lodge.

Energy self-sufficient with solar power for nine months of the year.

Eco lodge & B&B

	Kay & Kees Weytmans
tel	+64 (0)6 862 5444
fax	+64 (0)6 862 5006
email	kees@knapdale.co.nz
web	www.knapdale.co.nz

Entry 159

Photo: © Awaroa Lodge, Abel Tasman National Park, NZ

Awaroa Lodge

Awaroa Bay, Abel Tasman National Park, PO Box 163, Takaka 7172

Anyone lucky enough to discover the spectacular Abel Tasman coastal path will be seduced by the lure of this stylish hotel in the wildest part of the national park. Hardy adventurers may feel spoilt by the pampering (endless hot water tumbles out of the power showers), yet the deluxe charm doesn't detract from the natural beauty of the stunning setting. The lodge's green credentials are borne mostly out of its isolation as well as its dependency on the steady stream of kayakers and walkers drawn to the wild and remarkable Awaroa Inlet. Choose from superior studio suites with private decks, stylish deluxe rooms and standard family rooms that share a contemporary aesthetic – rattan and wood furniture, white walls and tiles, high spec aluminium fittings. The ebullient young team of mainly seasonal workers provide exceptional service and the restaurant is a delight – a range of Thai and Indian ingredients provide exotic and imaginative flavours.

- Hiking; kayaking; canoeing with Maoris from Motueka
- Abel Tasman National Park

rooms	26: 10 rooms for 2-3, 4 family rooms for up to 8, 12 studio suites.
price	NZ$235-$400.
meals	Full-board only.
closed	Never.
directions	By car from Nelson to Marahau or Motueka (1.5 hrs); boat transfer (arrange on booking). From Marahau on foot (3 days) or by sea kayak (1 hr from Totaranui, 2 days from Marahau - only for the experienced).

	Reservations
tel	+64 (0)3 528 8758
fax	+64 (0)3 528 6561
email	stay@awaroalodge.co.nz
web	www.awaroalodge.co.nz

Herbs, salads and spices used for cooking come from the lodge's own large organic garden.

Hotel

Entry 160

Tui Nature Reserve Wilderness Park

Private Bag, Havelock, Marlborough

See what just one family can do for New Zealand conservation, inspired by a landscape redolent with Maori mythology, a filigree of headlands, inlets, bays and forested peninsulas. All is exemplary, from solar-power cabins to food baskets that are a Pandora's delight of overflowing cheeses, homemade bread and vegetables fresh from the garden. Self-catering cabins offer a warm privacy in pine and soft-corn coloured walls, yet one of the reasons to stay here is getting to know Brian and Ellen, whose generosity, good humour and low prices mean that everyone is welcome. They take a vicarious pleasure in your holiday, not having taken their own in years, since all profits are invested local initiatives. More than likely it will be just a handful staying at any one time; it's an unalloyed sweetness to know that the only sound you'll hear at night is Marlborough Sounds. Best of all, it's only just beginning. *Minimum stay in the cottage two nights.*

- Tramping; kayaking; guided boat tours to see local wildlife
- Marlborough Sounds; Pelorus Sounds; Duffers Reef

rooms	1 cottage for 2-6; 2 cabins for 2-3.
price	Cottage NZ$135-$150; $20 extra person. Cabins $95. Singles $75.
meals	Self-catering. Food baskets NZ$35 p.p. on request.
closed	Never.
directions	Mail-boat/water-taxi from Havelock marina. Pick-up from wharf in Waitata Bay by 4x4/8-wheeler.

Significant pest control has allowed for major regeneration of native forest in the last ten years.

Brian & Ellen Plaisier

tel	0800 107 077 within New Zealand
mobile	+64 (0)27 448 3447
email	tuireserve@xtra.co.nz
web	www.ontopofthesounds.co.nz

Self-catering

Lochmara Lodge

Lochmara Bay, Queen Charlotte Sound, PO Box 172, Picton, Marlborough

It's an easy walk here along the Queen Charlotte Track, for native flax forests and the beaches of Marlborough Sounds are but a short tramp as the albatross flies. Prepare to be social, even in your own minimalist studio or chalet – there's a resident WWOOF population. The shared sitting room in the original farmstead is a good place to meet kindred spirits around the fire, and the television is blissful in its absence. Lovers of both art and nature are accommodated here, as annual artistic retreats run by owners Louise and Shayne have produced the dozens of sculptures dotted around the buildings. Detailed signs all over 11 acres of woods and farmland inform guests about local flora and wildlife recovery programmes; why lighting is kept to a minimum. If that's not enough, head for the aviaries to see endangered kakariki and weta being bred.

- Tramping, cycling, kayaking, fishing
- Over 50 bird species, incl. little blue penguin, white-faced storm petrel, northern royal albatross; geckos
- Marlborough Sounds; Motuara Wild-life Sanctuary tour

rooms	2 + 6: 2 doubles. 4 chalets for 2-4; 2 studios for 3-4.
price	NZ$80-$100. Studios $135. Chalets from $145.
meals	Breakfast $5-$15. Dinner $10-$30. Self-catering.
closed	June-September.
directions	Water-taxi next to Picton ferry terminal arranged on booking. Walk/mountain bike from Queen Charlotte track. Kayak, independent hire.

	Louise Bright, Shayne Olsen & Joe Walker
tel	+64 (0)3573 4554
fax	+64 (0)3573 4554
email	enquiries@lochmaralodge.co.nz
web	www.lochmaralodge.co.nz

Highly innovative sewage system – integrates both human & environmental systems.

Hotel & Self-catering

Entry 162

Lake Moeraki Wilderness Lodge
Private Bag 772, Hokitika, West Coast

Gerry and Anne have been in the eco-tourism business for years and their methods read like a manual for preservation and protection. Guests are encouraged to get their hands green and dirty controlling weeds and pests, as well as studying rare wildlife in the surrounding 7 million-acre reserve. Simple yet stylish rooms have been designed not to detract from the river and rainforest aesthetics outside, even as natural woollen carpets and inspired photography remind you of the best that's on offer. Glacial valleys, rainforest and the coast keep the hardiest tramper happy, while a night-sky walk will lead to the Southern Cross. Many proceed no further than the 'Red Dog Saloon' whose original wooden slabs can still be seen supporting tables made from wood pulled like your beer – cold and local – from Lake Brunner itself. You can almost taste the mantra: Reduce Reuse Recycle. *See also entry opposite.*

* Tramping (10 miles of lakes and river from lodge); night-walks; kayaking; swimming
* Crested penguins, seals, forest birds, freshwater ecology
* Fox Glacier, Fiordland, Tasman coast

rooms	28: 24 twins/doubles, 4 suites for 2.
price	Half-board NZ$290-$490. Singles from $380. Includes short guided activities daily.
meals	Half-board only.
closed	June & July.
directions	From Haast, Highway 6 north for 30km. From Fox Glacier Highway 6 south for 90km. Well-signed. Bus daily from Wanaka-Glacier. Cycling possible.

Lowland rainforest protected as World Heritage Area due to the McSweeneys & NZ Conservation Movement.

Eco lodge

	Dr Gerry McSweeney
tel	+64 (0)3750 0881
fax	+64 (0)3750 0881
email	lakemoeraki@wildernesslodge.co.nz
web	www.wildernesslodge.co.nz

Wilderness Lodge Arthur's Pass

PO Box 33, Arthur's Pass, Canterbury

Marvel at a 6,000-acre eco-triumvirate of nature protection, sustainable merino-sheep farming and responsible tourism. Mountains, beech forest, river valley – it's up to you what view you look at from your window in one of two lodges built from honest local stone, wood and iron. Rooms keep a natural integrity of wool, lanolin and New Zealand art, even manuka shampoo. Passionate conversation and nature adventures with campaigning owners, Gerry and Anne, will reveal how Wilderness Lodges have proven their rationale that money really does grow on trees. There are swathes of regenerating native forest – you may even be asked to help clear American pine seedlings or help them sheer sheep. The lodge makes a point of working in close consultation with the local Maori tribe at the Kura Tawhiti reserve. The gourmet food provides trampers with the perfect preparation for the Southern Alps.

- Independent or guided tramping in 30km of walking trails; kayaking; farm tours
- Kea parrots, endangered bush birds (incl. orange-fronted parakeet)
- Arthur's Pass National Park; glacial lakes; sheep station/nature reserve

rooms	20: 20 doubles, 4 suites.
price	Half-board NZ$290-$490. Singles from $380.
meals	Half-board only. Packed lunch available.
closed	June & July.
directions	130km from Christchurch, h'way 73; 16km east of Arthur's Pass township; signed. Trains & buses from Christchurch & Greymouth. Transfers. Cycling possible.

Ecotourism has been economically more successful than previous, exploitative sheep grazing.

	Dr Gerry McSweeney
tel	+64 (0)3318 9246
fax	+64 (0)3318 9245
email	arthurspass@wildernesslodge.co.nz
web	www.wildernesslodge.co.nz

Eco lodge

G & ♀ ✗ (Hello) 🍷 🍾 🚜 👟

Centre Hill Cottage Retreat

59 Howell Road, Totara Valley, Pleasant Point, Canterbury

A farmstay in the true sense of the word. Before you, the fertile land of the organic farm stretches into the Totara Valley and across to the dramatic Southern Alps in the distance. The self-contained cottage – one double room, one twin – is decorated in calm colours and wood and is stocked with everything you need to set up home, from a generous welcome hamper to wood for the stove. There are also enchanting surprises, such as an alfresco bathtub so you can soak under the stars (or a large indoor spa bath if it's chilly outside!). The surrounding farm has been run by Ian since 1968. He is as warm or as discreet as you wish, and for those wanting to learn about or discuss organic agriculture there is real expertise to be found here. If your interest is more passive – enjoying the organic produce, for example – there are plenty of other activities to immerse yourself in: swimming in the freshwater pool, cycling around the farm and surrounding countryside.

* Fishing rivers, tennis, farm walks, scenery good for sketching, painting
* An hour's drive from Lake Tekapo and the ski fields of Dobson or Fox Peak

It's just a short 50-metre walk to the certified Centre Hill Organic Farm.

rooms	1 cottage for 4.
price	NZ$250 for 2. $50 per extra person.
meals	Self-catering. Dinner on request. Restaurants 5-min drive.
closed	Never.
directions	2hr drive from Christchurch city, or flight (1.5 hrs) from Wellington to Timaru airport & 12-min drive. Pleasant Point on H'way 8; turn into Tengawai Road; follow signs.

Ian Blakemore

tel	+64 (0)3614 7385
mobile	+64 (0)27 420 1120
email	centre.hill@paradise.net.nz
web	www.centrehillcottage.com

Self-catering & Homestay & Working farm

Turtle Island Resort

Yassawas, Fiji, c/o Level 2, 38-40 Garden Street, South Yarra, 3141 Victoria

One of a group of 20 islands of the Yasawas, Turtle Island embodies 'paradise' in the most clichéd sense (*Blue Lagoon* was filmed here): an impossibly lush volcanic mound fringed by palm trees that stretch almost horizontally towards the water. American owner Richard Evanson bought the largely barren island in 1972 and set about complete re-forestation and adding a health clinic, secondary school and the spacious *bures* (Fijian cottages) scattered along the edge of one of the island's dozen beaches. All is sustainably managed, only 14 couples allowed at any one time, there's no swimming pool, and vegetables are grown on the island. There are fresh fruits salads (papaya, limes, mangos and pineapple) and adventurous and delicious dining (fresh lobster on a courgette fondue) – all locally sourced and overseen by Melbourne's chef du monde Jacques Raymond. Sumptuous. *Minimum stay six nights.*

- Hiking; horse riding; scuba diving, snorkelling, sailing & windsurfing; mountain biking; medicinal plant tours
- Green turtle, hawksback turtle, land & sea birds, reef fish, soft corals

rooms	14 cottages for 2. No singles bookings.
price	Full-board US$1,362-$2,390. Includes all activities.
meals	Full-board only.
closed	Never.
directions	By seaplane from Turtle Seaplane base on Wailoaloa Beach, 15min drive from Nadi International airport. Flight 30 mins.

	Andrew Fairley
tel	+61 (0)3 9823 8313
fax	+61 (0)3 9823 8318
web	www.turtlefiji.com

Employs 150 local villagers & runs a foundation that helps run a school, eye clinic & other local projects.

Eco lodge

The following places have been recommended to us but we have not yet inspected them. We'd love to hear about them so if you do stay at any, do let us know your experiences – good and bad! Your comments make a real contribution, be they on our report form, by letter or by email (see p.273).

South America

Argentina We did inspect Portal de Piedra in Provincia de Jujuy and we were impressed, but unfortunately there wasn't time to squeeze it in to this first edition. Do take a look: www.portaldepiedra.com

Brazil Amazonat Jungle Lodge www.amazonat.org

Ecuador Yachana Lodge www.yachana.com

Ecuador Sacha Lodge www.sachalodge.com

Central America

Costa Rica Bosque Del Cabo Eco-lodge, www.bosquedelcabo.com

Honduras Pico Bonito, www.picobonito.com

Nicaragua Finca Esperanza Verde (Green Hope Farm), www.fincaesperanzaverde.org

Panama Punta Caracol www.puntacaracol.com.pa

North America

USA A Stone Wall Inn, Vermont, www.astonewallinn.com

USA El Monte Sagrado Resort,

New Mexico, www.elmontesagrado.com

USA Papoose Creek Lodge, Montana, www.papoosecreek.com

Canada Trout Point Lodge, Nova Scotia, www.troutpoint.com

Canada Bathurst Inlet Lodge, North West Territory, www.bathurstinletlodge.com

South East Asia

Indonesia Bajo Komodo Eco Lodge, Komodo, www.ecolodgesindonesia.com

Indonesia Rimba Orangutan Eco Lodge, Tanjung Puting, www.rimbalodge.com/

Indonesia Sua Bali, Bali, www.suabali.com

Laos Kingfisher Ecolodge, www.kingfisherecolodge.com

Laos The Boat Landing Guesthouse, www.theboatlanding.com

Malaysia Nanga Sumpa Longhouse, Sarawak, www.borneoadventure.com

Africa

Botswana Duba Plains, www.wilderness-safaris.com

Ethiopia Bishangari Lodge, www.bishangari.com

Gabon Jale Ecolodge, Gulf of Guinea, praiajale.free.fr

Gambia Footsteps Lodge, www.natureswaygambia.com

Gambia Tumani Tenda Eco-tourism Camp, www.tumanitenda.co.uk

Kenya Camp Ya Kanzi, www.maasai.com

Kenya Shompole, www.shompole.com

South Africa Buffalo Ridge, Madikwe,
www.buffaloridgesafari.com

South Africa Grootbos Private
Nature Reserve, Western Cape,
www.grootbos.com

South Africa Soweto nights,
Soweto, www.sowetonights.com

South Africa Tswalu Kalahari
Reserve, Kalahari, www.tswalu.com

Tanzania Loliondo,
www.kirurumu.com

Tanzania Mwagusi Safari Lodge,
www.ruaha.org

Uganda Semliki Lodge,
www.safariuganda.com/
semliki_safari_lodge.htm

Europe

England The Eco-Lodge, Lincolnshire
www.internationalbusinessschool.net
/eco-lodge.htm

Italy Lama di Luna,
www.lamadiluna.com

Spain Andalucia Yurts, Andalucia,
www.andaluciayurts.com

Spain Las Alpujarras Retreat,
Granada,
www.lasalpujarrasretreat.com

South Asia

India Hilliya Resort, Kerala,
www.hiliyaresort.com

India Village Ways, Kumaon,
www.villageways.com

Sri Lanka Rainforest Edge,
www.rainforestedge.com

Sri Lanka Ulpotha,
www.ulpotha.com

Sri Lanka Yala Village,
www.yalavillage.com

Australasia & South Pacific

Australia Freycinet Lodge, Tasmania,
www.freycinetlodge.com.au

Australia Glass House Mountain
lodge, Queensland,
www.glasshouseecolodge.com

Australia Kooljaman at Cape
Leveque, Western Australia,
www.kooljaman.com.au

Travel
Conservation International is a
Washington-based non-profit
organisation whose focus is on
conservation. It runs an extensive
ecotourism programme to support
tourism projects that benefit
biodiversity, particularly within
community-based enterprises.
One of its showcase projects is
Chalalan Lodge (entry 11) in Bolivia.
ecotour.org +1 202 912 1000

The International Centre for
Responsible Tourism is a post-
graduate training and research
centre based at the University of
Greenwich. Runs a Masters degree in
Responsible Tourism Management as
well as distance learning courses.
www.icrtourism.org

The International Ecotourism Society
is a Washington-based membership
organisation whose aim is to help
provide information and guidelines
on ecotourism for academics,
architects, consultants, Eco lodge
owners, governments, tour operators
and travellers. Its web site is an
excellent source of information, and
includes a listing of national
ecotourism organisations worldwide
and an online library of books and
papers. ecotourism.org
+1 202 347 9203

The International Tourism
Partnership is a programme within

The Prince of Wales International
Business Leaders Forum (iblf.org),
with members from travel and
tourism companies around the
world. It focuses on the business
case for green tourism. +44 (0) 20
7467 3600 tourismpartnership.org

The Travel Foundation is a UK-based
charity that works with the travel
industry to encourage mores
sustainable practices in holiday
destinations. It was set up with help
from the Foreign and
Commonwealth Office and now
raises money via donations from
travellers and certain travel
companies to fund projects in
Cyprus, the Gambia, Mexico, Sri
Lanka and Tobago. (See p16-17).
thetravelfoundation.org.uk
+44 (0)117 9273049

Tourism Concern is a vociferous UK-
based charity that has campaigned
for ethical and fairly traded tourism
over the last 15 years. It has focused
particularly on human rights issues
and ran a concerted campaign to
protect mountain porters' rights.
Excellent reference library at its
offices in North London.
tourismconcern.org.uk
+44 (0)20 7133 3330

World Tourism Organisation is the
United Nations agency responsible
for tourism. It helped UNEP organise
the International Year of Ecotourism

in 2002, produced a Global Code of Ethics for the tourism industry, and launched a project known as ST-EP (Sustainable Tourism – Eliminating Poverty) at the Johannesburg World Summit for Sustainable Development in 2002 as a manifestation of the UN Millennium Development Goals. unwto.org +34 91 567 81 00

Other
Association of National Parks Authorities
www.nationalparks.gov.uk
Carbon Calculator
www.carboncalculator.com
Carbon Trust
www.thecarbontrust.co.uk
Centre for Alternative Technology
www.cat.org.uk
Climate Care www.climatecare.org
Convention on International Trade in Endangered species (CITES):
www.cites.org
Cyclists' Touring Club
www.ctc.org.uk
Ecological Footprint
www.ecologicalbudget.org.uk
Department for Environment, Food and Rural Affairs www.defra.gov.uk
Department for International Development www.dfid.gov.uk
Energy Saving Trust www.est.org.uk
Fairtrade Foundation
www.fairtrade.org.uk
Forum for the Future
www.forumforthefuture.org.uk
Friends of Conservation
www.foc-uk.com

Friends of the Earth www.foe.co.uk
Global Action Plan
www.globalactionplan.org.uk
Good energy www.good-energy.co.uk
Green Score www.greenscore.org.uk
G-Wiz (electric cars)
www.goingreen.co.uk
Gold Standard carbon credits
www.cdmgoldstandard.org
International Institute For Environment and Development:
www.iied.org
Marine Stewardship Council
www.msc.org
One: The Campaign to Make Poverty History www.one.org
Overseas Development Institute
www.odi.org.uk
Pan Parks www.panparks.org
Renewable Energy Foundation
www.ref.org.uk
Soil Association
www.soilassociation.org
Sustrans www.sustrans.org.uk
The Climate Neutral Company
www.carbonneutral.com
The World Conservation Union
www.iucn.org
United Nations Environment Programme-World Conservation Monitoring Centre
www.unep-wcmc.org
United Nations Millennium Development Goals
www.un.org/millenniumgoals
WaterAid www.wateraid.org
World Wide Fund for Nature
www.wwf.org

Certification

Green Tourism Business Scheme certifies tourism-related businesses in the UK, such as hotels, travel companies and conference venues that are making strides (some larger than others) to be eco-friendly. www.green-business.co.uk

Blue Flag identifies environmentally sound beaches and marines – over 3,000 in 36 countries across Europe, South Africa, Morocco, New Zealand, Canada and the Caribbean.

Fair Trade in Tourism South Africa is a stringently applied trademark awarded to ethical South African tourism businesses that provide fair wages and working conditions, such as Umlani Bushcamp (entry 118) and Hog Hollow Country Lodge (entry 121). www.fairtourismsa.org.za

Costa Rica's Certification for Sustainable Tourism has pioneered sustainable tourism certification in Central America; important for a region swimming in greenwash. The only two with 'five green leaves' are Finca Rosa Blanca Country Inn (entry 47) and Lapa Rios (entry 52). www.turismo-sostenible.co.cr

Ecotourism Australia recognises genuine ecotourism and nature tourism operators in Australia. It is particularly hot on interpretation and awards a separate certificate for ecotourism guiding. Hilary Hughes at Kanimbla View Clifftop Retreat (entry 154) has an advanced certificate. www.ecotourism.org.au

Green Globe is the closest there is to a worldwide green certificate in the travel industry, with members in over 50 countries. It was criticised in its early days for not differentiating clearly enough those members that made a commitment to being green from those that were actually practising green, but on our inspections we found many good certified examples such as Udayana Eco Lodge (entry 149) in Bali. www.greenglobe21.com

Awards

IH&RA Green Hotelier of the Year once promoted environmental awareness among hotels but now questions wider issues in sustainable development. Highly commended in the Independent category was Three Rivers Eco Lodge (entry 26) in Dominica. www.ih-ra.com/awards

Tourism for Tomorrow Awards select travel industry organisations and projects as role models for sustainable tourism. There are four categories, including an 'Investor in People Award' and a 'Conservation Award' won in the past by Damaraland (entry 114) in Namibia. www.tourismfortomorrow.com

First Choice Responsible Tourism Awards ask travellers to nominate tourism companies and organisations that are acting more responsibly towards the environment, conservation and local people. There are 12 categories, including 'Best

Small Hotel', 'Best for Poverty Alleviation' and 'Best for Innovation'. Previous winners include Nihiwatu (entry 150) on Sumba Island, Indonesia, Kasbah du Toubkal (entry 99) in the High Atlas, Morocco, Chumbe Island (entry 107) on Zanzibar and Whitepod (entry 88) in the Swiss Alps.
www.responsibletourismawards.info

Directory of green tour operators

A growing number of tour operators publish a policy or 'code of conduct' that sets out how their holidays minimize their impact on the environment, contribute to conservation and provide real benefits for local people. Here is a selection of companies that go the extra mile:

Discovery Initiatives, Cirencester, runs nature holidays, wilderness tours and safaris in 35 countries. Founded in 1997 by Zimbabwe-born Julian Matthews, the company has worked with over 40 conservation organisations worldwide and has contributed over £600,000 to projects that help communities and conservation. In the Galapagos, it runs trips on board Ecoventura Yachts (entry 4) and contributes annual membership to the Galapagos Conservation trust (www.gct.org) for every client. +44 (0)1285 643333. www.discoveryinitiatives.co.uk

Expert Africa, Old Isleworth, Middlesex, specialises in organising trips to sub-Saharan Africa. Formerly Sunvil Africa, it is run by Chris McIntyre, author the informative Bradt Travel Guides to Zambia, Namibia, Botswana, Zanzibar. Among the many environmentally friendly and socially responsible places the company features are Shiwa Ng'andu Mansion House (entry 110) in Zambia and Chumbe Island (entry 107), in Zanzibar. www.expertafrica.com, +44 (0)208 232 9777.

Tribes Travel, Woodbridge, Suffolk, is run by Amanda and Guy Marks who have pioneered the principles of fair trade in travel. Included on their list of recommended places are Dana Guesthouse (entry 123) in Jordan and Posadas Amazonas (entry 9) in Peru. Tribes worked with Twin and CaféDirect to help set up Kahawa Shamba (entry 106) in Tanzania. www.tribes.co.uk +44 (0)1728 685971.

Rainbow Tours, London, is run by Roger Diski and provides tailor-made tours to Africa and the Indian Ocean. It has a strong commitment to community empowerment and sustainable rural development, and focuses on owner-run places, such as Guludo Beach Lodge (entry 113) in Mozambique and Bird Island Lodge (entry 125) in the Seychelles. www.rainbowtours.co.uk +44 (0)20 7226 1004

For information on planning your journey by bus, coach or train... You may have to dig deep into some of these sites to find the relevant information.

General
www.seat61.com
www.fahrplan.ch
www.thomascookpublishing.com
www.nationalrail.co.uk

South America
Argentina
Train: www.sateliteferroviario.com.ar (in Spanish only)
www.ferrobaires.gba.gov.ar
Bus: www.solobus.com.ar
www.viabariloche.com.ar
Brazil Train: www.supervia.com.br
www.transportes.gov.br (both Portugese only)
Bus: www.novorio.com.br
Chile Train: www.efe.cl
Bus: www.turbus.com
Peru Train: www.perurail.com
www.ferroviasperu.com.pe
Bus: travel.peru.com

Central America
Belize Bus: www.enjoyguatemala.com
Costa Rica Bus: www.ticabus.com, www.infoturistica.com
www.costaricabustickets.com, www.monteverdeinfo.com
Mexico
Train: www.mexlist.com
Copper Canyon train service see
www.chepe.com.mx
Bus: mexico-connect.com

North America
Canada Train: www.viarail.ca
Bus: www.greyhound.ca

Europe
Train: www.interrailnet.com
www.raileurope.co.uk
www.europeonrail.com
Bus: www.eurolines.com
www.nationalexpress.com
www.busabout.com
www.busstation.net
UK
All: www.traveline.org.uk
Ireland Train: www.irishrail.ie
Bus: www.buseireann.ie
Norway Train: http://www.nsb.no/
Bus: motorbus.net
Greece
Train: www.ose.gr (click orange "EN" button in right corner for English)
Bus: www.diadiktion.com
www.ktel.org www.hri.org

Australasia
Australia www.trainways.com.au
Bus: www.greyhound.com.au
www.premierms.com.au (East coast)
www.integritycoachlines.com.au (West coast),
www.redlinecoaches.com.au
www.tigerline.com.au (Tasmania)
New Zealand
Train: www.tranzscenic.co.nz
Bus: www.intercitycoach.co.nz

This calculator is designed to make it easy to work out your personal carbon dioxide emissions from different forms of transport. Fill in the white boxes with your numbers. Simply follow the instructions in the title for that box, e.g. a x b = c.. You can use the following table to list your journeys made in the last year. Enter the distance (or journey-time for flights), the number of ways, i.e. "1" for 1-way or "2" for 2-way, make a guess at your "share" of the car's use, and enter this in the table below, as a decimal (for example, if you are the sole user of the car, enter your "share" as 1. If your share is 50%, enter 0.5; for one third enter 0.33, for 25% enter 0.25, etc.), and the times you make the journey. If you need more space, simply list your journeys separately, add up the miles, and enter them into the table.

A Distance (miles)	B 1 or 2-way	C Miles C=AxB	D Share	E Times a year	Total CxDxE

Car & Taxi journeys   Total

x conversion factor   0.36

CO_2 emissions (kg)

A Distance (miles)	B 1 or 2-way	C Miles C=AxB		E Times a year	Total CxE

Train & Bus journeys   Total

x conversion factor   0.1

CO_2 emissions (kg)

A Journey time	B 1 or 2-way	C Hours C=AxB	D Miles =Cx500	E Times a year	Total DxE

Air journeys   Total

x conversion factor   0.87

CO_2 emissions (kg)

Information provided with the kind permission of Mukti Kumar Mitchell and Resurgence Magazine, www.resurgence.org.

Sources include: The National Energy Foundation (www.natenergy.org); The Department for the Environment, Food and Rural Affairs (www.defra.gov.uk); The National Office of Statistics (www.statistics.gov.uk).

South America
Argentina (-3)
Bolivia (-4)
Brazil (-3)
Chile (-4)
Ecuador (-5)
Galapagos Islands (-6)
Guyana (-4)
Peru (-5)

Central America
Belize (-6)
Costa Rica (-6)
Guatemala (-6)
Mexico (-5 to -6)
Nicaragua (-5)

Caribbean
Dominica (-4)
Guadeloupe (-4)
Jamaica (-5)
St Lucia (-4)
US Virgin Islands (-4)

North Ameria
Canada (-5 to -8)

Europe
Britain (0)
France (+1)
Greece (+2)
Iceland (+1)
Ireland (0)
Italy (+1)
Norway (+2)
Portugal (0)

Spain (+1)
Switzerland (+2)

Africa & Middle East
Botswana (+2)
Egypt (+2)
Jordan (+2)
Kenya (+3)
Morocco (0)
Mozambique (+2)
Namibia (+1)
South Africa (+2)
Tanzania (+3)
Zambia (+2)

Indian Ocean
Maldives (+5)
Madagascar (+3)
Seychelles (+4)

South Asia
India (+5.30)
Nepal (+5.45)
Sri Lanka (+5.30)

South East Asia
Indonesia (+7)
Malaysia (+8)

Central Asia
Mongolia (+8)

Australasia & South Pacific
Australia (+8 to +10)
Fiji (+12)
New Zealand (+12)

Suggested reading

Books

Rough Guide to a Better World:
a free guide to how activism, giving to charity, volunteer work, ethical shopping and tourism can all help with problems faced by the developing world. The introduction contains the immortal line: "If you think you are too small to make a difference, try sleeping with a mosquito." Foreword by Bob Geldof. (Rough Guides and DFID, www.roughguide-betterworld.com)

Ecotourism And Sustainable Development : Who Owns Paradise?: the seminal work on the ecotourism industry and a first-hand account of ecotourism projects around the world. By Martha Honey, now Executive Director of the International Ecotourism Society. (Island Press, www.islandpress.org)

The Ethical Travel Guide: a directory of 300 community-based holidays worldwide, vetted by Tourism Concern (see pp.22). Contains a thorough introduction to current ethical issues in the travel industry by Polly Pattullo. (Earthscan, www.earthscan.co.uk)

The Times Holiday Handbook – The Essential Trip-Planning Guide: includes the latest advice on travel money, insurance, renewing your passport and resolving holiday problems. By *The Times* travel editor, Cath Urquhart. (Navigator Guides, www.booksfirst.co.uk)

Magazines

Green Hotelier: an excellent source of information for all things green in the hotel industry. It provides practical tips on how hoteliers can incorporate eco-friendly technologies and includes useful case notes on best practice. www.greenhotelier.com

Green Futures: the very latest news and debates on how society and companies are progressing towards sustainable development. Published by Forum for the Future, which was founded by green gurus Jonathan Porritt and Sara Parkin. www.greenfutures.org.uk

Ethical Consumer: the consumer watchdog of the eco world, a magazine that digs behind brand names to differentiate between the green and the greenwash. www.ethicalconsumer.org

The Ecologist: the stalwart of the old environmental guard and a magazine that still likes a good rant. Carries probing and thorough articles on a huge array of topics, from exposés of well-known brands to globalisation and nanotechnology, and has a fantastic guide to green shopping. www.theecologist.org

New Consumer: a fresh, new magazine with a focus on ethical and sustainable lifestyles. Though its articles tackle grave issues, *New Consumer*'s celebration of the positive, its focus on offering everyday solutions to sustainability problems and its crisp, modern design lift this magazine out of the realms of hair shirts and sandals. www.newconsumer.org

Resurgence: the spiritual voice of current positive green thinking, edited by the inspirational Satish Kumar. You'll happen across entertaining and thoughtful articles from an eclectic bunch, from Noam Chomsky to Andrew Marr, David Nicholson-Lord, James Lovelock, Prince Charles and The Dalai Lama. www.resurgence.org

The World Wide Web is big – very big. So big, in fact, that it can be a fruitless search if you don't know where to find reliable, trustworthy, up-to-date information about fantastic places to stay in Europe, India, Morocco and beyond...

Fortunately, there's www.specialplacestostay.com, where you can dip into all of our guides, find special offers from owners, catch up on news about the series and tell us about the special places you've been to.

www.specialplacestostay.com

Discover your perfect self-catering escape in Britain... With the same punch and attitude as all our printed guides, Special Escapes celebrates only those places we have visited and genuinely like.

www.special-escapes.co.uk

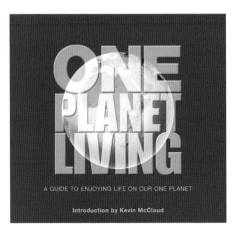

If everyone in the world consumed the planet's natural resources at the same rate as people in the UK, we would need THREE planets to support us

The Solution?
One Planet Living

One Planet Living   Edition 1, £4.99

A practical guide providing us with easy, affordable and attractive alternatives for achieving a higher quality of life while using our fair share of the planet's capacity. Two environmental organisations, BioRegional and WWF, have come together to promote a simple set of principles to make sustainable living achievable.

The Little Earth Book   Edition 4, £6.99

By James Bruges

A little book that has proved both hugely popular – and provocative. This new edition has chapters on Islam, Climate Change and The Tyranny of Corporations.

The Little Food Book   Edition 1, £6.99

By Craig Sams, Chairman of the Soil Association

An explosive account of the food we eat today. Never have we been at such risk – from our food. This book will help clarify what's at stake.

The Little Money Book   Edition 1, £6.99

By David Boyle, associate of the New Economics Foundation

This pithy, wry little guide will tell you where money comes from, what it means, what it's doing to the planet and what we might be able to do about it.

www.fragile-earth.com

Order form

All these books are available in major bookshops or you may order them direct. Post and packaging are FREE within the UK.

Bed & Breakfast for Garden Lovers	£14.99
British Hotels, Inns & Other Places	£14.99
British Bed & Breakfast	£14.99
French Bed & Breakfast	£15.99
French Hotels, Châteaux & Other Places	£14.99
French Holiday Homes	£12.99
Greece	£11.99
Green Places to Stay	£13.99
India	£11.99
Ireland	£12.99
Italy	£14.99
London	£9.99
Morocco	£11.99
Mountains of Europe	£9.99
Paris Hotels	£9.99
Portugal	£10.99
Pubs & Inns of England & Wales	£13.99
Spain	£14.99
Turkey	£11.99
One Planet Living	£4.99
The Little Earth Book	£6.99
The Little Food Book	£6.99
The Little Money Book	£6.99
Six Days	£12.99

Please make cheques payable to Alastair Sawday Publishing   Total £

Please send cheques to: Alastair Sawday Publishing, The Old Farmyard, Yanley Lane, Long Ashton, Bristol BS41 9LR. For credit card orders call 01275 395431 or order directly from our web site www.specialplacestostay.com

Title   First name   Surname

Address

Postcode   Tel

If you do not wish to receive mail from other like-minded companies, please tick here ☐

If you would prefer not to receive information about special offers on our books, please tick here ☐

Report form

If you have any comments on entries in this guide, please let us have them.
If you have a favourite eco lodge, hotel or other new green discovery, please
let us know about it. You can return this form, email info@sawdays.co.uk, or
visit www.specialplacestostay.com and click on 'contact'.

Existing entry

Property name:_____

Entry number: _____ Date of visit: ___ / ___ / ___

New recommendation

Property name:_____

Address: _____

_____

Tel: _____

Your comments

What did you like (or dislike) about this place? Was it environmentally
friendly? What was the location like? What sort of food did they serve?

_____

_____

_____

_____

_____

_____

_____

_____

Your details

Name: _____

Address: _____

Postcode: _____ Tel: _____

Quick reference indices

Cultural integration
Activities organised that
involve integration with
local cultures.

Quick reference indices

Quick reference indices

Quick reference indices

Quick reference indices

Flora
Good for garden lovers or
people who love wild
plants/trees.

Quick reference indices

Quick reference indices

Photo below Nihiwatu, entry 150

Beautiful as they were, our old offices leaked heat, used electricity to heat water and rooms, flooded whole rooms with light to illuminate one person, and were not ours to alter. We failed our eco-audit in spite of using recycled cooking oil in one car and gas in another, recycling everything we could and gently promoting 'greenery' in our travel books. (This book and our Fragile Earth series take a harder line.)

After two eco-audits we leaped at the chance to buy some old barns closer to Bristol, to create our own eco-offices and start again. Our accountants thought we were mad and there was no time for proper budgeting. The back of every envelope bore the signs of frenzied calculations, and then I shook hands and went off on holiday.
Two years later we moved in.

As I write, swallows are nesting in our wood-pellet store, the fountain plays in the pond, the grasses bend

Photos above Quentin Craven

before a gentle breeze and the solar panels heat water too hot to touch. We have, to our delight, created an inspiring and serene place.

The roof was lifted to allow us to fix thick insulation panels beneath the tiles. More panels were fitted between the rafters and as a separate wall inside the old ones, and laid under the under-floor heating pipes. We are insulated for the Arctic, and almost totally air-tight. Ventilation is natural, and we open windows. An Austrian boiler sucks wood-pellets in from an outside store and slowly consumes them, cleanly. Rain-water is channeled to a 6000-litre underground tank and then, filtered, flushes loos and fills basins. Sun-pipes funnel the day-light into dark corners and double-glazed Velux windows, most facing north, pour it into every office.

We built a small green-oak barn between two old barns, and this has become the heart of the offices, warm, light and beautiful. Wood plays a major role: our simple oak desks were made by a local carpenter, my office floor is of oak, and there is oak paneling. Even the carpet tiles tell a story; they are made from the wool of Herdwick sheep from the Lake District.

Our electricity consumption is extraordinarily low. We set out not to flood the buildings with light, but to provide attractive, low background lighting and individual 'task' lights to be used only as needed. Materials, too, have been a focus: we used non-toxic paints and finishes.

We have a building of which we are proud and which has helped us win two national awards this year. Architects and designers are fascinated and we are all working with a renewed commitment. But, best of all, we are now in a better position to encourage our 'owners' and readers to take 'sustainability' more seriously.

I end by answering an obvious question: our office carbon emissions will be reduced by about 75%. We await our bills, but they will be low and, as time goes by, relatively lower – and lower. It has been worth every penny and every ounce of effort.

Photo above Paul Groom
Photo below Tom Germain

Kasbah du Toubkal

BP 31, Imlil, Asni

Below North Africa's highest peak the Imlil valley soars away on wings of fertile terraces and red villages. This exceptional mountain retreat is a Berber-European union born of the desire to share Jbel Toubkal's splendours with like-minded visitors without destroying them. Painstakingly rebuilt by entrepreneur Mike McHugo and tireless Hajj Maurice, their 'Berber Hospitality Centre' provides two-budget sleeping: Berber salons (cushioned sitting/sleeping benches round double-height rooms), or good double rooms with bathrooms plus one superb cliff-hanging apartment. Hospitality is a Berber talent: big open smiles, intelligent local knowledge, deep respect for people and animals, and wonderful tagine! Enjoy fascinating glimpses of their culture while walking and mule-trekking; and soothe aching limbs in the hammam. Only 90 minutes from Marrakech, it's another world. *Sole occupancy possible.*

- Rambles around Berber villages; guided ascent of Jbel Toubkal (crampons & ice-picks in winter); ski mountaineering

rooms	14: 11 doubles; 1 apartment for 6; 3 Berber salons for 3-10, sharing bathrooms.
price	€140-€400. Apt €700. Salons €110-€140 for 3-4.
meals	Lunch €15. Dinner €20. BYO.
closed	Rarely.
directions	From Marrakech for Asni then Imlil (65km). Park in village (guarded); 500m walk or mule ride.

	Hajj Maurice
tel	+212 (0)24 485611
fax	+212 (0)24 485636
email	kasbah@discover.ltd.uk
web	www.kasbahdutoubkal.com

5% is added to your bill to help fund local community projects.

Hotel

Entry 99